FILM REVIEW

1977–78

FILM REVIEW
1977–78

edited by F. Maurice Speed

W. H. Allen · London
A Howard & Wyndham Company
1977

All rights reserved, including the right
of reproduction in whole or in part in any
form whatsoever.
Printed in Great Britain by
Fletcher & Son Ltd, Norwich
for the publishers
W. H. Allen & Co. Ltd,
44 Hill Street, London W1X 8LB
Bound by Richard Clay (The Chaucer Press) Ltd,
Bungay, Suffolk

ISBN 0 491 02211 5

CONTENTS

INTRODUCTION

After a year in which extreme violence, bestiality and (literally in the case of *Carrie*) buckets of blood deluged the screens of our cinemas it is, perhaps, a good moment to pause and question what harm this flood of so-called 'exploitation' films may be doing to film business in general and what share they must accept for the depressing story of further falls in the numbers of people going to see the movies.

It is not easy to get relative, comparable figures for the same period from, say, a dozen countries. Nor is it really necessary to prove the decline. Various news stories and statistics that have appeared from time to time during the year add up to weighty and, indeed, incontestable evidence that the falling-off is more or less world-wide.

For instance, here in Britain* during the first half of 1976 cinema attendances dropped to 55·86 million, as against 68·10 million for the same period in

1975, a drop of 18% and part of the long-term fall from 291 million admissions in 1966 to 124 million in 1975. (Though it is interesting to note that while fewer people are going to the cinema, their choice of cinemas grows: 1,590 were operating in 1975 against 1,510 in 1971, this coming about largely, one would guess, from the current trend of converting one large cinema into several small ones. In France† it was announced that during the past fifteen years audiences have halved in numbers from 160 million to a mere 80 million. In America,‡ too, after a heartening upsurge at one point in 1975, figures during 1976 and 1977 have again been falling, with an overall 14% decrease during the last three years.

In Germany during the first quarter of the year there was a drop of 8·6% and in Italy, too, they have been increasingly concerned by a withering in cinema attendances, blamed there on the higher admission prices caused by the country's galloping inflation, proliferation of television choice and falling standards in output (in this context it is relevant to point out that the deaths of such outstanding figures as De Sica, Visconti, Germi and Pasolini all occurred within the year, coinciding with a sharp drop in both quantity and quality of production). The search for reasons for this continual decline in the fortunes of the cinema are constant and the suggestions many and varied. Obviously valid contributory factors include the increasing addiction to television and the ever-wider public that it is reaching; the increasing diversity of other forms of public entertainment, all competing with the

cinema for the less amount of money in the purse caused by inflation.

But none of this is the entire answer, for once again this year the old cinematic adage that there is nothing wrong with the cinema that good – or should I say attractive – films will not cure has been proved once again. It is not just a lucky break that has made *Jaws* the biggest money-maker in the whole history of the movies. It is because it was exciting – sensational if you like – first-class entertainment.

But all that a *Jaws* and like movies will do to bring the people back into the cinemas is immediately negated by the far larger number of variously pornographic films which are driving them away; though films exploiting explicit and devious sex, bloody violence and the use of the foulest language may in the short term attract sensation-seeking audiences, at the same time they are driving away, often for good and all, other, larger audiences – more intelligent, discriminating patrons who have always been the backbone of the cinema and its greatest asset by their enthusiasm and consequent communication of their enjoyment to others. It is these patrons, rather than the kinkies and sensation-seekers, who will be the reason why the cinema fails completely or takes on a new lease of life in the future.

You may find it, I hope, as significant as I do that when some time ago advertising agents J. Walter Thompson took a poll on the subject of screen violence it emerged that 35% of those questioned actively avoided violence and 25% even went as far as to say they would like the government of the day to take action to

---

British filmgoing figures: The figure for the complete period, announced after the above was written, was 107 million admissions for the year 1976 as compared with 125 million for 1975. The actual figures of admissions for the past ten years are as follows: 1966 – 288m; 1967 – 264m; 1968 – 237m; 1969 – 214m; 1970 – 193m; 1971 – 176m; 1972 – 156m; 1973 – 142m; 1974 – 143m; 1975 – 125m. And the figure for 1954 was 1,275m!

† *French filmgoing figures:* With French film production figures more or less stable (214 films made in 1976 as against 222 in 1975) there was a drop of 2·58% in attendance numbers, with just over 176 million admissions registered during 1976.

‡ *American filmgoing figures:* But *Variety* published (in March) a remarkable upsurge for the American box-office for February 1977, which saw an all-time record with a 22% rise over the same month last year and a 5½% rise over January (1977). Even allowing a 5·2% inflation figure the January statistic represents a 17% rise over the previous February!

control it. (The poll, incidentally, was aimed primarily at the television viewer but is surely equally applicable to moviegoers.)

Additional support for the claim that the public is increasingly rejecting screen violence comes from the published results of the box-office returns of films in the United States. There in the list of the first ten biggest money-spinners of the year half were comedies, two were spectaculars (*Jaws* and *Battle of Midway*) and none were motivated by extreme violence or explicit sex.

Though in the short term sensational films like *The Texas Chainsaw Massacre* and *Death Weekend* may do well because of (largely unhealthy) curiosity, in the long term it is my contention that they are doing a great deal of harm to the cinema. Though I have met patrons (mostly, alas, in the younger age groups) who have professed enjoying (!) this kind of blood-letting bestiality, I have also met, both personally and through letters of protest, a considerably greater number who have been shocked and disgusted by them to the extent of saying that they had put them off moviegoing for good. I mention these two films simply because the titles spring to mind, but during the year there have been many others, sometimes worse, exploiting all the baser human instincts, and dwelling on those less pleasing functions of the human body which should be kept private.

All of which brings us back to the perennial subject of censorship in the cinema.

The controversy which surrounded the new censor James Ferman almost as soon as he took over the job last year has

continued unabated all through this. Sniped at from all sides, he has continued resolutely on the course he chose at the outset and let nothing deter him. And there are plenty both in and out of the industry who think that he continues to do a pretty good job in view of the almost insurmountable difficulties which come with the position.

Everyone must surely agree that in theory, and too often in practice, censorship, all censorship, is a bad thing and can easily be an evil one. But in view of what is getting through today with the X-certificate label, can anyone really suggest that we would be better off without any sort of restraint on those fast-buck moviemakers who will stoop to any depths and exploit any kind of sensation in order to make money?

Against censorship as I am in the final analysis, aware of its many imperfections, dangers and whatever, I must say that at this point of time I stand beside Ferman when – as a television producer he supported freedom in all kinds of programmes – he now says: 'But I have always said there have to be some limits based on the standards we want in our society.' And on this rule he has based his complete rejection for public showing of a number of films, including the late Pasolini's last, *Salo*, *The Story of O* and *Deep Throat*.

In connection with this censorship argument, the anti-censorship lobby had a fine old time in early 1977 when Danish producer Jens Thorsen was refused entry into this country. He had come, he said, merely to help launch *The Story of Thirteen* in the making of which he had a hand, but quite obviously the

authorities were aware of his previously announced ambition of making his film about the sex life of Jesus Christ in this country, facilities for the project having already been refused in his own and other countries.

This action drew a chorus of outrage and, indeed, in some ways Thorsen might have felt justified in his feeling that he was being treated unfairly, in view of the fact that nobody seems to have tried to stop Wolf Schmidt making his film *The Passover Plot* in which it is said Jesus Christ is depicted as a left-winger planning a phoney crucifixion as a political plot against the Romans!

Turning now to a completely different subject, I think figures published in *Variety* with regard to the financial returns of American films shown throughout the world are both surprising and interesting. From these it appears that Canada is Hollywood's best customer, contributing some $63 million to the kitty last year; Japan with $56 million came next, then Italy, France and Germany, with Britain sixth with a figure of just over $37 million, almost identical with that contributed by Australia.

Incidentally, Hollywood appears to be heavily backing re-makes and sequels to previous successes for the immediate future. Among the former will be *Grand Hotel*, while sequels and follow-ups include *Gone With the Wind*, *Jaws 2*, *Airport '77*, *Rosemary's Baby Part 2*, *The Heretic* (subtitled *The Exorcist Part 2*) and *Freebie and the Bean Part 2*. There are hints and rumours that MGM are already working on *That's Entertainment Part 3*, and that as long as the new *King*

Kong is as successful as they hope it will be, there'll be a *King Kong* carry-on for 1978.

In connection with *Kong*, the company that made the original film, RKO Radio, which long ago went out of the film distribution business, now appears likely to make a come-back and within the next year or so we may well be seeing again that once familiar trademark of a Radio Tower transmitting morse signals (or its equivalent) on our screens. The new RKO General Pictures Company is negotiating with producers not only to produce re-makes of some of the old company's past successes, but also to produce film stories of which they hold the screen rights but which have never been made, including a William Faulkner short story and scripts by Billy Rose, Edgar Wallace, Irwin Shaw, Charles MacArthur and other famous names – apparently a golden hoard which includes some 400 'properties' in all.

In Britain we saw the completion of the British Lion/EMI merger, with the latter taking over the former, and the ending of the 20th Century-Fox and Rank collaboration in various departments of their organisations. In America, though, Fox did a collaboration deal with United Artists by forming a joint company called Hollywood Home Theatre to make complete programmes, including movies, for the Cable TV home entertainment industry. This Cable TV business, which relies very heavily on the telecasting of films, is flourishing in America and new stations are opening, or are planned to open, at an increasing rate throughout the United States.

It was EMI who at the end of 1976 announced an interesting experiment in the way of showing films otherwise unlikely to have anything like a wide release. When the Walter Reade Organisation opened their Bloomsbury Cinema in London a few years back it was with the idea of showing just this kind of specialist and so-called minority interest movies. The plan failed. Taken over by ABC circuit, it remained something like a celluloid white elephant. Now the programming at the cinema has been handed over to that astute and highly successful specialist cinema owner/manager Kenneth Rive (two of his own three cinemas having been closed down for redevelopment) who plans to present seasons of internationally prestigious 'art' films (he started with the delightful and highly successful French movie *A Nous Les Petites Anglaises*), the success or failure of which will be closely watched by EMI, who say that if the Bloomsbury takings justify it, they will be prepared to give some of these films a far wider release than they would ever have otherwise had.

Rive plans to exploit the cinema itself to the fullest extent, including the presentation of occasional lectures, special lunch-time and late-night screenings and other relevant entertainment. And he is putting in a coffee-bar for patrons, something quite common, apparently, in American cinemas but hitherto more or less unknown in this country. What could emerge from all this – and one hopes fervently that it will – is a wide release of some of those subtitled foreign films which, though often among the best we see during a year, seldom get more than two or three isolated showings after their premier London run.

Another experiment coming to Britain in 1977 (it will probably be in operation by the time you read this) is electrovision, the so-called multi-sensory entertainment already a success (of several years' standing) in cities like New York, Honolulu and San Francisco. Called 'The London Experience' it will be presented by EMI in the premises formerly occupied by the Lyons Corner House in Coventry Street, W.1. It's a multi-media audio-visual show which will include slides, films and multi-channel sound. On a screen of some 700 square feet of stretched nylon, with five sound channels and some 42 slide and film projectors – all controlled by micro-computers – it will present the story of London past and present, spectacular sequences including the Great Fire of London and the London Blitz. Unlike any other cinema ever built it will have only 300 seats in an area of 4,000 square feet. Something like ten one-hour shows each day are planned.

Another note of considerable technical interest has been the announcement of a new camera which it is claimed will revolutionise 3-dimensional moviemaking. Patented in the US as the 'Depix' camera, it consists of a convertor in front of the single lens of a conventional camera. Two pictures are taken, one right and one left, separated horizontally and then placed vertically one above the other within a single frame of the standard film. It is claimed that by using the Depix camera 3-D filming is as simple as standard filming methods and the inventors say that it can be used with equal ease and success by both large and small screen cameras, pointing to possible 3-D TV at some future date.* By the beginning of 1977 the makers claimed their cameras were already being leased to a number of Hollywood production companies. So watch for further developments!

The film industry in this country got little sympathy from the March-published Annan Report on television, a report which apparently cost £315,000 and two years to produce. Said the report: 'There was, running through much of the evidence we received from those with an interest in the film industry, an understandable, but we believe wrong-headed, feeling that television, having stolen the mass audience away from the cinema, should now be required to allow the film industry a share of the profits of the television industry's popularity.

'It was argued that since some of TV's popularity is based on the televising of cinema films, and since TV shares some of the same creative skills and creative artists, then, like an aged parent, the film has a right to expect TV to support it in its old age.

'We do not believe such a relationship between the film and television industries would ensure the rejuvenation of the British film production industry. Nor would it be in the interest of either the cinema-going public or the TV audience.' After this quiet kick in the teeth the industry had little reason to expect too

*News is that a certain Frank Wong will be bringing from Taiwan two new 3-D films to show at the 1977 Cannes Film Festival (*Dynasty* and *Thirteen Nuns*) but it appears that these are the familiar stereoscopic films needing those special glasses to be worn by the viewing audience.

much from the interim action committee recommendations, so long overdue.

Hardly cheering for the British studios was the news early in 1977 that producer Cubby Broccoli, a long-time British-residing American responsible for most of the James Bond films, announced that with the tax situation in Great Britain driving him back to America, his next Bond film would be made there instead of here.

News from the British studios isn't in any case all that bright. After celebrating forty years of existence in 1976, Pinewood found itself without a single film on the floor at one point early in 1977. Obviously after having read the list of forty-four films planned for British production during 1977 published in *Cinema International* they are looking forward to better times, including the four big feature films that Rank are themselves planning to make, in association with Michael Klinger (at a cost of something over £11 million), during the next two years, along with several television series. But one wonders how many of these other forty-four films will ever get on to the studio floor!

November rumours that Shepperton Studios were about to be sold brought a hot denial from the board's chairman, who claimed that, on the contrary, he and his board were intending to spend a lot of money on the studios under a five-year improvement plan. All this came after the stories about Harry Saltzman's bid to take over Shepperton and the – definitely considered, it appears – May offer by the local council to buy the land for building development, they having previously purchased thirty-four acres of

the studio grounds for this purpose. Incidentally, the last Shepperton balance sheet showed a pre-tax profit of £28,000 for the year.

Twickenham Studios changed hands (for £360,000) in the summer of 1976, the new owners being Humphries Holdings (who already controlled the De Lane Lea, Humphries Laboratories and Filmatic companies). With a £37,000 profit for the last financial year and a number of films due in for production, there was a healthy atmosphere of optimism in this celluloid workshop by the Thames.

The year has produced its usual crop of odd and amusing stories. There was the one about the American cinema – the Capri at Columbia – which introduced topless usherettes but subsequently had to shelve the idea because of a shortage of girls prepared to bare their bosoms for the sake of increasing the cinema's takings! Then there was the critic, also in America, who sued a cinema for $150,000 because a rat bit him at a press show. The critic complained: 'I suffered considerable mental anxiety, pain, suffering and revulsion.' And you can add your own comments to that one.

Sueing MGM for a cool million dollars damages because they used extracts from her old films without her permission (in *That's Entertainment*) Esther Williams revealed that she was only paid the equivalent of £25 a week when she signed her original contract with Metro and, even after several years, she was only getting a little over £100 a week while making those big swimming spectaculars. And of the more unlikely subjects to be filmed in 1977, Bill

Cayton's plans to make a movie based on *The Guinness Book of Records*, is one of the oddest though, come to think of it, it could turn out to be the comedy movie of the century.

One wonders how many films a year are made in Poland in view of the fact that it appears that more than 200 a year are made just for children and teenagers – a figure that must turn our own highly effective Children's Film Foundation green with envy!

What of the films? Well, I've already mentioned the slide towards greater bloody violence but also worth mentioning is the increasing tendency to use, either as a theme or at least as part of the content, the formerly taboo subject of homosexuality – seldom with good taste. Hollywood's past itself inspired several movies, all somewhat significantly below their obvious potential, films like *Silent Movie*, *Inserts* and *Nickelodeon*. But among the good things were Hitchcock's vintage *Family Plot*, the highly original musical *Bugsy Malone* and John Wayne's *The Shootist*, in which he gave one of the finest, most deeply felt performances of his long career. We had some fine films from Australia, too, including *Sunday Too Far Away* and *Picnic at Hanging Rock*. And we had *The Omen* to break all kinds of records. Spectaculars were comparatively few and far between with *King Kong* chasing *Jaws* in terms of box-office revenue and, at the time of writing, only one resort to Sensurround, in *Battle of Midway*.

To anyone like myself who sees anything from two to eight films a week it has been a year of a lot of rubbish and some small delights, gold occasionally glinting among the dross. It has in fact been a year very much like any other. And, as usual, as one looks ahead there appears so much more promise for the future; promise, alas, too seldom fulfilled. However, I still find it well worthwhile to sit through a dozen bad, indifferent or normal-standard movies for the sake of the good and even great ones which space them out and give renewed hope for the future. And the cinema, with hope, faith and charity, has a great future so let's hope that those within the industry don't sell it short by either voice or deed.

The films which took the most money at the box-office in the United States and Canada during 1976 were:

1. *Jaws*
2. *One Flew Over the Cuckoo's Nest*
3. *All the President's Men*
4. *The Omen*
5. *Bad News Bears*
6. *Silent Movie*
7. *The Battle of Midway*
8. *Dog Day Afternoon*
9. *Murder By Death*
10. *Blazing Saddles*

In Sweden:

1. *Jaws*
2. *One Flew Over the Cuckoo's Nest*
3. *Let the Prisoner Loose*
4. *A Lover and his Lass*
5. *The Man on the Roof*
6. *Buddies*
7. *Godfather 2*
8. *Flaaklypa Grand Prix* (Norwegian)
9. *Sven Klang's Quintet*
10. *Sign of Twins* (Danish)

*(Swedish)

In Italy:

1. *Jaws*
2. *One Flew Over the Cuckoo's Nest*
3. *Three Days of the Condor*
4. *1900 Part 1*
5. *Di Chei Segno Sei?*
6. *Godfather II*
7. *L'Anatra All'arancia*
8. *Taxi Driver*
9. *Bluff*
10. *Salon Kitty*

*(Italian)

In France:

1. *Jaws*
2. *A Nous Les Petites Anglaises*
3. *L'Aile Ou La Cuisse*
4. *One Flew Over the Cuckoo's Nest*
5. *Un Eléphant Ça Trompe*
6. *Dr Françoise Gailland*
7. *Barry Lyndon*
8. *Le Corps de Mon Ennemi*
9. *Corps Après Moi . . .*
10. *Police Python 357*

(*French)

As a kind of footnote to this Introduction I would like once again to express my thanks – and some years I regret to say I have forgotten the courtesy – to the various film companies who for the past thirty-four annuals have so unfailingly assisted me in every possible way. Without their co-operation and help there never could have been, nor would now be a *Film Review* annual! Obviously my warmest feelings are towards the several publicity directors who for all or nearly all those years have given me unfailing service, but equally warm thanks to many others, more lately on the scene but always helpful, providing me with everything I have asked for.

In any achievement record of the period that of Alfred Hitchcock should be underlined. In his seventy-seventh year, his fifty-third film *Family Plot* turned out to be one of his best; a deftly plotted thriller with plenty of typical Hitchcock comedy touches and oblique references to past successes. And below he made his usual witty brief appearance in his movie, on this occasion remaining in the shadows!

Another 1976 achievement was that of John Wayne, who in his seventieth year gave one of the finest performances of his career in *The Shootist*, playing a gun-fighter who is suddenly told that he has cancer and only a few weeks to live. Perhaps because it was so reminiscent of his own – won – fight against the disease it was certainly a far more subtle, deeper and moving characterisation than that normally given by Big John.

At the other end of the age scale, the 1976–77 period was something of a triumph for sixteen-year-old Jodie Foster, who came up with three remarkably mature and critically commended performances in *Taxi Driver*, *The Little Girl Who Lives Down the Lane* and *Bugsy Malone*.

With considerably fewer new films on offer, the cinema during the 1976–77 release period turned to revivals of old classics and old successes. These included MGM's spectacular $15,000,000 1959 re-make of *Ben Hur* (with the famous chariot race spectacle), Walt Disney's *Bambi* and Chaplin's *Monsieur Verdoux* (though the last appears to have something less than the anticipated wide release success).

The Releases of the Year in Pictures

The films illustrated in this section are those from England, America, Canada and Australia (those from mainland Europe and other countries will be found in the following section, 'The Continental Film') which have had a general (or circuit) or floating release at any time between the beginning of July 1976 and the end of June 1977.
You will find more detailed information about the films illustrated in 'The Releases of the Year in Detail' in between pages 124 and 147.

A few years back Merian Cooper, one of the three men behind the original, 1933, *King Kong*, having said he made the film for less than half-a-million dollars, estimated that to re-make the movie would cost all of seven million dollars! And he wasn't so far out either, as producer Dino de Laurentiis found when he made the new version of this classic old monster movie for 1977 release. Following the old film pretty faithfully in outline, the new *King Kong* (EMI) was spectacular, thrilling and technically as brilliant as its predecessor, then, in 1933, far in advance of its time. Jessica Lange was the pretty new beauty taming the beast, standing up well to the competition offered by Fay Wray in the same part in the original film.

Bruce Dern wakes Barbara Harris in Alfred Hitchcock's *Family Plot* (CIC). Made in his seventy-seventh year, this thriller about two couples, one who make kidnapping their business and the other who are searching for a missing heir, was one of Hitchcock's best; a deft mixture of thrills and chortles, with many a witty reference to past successes and always technically superb.

On novelty value alone, *Bugsy Malone* (Fox–Rank) deserves credit as being one of the outstanding films of its year. Taking the classic old gangster formula of the 1920–30s, it deleted all the violence, added a series of musical numbers and then handed the whole thing over to a cast of children to interpret. A difficult recipe, but one which in the hands of director-writer Alan Parker became a real fun film. In scene 1, Fat Sam (John Cassisi) gives instructions to girl gang member Tallulah (Jodie Foster). In scene 2 the opposition, led by Dandy Dan (Martin Lev, centre), prepare to do battle with their custard pies.

Fred Astaire and Judy Garland in their classic 'Couple of Swells' number from the 1948 musical *Easter Parade*, one of the extracts from famous MGM 'Golden Age' movies packaged in *That's Entertainment, Part 2* (MGM/EMI), which proved equally, if not actually, more entertaining than the previously released Part 1.

Made a year or so back, but only reaching Britain in late 1976 (and then getting a ridiculously restricted release) Orson Welles's masterly documentary *F for Fake* (Essential Cinema) revealed him again as the great magician of the cinema which he is, and made one aware how sadly wasted is his vast talent. Basically about master painter-forger Elmyr de Hory and his biographer Clifford Irving (himself the famous forger of Howard Hughes's autobiography) the film wittily digressed to examine the whole relationship of deception, truth, art and life.

Robin and Marian (Rastar–Columbia) – Sean Connery and Audrey Hepburn – presented a new-look version of the old Robin Hood legend, making Robin an ageing outlaw who is getting past the sort of larks one reads about in the usual stories about him. And Marian is shown as a Sister of Mercy who kills her old love out of kindness! And it was all something of a new and more serious departure for director Richard Lester. Both the stars, by the way, gave performances superior to their material. Left: Robin with his faithful follower Little John (Nicol Williamson).

Although superior of script, authentic in background and well served by the acting, it is doubtful if Scotia-Barber's Italian-made, English-speaking biblical effort *Moses* had the sort of success at the box-office that its producers may have hoped for! Burt Lancaster played the man called by God to lead the Children of Israel into the Promised Land.

Whatever other criticism one may level against Stanley Kubrick's very long and lavish epic *Barry Lyndon* (Warner), there was no question about the beauty of the film, which often looked like classical picture-landscapes brought to life, as this Thackeray story about a young Irish lad who climbs and falls unrolled. A multi-million, three-hour period piece, the film had a very good critical reception on the whole, though amid all the acclaim there were some sour notes, particularly about over-length and slow pace. Ryan O'Neal (boating with Marisa Berenson) played anti-hero Barry.

Chief Dan George beats *The Outlaw Josey Wales* (Malpaso–Warner) to the draw in an earlier scene from this fascinating Western in which, as well as directing, Clint Eastwood played the title-role of a farmer who turns into a cold killer when at the outbreak of the American Civil War his wife and child are callously murdered and his home burnt down.

John Wayne gave one of the finest performances of his career in *The Shootist* (Paramount–CIC), a sort of chamber Western about an ace gunslinger and his last days – he's dying of cancer – in Carson City. Perhaps because he himself has suffered from the disease (but won through at the cost of a lung) Big John's performance seemed like a valediction. In the background of this scene, Lauren Bacall, as the rooming house keeper, who brings him friendly consolation in his last days.

18

Arthur Penn's *The Missouri Breaks* (United Artists) had plenty of classic Western ingredients in the story of a horse-ranch owner who brings in a hired killer – 'The Regulator' – when all else fails to stop the thefts from his herd by an outlaw gang (led by Jack Nicholson) which also murders his foreman: a situation complicated by the rancher's daughter (Kathleen Lloyd) falling in love with the outlaw leader! By far the most remarkable point about the movie was Marlon Brando's eccentric and completely out of context performance as 'The Regulator' (below).

Another classical Western situation in the Fox film *The Last Hard Men*, with Charlton Heston as the 'retired' lawman forced to strap his pistols on again when he hears that a killer he sent to jail some years back has broken out and is on the way to kill him. Directed by Andrew McLaglen, this superior sagebrusher was beautifully photographed, had magnificent backgrounds, and a kind of Greek tragedy atmosphere. Villain was James Coburn (below), with fellow escapee Jorge Rivero.

One of the busiest husband and wife star teams (they've now made eleven films together), Charles Bronson and Jill Ireland played lovers in Mike Frankovich's comedy Western *From Noon Till Three* (UA). Having created a legend of their passion, the pretty widow refuses to kill it, when her lover turns up again to prove he isn't, as everyone thought, dead, and kills herself in order to keep the legend unsullied! And all good clean fun it was, too.

The particularly fascinating facet of UA's *Trackdown* – another of these somewhat disturbing movies with a motif of the private citizen taking things into his own hands when the forces of law and order seem unable, or unwilling, to right wrongs – was the appearance in the hero's role of Robert Mitchum's son Jim, so like his dad it was almost uncanny! Helping him to fight the villains, Erik Estrada.

But easily the funniest sagebrusher of them all was MGM–CIC's *Hollywood Cowboy*, which convincingly created the atmosphere of those wonderful old 'B' Westerns of the 30s. Against this background Jeff Bridges gave a good performance as the Iowan farm boy, smitten with the movies, who comes to Hollywood and by lucky chance soon finds himself a cowboy star of the period.

Somewhat less successful was Robert Altman's *Buffalo Bill and the Indians or Sitting Bull's History Lesson* (EMI), a highly stylised affair in which, set against the background of the show which Cody starred in during his somewhat less active, later years, told the story of the ex-buffalo hunter's devious dealings with his old foe Chief Sitting Bull. And within this framework Altman attempted to portray something of America's reprehensible treatment of her Indians.

Never was there a more convoluted (or crazy) detective plot than that dreamed up by Neil Simon for Columbia's *Murder by Death*, in which an eccentric millionaire invites five of the world's most famous (fictional) detectives to solve a murder during a weekend in his old and creepy mansion. The fatal five are Charlie Chan (Peter Sellers), Hercule Poirot (James Coco), Miss Marples (Elsa Lanchester), Sam Spade (Peter Falk) and Nick Charles and Nora (David Niven and Maggie Smith). Above: Poirot, Chan and Spade discuss theories! And all very amusing it was, too.

Twenty-eighth in record-breaking line, *Carry On England* (Rank) may not have been the funniest of the series but it still carried plenty of broad and true-blue British humour in a story about a mixed-sex R.A. battery during the war, and the efforts of newly posted Captain Kenneth Connor to bring more order and less larking to the camp – but finds the more than ample proportions of Diane Langton complicating his task!

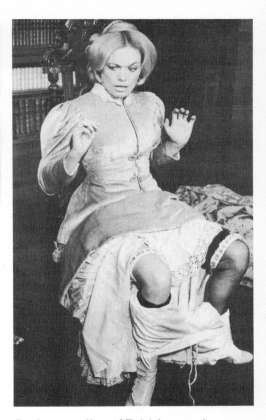

Something of a comedy novelty film (made 1966 but only now seen in Britain), *What's Up Tiger Lily* (Focus Films) was a typical Japanese action thriller about spies, dubbed with Woody Allen's idea of suitable English dialogue, which his fans found highly hilarious, some others less so.

Third of the new British comedy 'Confessions' series of films *The Confessions of a Driving Instructor* (Columbia) again featured the young hero (Robert Askwith) whose – astonishing! – appeal to the fair sex leads to all sorts of complications in his jobs, in this case spending a great deal of his time trying to prevent his clients from driving him into their beds! All basic British comedy stuff – and highly successful at the box-office, it appears.

More of the same kind of thing was to be found in Salon's *Adventures of a Taxi Driver*, with Barry Evans as the young cabbie who spends most of his time avoiding the amorous advances of his clients. And, again, it appears to have proved a successful money-maker if nothing else.

In the same line of British comedy country was EMI's *Keep It Up Downstairs* – though this young lady seems to be taking it down upstairs!

Though denied, the reference in the title of Michael Winner's *Won Ton Ton, the Dog who Saved Hollywood* (Paramount–CIC) was obvious. Always amusing, and often very funny indeed, this comedy about film-making in Hollywood in the 20s offered an incidental 'spot the stars' exercise, for many of them, retired, forgotten and otherwise absent from the screen for many years, made fleeting appearances. As the girl who reaches stardom through the dog, Madeline Kahn gave a delightful performance; while Art Carney (centre) played the director, Bruce Dern (right) with Phil Silvers in the background, the opportunist and Gloria de Haven (left) the star.

Another attempt to recapture Hollywood's past was in *W. C. Fields and Me* (Universal–CIC) in which while failing to catch anything like all the full inimitable personality of the old comic, Rod Steiger did present a very passable interpretation of him, warts and all! The film was based on a book by Carlotta Monti, who actually shared the last days of the bibulous W.C.

Inventor professor Peter Cushing and financier/assistant Doug McClure concentrate on the controls of their 'Iron Mole' as it burrows its way towards the fantastic world *At the Earth's Core* (British Lion), where they find some real odd beasties, pretty girls and high adventure. Grand cinematic hokum based on the book by Edgar Rice Burroughs.

Remember *Westworld*, that film about a pleasure resort serviced by robots which was smashed up in their final uprising? Well, it comes back to the screen, rebuilt and re-roboted (with Phase Two automatons) in *Futureworld* (Brent Walker), an amusingly daft story about yet another scientist planning a world take-over from behind the front offered by the resort. Luckily he's rumbled by a couple of nosey reporters, one of them (Blythe Danner) shown dallying with the only old, Phase One, robot left in action (Yul Brynner).

Nearly every film that attempts to take a look into the future finds it, to say the least, a forbidding prospect! No exception was *Logan's Run* (MGM–CIC), which presented twenty-third century life as being forcibly terminated on one's thirtieth birthday, when the unfortunates reaching that advanced age are 'exploded' on the 'carousel'! It is left to cop Michael York to venture outside the pleasure-dome living space and find old man Peter Ustinov and enlightenment!

Brutal rape and its consequences were the motivation of Paramount–CIC's release *Lipstick*, in which newcomer Margaux Hemingway gave an impressive performance as the victim. And playing the girl's kid sister, Margaux's real sister Mariel was also good.

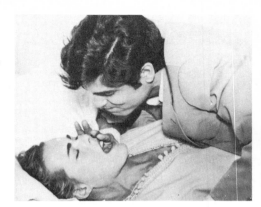

You'd have to be a pretty intuitive character, if at first seeing you'd be able to sort out all the confusing intricacies of the plot of *Len Deighton's Spy Story* (Gala), in which dour Michael Petrovitch (facing one of the baddies – Nigel Plaskitt) played a nuclear sub. officer who becomes involved with opposing spy factions as they play their 'War Games'!

Along genuine Hitchcock lines, Columbia's *Obsession* was a real puzzler as it related the story of a man whose wife and daughter are killed in a ransom plot that goes sour and is faced some fifteen years later with what appears to be a complete replica of the situation! A good script, genuine thrills (enough to make one happily overlook all the obvious improbabilities), sure direction (by Brian de Palma) and neat performances (Cliff Robertson and Genevieve Bujold) added up to one of the best thrillers of the period.

Michael Klinger believes in giving the moviegoers value for money, and so far his policy has paid off in quite a big way as it did again in his Hemdale release *Shout at the Devil*, a rumbustious adventure melodrama – supposedly based on truth – set in Africa during the First World War, when a fine young Britisher (Roger Moore) and a roistering Irish adventurer (Lee Marvin) declare their own personal war on the local sadistic German Commissioner (Barbara Perkins is the girl sheltering in Moore's protective arm). Below: one of the many spectacular scenes in the film.

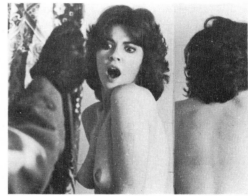

Quite as, if indeed not more unlikely was Edward Dmytryk's exciting, brutal thriller *The Human Factor* (Rank) in which computer expert John Mills (foreground) uses his machine to help his pal (George Kennedy) take revenge on those responsible for the apparently motiveless killing of the latter's wife and family.

Also in the Chamber of Horrors collection, Pete Walker's hardly less horrifying (in part) *Schizo* (Warner), in which only at the end do we learn (if we haven't guessed quite a while previously) the true identity of the split-personality killer.

Somewhat understandably annoyed, Kris Kristofferson – as *The Sailor who Fell from Grace with the Sea* (Avco–Embassy–Fox) – and Sarah Miles, his mistress, discover that her small son has been entertaining himself by watching them love-making through a hole in the wall. From a Japanese original, it was not a completely happy blend of love and horror which ends in ritual murder by a gang of schoolboys led by a little monster.

Aces High (EMI) took the classic old R. C. Sherriff First World War story *Journey's End*, transferred it from the Army to the R.F.C. – and did a remarkably good job of it. Movingly and excitingly it told the story of the young replacement pilots whose average life at this crisis time on the Western Front was about two weeks! Here the sage old commander (Christopher Plummer) listens to the exchanges between youngster Peter Firth (a most commendable performance) and his young veteran flight leader Malcolm McDowell. And the aerial dog-fights between the old biplanes were magnificently organised and flown.

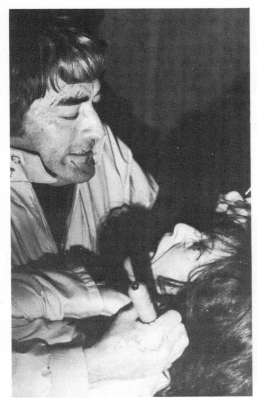

Not seen either side of the cameras for some time, Ida Lupino turned up to fight – with William Shatner – the devils in Fox–Rank's spine-chiller *The Devil's Rain*, a rather confused affair which presented a heavily disguised Ernest Borgnine (left) as the leader of the Satanic sect.

Fox's English-made *The Omen*, one of the better post-'Exorcist' efforts, was all the more compelling for the performances of its stars; Gregory Peck as the American Ambassador caught up in some devilish business – here he stabs his housekeeper, Billie Whitelaw, with the kitchen fork! – and Lee Remick as his wife.

An increasing number of impressive films are now coming out of Australia and one of the most impressive this session was Warner's *Sunday Too Far Away*, which brought to vivid and convincing life the way of the sheep-shearers in the dry and isolated outback some twenty years ago. Wonderfully captured atmosphere and remarkably good performances all helped towards making this one of the most sadly underrated movies of the year.

Another quite outstanding Australian effort was Peter Weir's (he directed that other very interesting movie *The Cars That Ate Paris*) *Picnic at Hanging Rock* (GTO) which was set in the beginning of the twentieth century and told a chilling story of some teachers and schoolgirls who went for a picnic at the beauty spot of the title, a picnic from which some of them never returned. Here one of those that did return (Margaret Nelson) is quizzed by a mistress (Helen Morse) and a policeman (Whyn Roberts).

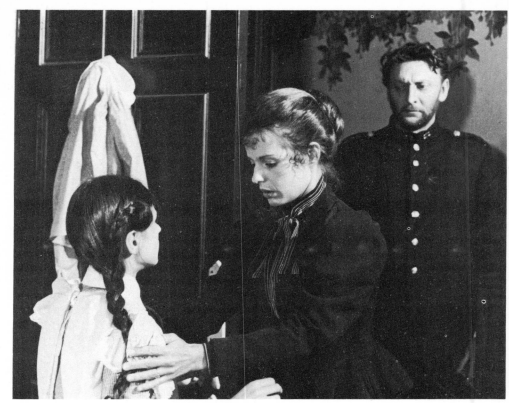

Though it did do good business at the box-office EMI's *Mandingo* was neither a pleasant nor a particularly well-made movie, with its brutal hot-house Deep South atmosphere of degradation. But the sequel *Drum* was even less well-made and certainly had a less salubrious story of violence, sex and sadism against the background of all the most horrifying facets of slavery. Warren Oates and Isela Vega were among those unhappily involved.

Shades of *Madame Butterfly* – yes, they were easily observable in EMI's *Seven Nights in Japan*, a rather weak little confection about a handsome young Prince – George, played by a rather wan-looking Michael York – and a pretty little commoner (a Japanese bus conductress, played by genuinely pretty little Hidemi Aoki) who meet, love and part in the sad old way. . . . Only Puccini's music was missing!

The terrible choice to be made by *Lifeguard* Rick (Sam Elliott – extreme right) in the Paramount–CIC film of that title was whether, though now nearing the elderly mid-thirties, he should stay on the sunny Californian beaches with the girls crying to share his bed and (surf)board, or wave a sad farewell to this good life and go for the money – and wealthy widow who woos him, too – in the city. And anyone should be able to guess the answer to that one! Anyway, a silly story but first-class atmosphere and pleasant performances.

31

If several films were critically underrated during the year, one that seemed the reverse, to be overrated, was the Cannes Festival Prize-winner *Taxi Driver*, a particularly violent, bloody and unpleasant story about a psychotic who develops a terrible hatred for the sleazier characters of the district of New York in which he plies for hire, and eventually guns down three of them – one quite innocent – for which episode he becomes something of a hero! Martin Scorsese (psychedelically) directed; and Robert De Niro was certainly impressive as the nutty thug – shown enjoying himself! Obviously encouraged by the success of this Scorsese, Gate released for the first time this side of the Atlantic a much earlier (1969) film of his called *Who's That Knocking at my Door*, which might have been a sketch for some of his later successes. Harvey Keitel was the leading player in this.

The familiar, stony face of Charles Bronson, looking out from his bullet-splattered car in Columbia–Warner's *St Ives* as he doggedly follows the clues to the mysteriously stolen ledgers which he has been employed to recover.

Apart from being more serious in story and theme than most Disney films, *Escape from the Dark* was sadly noteworthy in being the last film in which Alastair Sim appeared, as the coalmine owner who brings a happy ending to this story of a trio of youngsters who, when the local pit is mechanised, carry through a plot to rescue the otherwise condemned pit ponies. In the first scene old-timer Joe Gladwin agrees to help the expedition's leader, Andrew Harrison, while in the second Chloe Franks, as the second of the children, waits with mother (Prunella Scales) after the warning has been sounded, announcing an underground disaster.

More familiar Disney comedy, *No Deposit, No Return* was all about two youngsters who are kidnapped when on the way to visit their grandfather. Here detectives Herschel Bernardi and Charlie Martin Smith come to the end of the road . . .

One of the best, funniest comedies of the year, Paramount–CIC's *The Big Bus* told the story of the eventful trip of the first nuclear-powered bus, scheduled to run non-stop between New York and Denver but halted, balanced over a ravine, and otherwise bombed and be-devilled *en route*. With its satirical references to other movies – in particular the air disaster thriller – it was a judicious mixture of laughs and chills. And as the inventor's daughter, in charge of the trip, Stockard Channing was delicious!

Carol White and Veronica Anderson as the two girls who act out the odd fantasies of the rich young man they live with in James B. Harris's (he wrote, directed and produced) *Some Call It Loving* (Pleasant Pastures), a real weirdie of a film which had some pretence of poetry (but also plenty of plain pretentiousness) as it told a tale about a Sleeping Beauty who is temporarily awakened but eventually sent back to her – drugged – sleep.

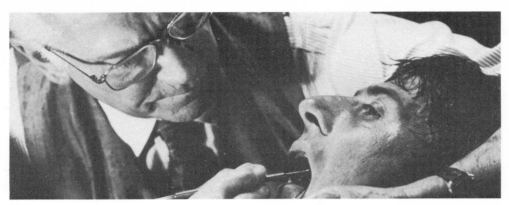

Though horribly confusing in its early stages, John Schlesinger's *Marathon Man* (Paramount–CIC) eventually settled down into a finely-acted thriller about a Nazi criminal who after years of hiding in South America comes to New York to pick up his ill-gotten gains, stored in a bank there. Lots of agents and double-agents, murders and chases – with an innocent athletic student brother of one of the agents (Dustin Hoffman), here getting the treatment – and, later, returning it – from the Nazi (Laurence Olivier), finding his training standing him in good stead when mistakenly suspected of having information about the case.

Nothing quite like *The Scarlet Buccaneer* (Universal–CIC) has been seen on the screen in years: a roistering, hokumish tale of a brave pirate (happy Robert Shaw) defeating the evil governor and – don't let this scene fool you – winning the heart and hand of lovely, if militant, Genevieve Bujold in Jamaica. Above: one of the more spectacular stunts in the movie.

Two Up and One to Go! That's the story of the rush – race in fact – to present the film reconstruction of the bold and exciting raid on Entebbe airport in Uganda by Israeli commandos in the summer of '76 in order to rescue a plane load of their hijacked nationals held under joint Arab and Amin guard. Warner's *Victory At Entebbe* won by a head from Hemdale's *Raid On Entebbe* in terms of time, but in fact the latter was the better film of the two in the sense that it was the somewhat more convincing. But both films showed little visual evidence of the remarkable speed of their production, having been planned, written and completed within a period of six months. *Victory* (*a*) starred Burt Lancaster as the Israeli War Minister and Anthony Hopkins played the prime Minister – seen putting their respective points of view at a cabinet meeting – and in *Raid* Peter Finch (*b*) in his last performance played the latter role. The airport scene from *Raid* (*c*) shows the actual rescue taking place. The 'one to go' is a third film on the subject, titled *Operation Thunderbolt*, made with very close co-operation of the Israeli government and at this point still unreleased.

Pretty but unlikely candidate Linda Lovelace in the quite crazy comedy *Linda Lovelace for President* (New Realm) which had as a bonus plenty of sex and nudity as it gained its fun from guying the whole business of the American Presidential elections.

The second to last performance of Peter Finch, prior to his death (see 'In Memoriam' section), was in the highly acclaimed and Oscar-winning Paddy Chayefsky MGM–UA release *Network*. In this bitingly satirical comment on American television Finch played a kind of TV Messiah who, having withdrawn his threat to kill himself on his last programme when as a result his 'ratings' rise dramatically and he is reinstated, finally bites the hand that feeds him too often and is assassinated 'on camera' by his bosses. Three other good performances in the film came from (Studio Boss) Robert Duvall, (power-hungry programmer) Faye Dunaway and (news department head) William Holden.

That man of screen violence Sam Peckinpah turned to the violence of war for his EMI release *Cross of Iron*, a British–German co-production set on the Eastern front and considerably concerned with the feud between the veteran German Sergeant Steiner (James Coburn, far right) and the ruthless, distinction-seeking Captain Stransky (Maximilian Schell, seen left with the Colonel, James Mason, centre, and the cynical Captain Kiesel, David Warner).

Based on the novel by Jack Higgins, ITC–CIC's *The Eagle has Landed* was an original war thriller about a German plot to kidnap Sir Winston Churchill during his weekend stay with friends in the country. Michael Caine played the leader of the Nazi commando squad who, when the local vicar (John Standing) stumbles on the true identity of the 'Polish' visitors, rounds up the local community and locks them in the church. Above: Jenny Agutter as the local girl who develops an 'instant' crush on the Irish spy sent to prepare the way for the German parachutists.

Cop Captain Charlton Heston takes a close-circuit television look at the crazy sniper who has installed himself in an almost impregnable tower of a Los Angeles sports stadium with the idea of assassinating the visiting US President but, when the President is warned and doesn't turn up, starts to shoot casually into the terrified crowd. In CIC's exciting and bloody thriller *Two-Minute Warning*.

Worried Energy Minister, Ian Bannen, discovers the body of his murdered girlfriend and his double-crossing Public Relations Officer, Barry Foster, promises he'll do a cover-up (having previously organised the girl's death so that he can get the Minister into his hands and force him into changing his political attitude to the oil lobby which is trying to stop a bill being passed to keep up prices). From EMI's tough, rough detection thriller with a political background, *Sweeney*.

The remarkable young Jodie Foster with Martin Sheen as the young cripple who becomes her lover in the Rank release *The Little Girl who Lives Down the Lane*, an adaptation of the Laird Koenig thriller about a little girl who lives alone in a house by the sea and uses an imaginary father to keep her visitors from becoming too inquisitive and finding the body in the cellar!

Charles Manson and shaven girl followers in dock during the trial of the members of this hippy community who, charged with several killings, admitted thirty-five. Hemdale's *Helter Skelter* proved to be a remarkably factual and careful reconstruction of the events that followed the murder of film-star Sharon Tate and some of her guests in Hollywood in 1969. As the evil Manson, Steve Railsback gave a remarkably magnetic performance.

'Dirty Harry' (the nickname for tough New York cop Harry Callahan, played by Clint Eastwood) returned to the screen in Columbia–Warner's crime thriller *The Enforcer*. Suspended because of the strong-arm methods he uses against the local villains, Harry persists in his fight in a private capacity and comes back into official favour when he rescues the kidnapped Mayor – though only at the cost of the life of his woman cop partner.

William Elliot as the coloured half of a team of Los Angeles Narcotics Bureau Cops who bring the dope-pushers to justice in Scotia–Barber's *Hang Up*.

In Fox's Canadian crime-thriller *Breaking Point* Lieutenant Robert Culp promises judo expert Bo Svenson and wife Linda Sorenson protection from the local Mafia, who are determined to have revenge on the man who has testified against them. Incidentally it proves an empty promise and in the end Mr Svenson is forced into taking the law, and war, into his own hands.

It didn't take much imagination to see Hemdale's *Abduction* as a fiction-veneered account of the Patty Hearst abduction case, with Judith-Marie Bergan as a young student, who, held prisoner by a gang of black and white revolutionaries, gradually becomes involved with, and is soon helping, her captors in their crimes.

There were two extremely good performances in UA's bloody though well-made piece of celluloid Grand Guignol, *Carrie*. The first was from Sissy Spacek (far left, with William Katt in the scene of their crowning as King and Queen of the Ball, a moment of joy that is followed by a deluge of blood and horror) as the girl with strange powers who creates a holocaust, and the second was from Piper Laurie (left) as her fanatical mother who gets her come-uppance when the local cutlery at the command of Carrie flies through the air, and into her.

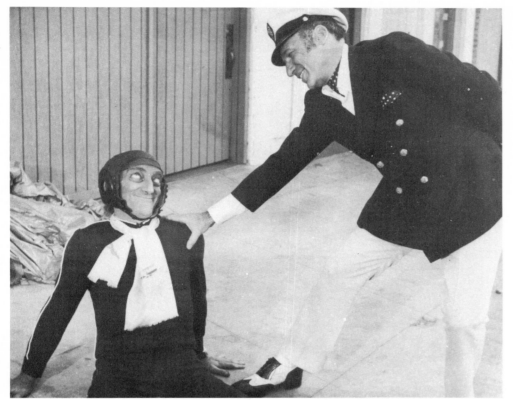

The novelty about Mel Brooks' Fox film *Silent Movie* was that in fact it had only one word of dialogue along its entire length, the De Gaullist 'No!' But this generally affectionate attempt to recapture the rapture of the old silent comedies was never quite on, although there were some good visual gags along the way. Mel Brooks himself played the director whose idea of making a modern silent movie saves his boss's job and the studio from a takeover; Marty Feldman (left) played one of his eccentric companions.

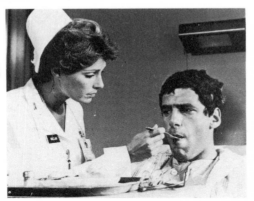

Though increasingly amusing towards the end, the Scotia–Barber comedy *C.A.S.H.* was never likely to win the success of its predecessor *M.A.S.H.* Elliott Gould played the Army's guinea-pig who after so many experiments with various gases becomes useless to them for the purpose and is discharged – to turn to crime. He uses his specialised knowledge to render a whole town unconscious while he and his pal rob the banks! The girlfriend nurse, by the way, is Jennifer O'Neill.

Sometimes funny, sometimes tasteless, sometimes vulgar, Warner's *The Ritz* had as its central situation that of a normal man taking refuge from his murderously inclined brother-in-law in a hotel which is full of homosexuals. The film has two very good performances, those of Jack Weston and Rita Moreno.

The gay, and not so gay, companions in Fox's comedy-drama *Next Stop Greenwich Village*, which against the background of the 'Village' and its varied inhabitants told the story of a Jewish lad (Lenny Baker, in a beret) and his struggle to become a film actor; this against the wishes of his Momma (Shelley Winters – with husband Mike Kellin, left).

Barry Humphries was one of the contributing comics in Essential's *Pleasure at Her Majesty's*, a straightforward film record of some of the rehearsals and part of the actual show of the special production staged in London in 1976 in aid of Amnesty International. Other funny men taking part included Peter Cook, The Goodies, some of the Monty Python team, and many others.

Gene Wilder and Jill Clayburgh race to safety from a train crash in Chicago's rail terminus in the consistently entertaining Fox comedy-thriller *The Silver Streak* – the film chosen as the 1977 Royal Film Performance attraction.

Homosexuality was increasingly employed as a comedy motif last year, one such film being CIC's *Norman . . . Is That You?* an adaptation of a New York stage comedy (which apparently was considerably less than a major hit). Red Foxx played the old negro (with statuesque Tamara Dobson) who comes to town and finds to his horror that his son is living with a white man.

Visiting his former chief Inspector boss (Herbert Lom) on the eve of his release from a mental asylum, his successor, Chief Inspector Clouseau (Peter Sellers), soon achieves a violent relapse for his old enemy in UA's third Pink Panther comedy *The Pink Panther Strikes Again*, in which the bumbling, accident-prone French detective has only his incredible luck to save him from deserved disgrace!

That old plot about the couple who divorce but find they can't live without each other was dusted off and used for Scotia–Barber's mild little comedy *I Will, I Will . . . For Now*, in which Elliott Gould and Diane Keaton illustrated the humours of sexual incompatibility.

There was a great hoo-haa about Woody Allen playing his first 'straight' role in Columbia's *The Front* but in fact he played the part in his usual comedy style, adding a rather incongruous note to what was basically a dramatic story about an unpleasant chapter in American political history, the period when Senator McCarthy instituted his ('Red') witch-hunts in the late 40s and early 50s and caused so many of Hollywood's best talents to be blacklisted and refused work.

Baseball as a background to or motivation of a film has never been previously successful (in GB) and CIC's rather jolly little comedy *The Bingo Long Travelling All-Stars and Motor Kings* proved to be no exception, though it included in the cast two popular coloured stars in Billy Dee Williams and James Earl Jones.

Then along came CIC's *The Bad News Bears* to prove that all rules have exceptions. For this delightful little comedy about a second-rate kids' baseball team taken in hand by a boozey coach (Walter Matthau at his best) and with the help of a juvenile delinquent and a gifted girl (Tatum O'Neal) made into top-of-the-league material, was a, deservedly, great success.

Walt Disney's *Treasure of Matecumbe* provided one of the ever-lessening number of U-certificated family films of the period, a highly entertaining story of two boys and their search for hidden treasure among the Florida Keys about a hundred years ago.

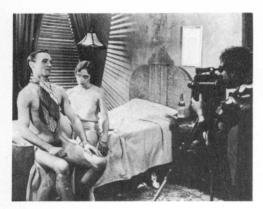

The 'Boy Wonder' (Richard Dreyfuss) shoots a scene from one of his blue movies in UA's *Inserts*, his stars being Jessica Harper and Stephen Davies. A story about an alcoholic former silent director of great promise who now pays the rent by doing this kind of work for a gangster producer, *Inserts* attempted to be a sex film with significance, and at times promised that it could be. But in the end that promise was never quite realised.

Brent Walker's *Emily* followed closely the *Emmanuelle* tradition by giving what was basically just another sex film some top standard production qualities. This particular piece of (British) 'posh porn' illustrated the sexual education of the young lady of the title, who at one point finds out that her mother (Sarah Brackett) is a high-class tart. The gentleman 'customer' is Victor Spinetti.

The only really good thing in CIC's *The Incredible Sarah*, a biographical picture of Sarah Bernhardt, was Glenda Jackson's memorable performance in the title role. So far the film has had only a very limited release and is now, almost certainly it seems, unlikely to have a much wider one.

Following up the success of the 1971 film *A Man Called Horse*, UA came up with a 1976 sequel, *The Return of a Man Called Horse*, in which British milord Richard Harris returns to the Indian tribe which made him first a slave and then a brave, to help them regain the lands from which they have been driven by white men villains. Left: Gale Sondergaard – and some old-timers may recall her in very different roles!

Henry Fonda, as the old-timer gunman who wants to put his feet up with his guns, shows admirer Terence Hill that he still has his 'shooting eye' in this scene from *My Name is Nobody*, Sergio Leone's witty send-up of his own particular kind of Western, the mixture of bloody brutality, fine photography and style which he introduced to the screen with the first of his 'Man With No Name' films. Leone produced; the director here was Tonino Valerii.

CIC's *Mustang Country* may not have been an outstanding Western but it was extremely pleasant to see in it old-timer Joel McCrea back in the saddle again in a quiet story about a rancher who's determined to win the reward offered for the capture of a particularly fine wild mustang.

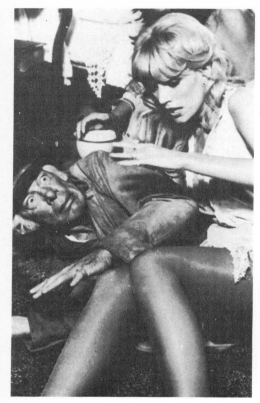

James Coburn was the commentator and participant in EMI's *White Rock*, the somewhat unusual film of the 1976 Winter Olympics, which had a special musical content provided by Rick Wakeman.

Erna May lets it rip in Fair Enterprises's *Moon Over the Alley*, a brave and interesting, if modest, black-and-white attempt to show several layers of life in Notting Hill. And the songs and musical background were provided by Galt Macdermot, possibly best known as the composer of that famous musical show *Hair*.

In the *Cat Ballou* tradition but well below the high standard of that comedy-Western classic, Brent Walker's *The Great Scout And Cathouse Thursday* was a broad and bawdy comedy with Lee Marvin as the Scout and newcomer Kay Lenz as the little whorehouse girl who determinedly adopts him and installs herself as his personal camp follower.

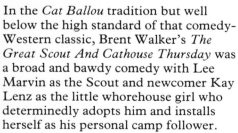

Glenda Jackson in the title-role, and Timothy West as Judge Brack, in Scotia–Barber's *Hedda*, the film of the Henrik Ibsen stage classic in which Miss Jackson has previously enjoyed a successful tour of British theatres.

Bowing to Muslim pressure, the producers of 'Mohammad – Messenger of God' changed the title to *The Message* for the London première in both English and Arabic versions; but that didn't stop a protest which ended in murder and mayhem during the American showings of the movie, which was a most decorous and sincere, slow and spectacular story of the triumph of Mohammad, whose seventh-century preaching was to eventually result in some 700 million followers all over the world. With the Prophet never shown, Anthony Quinn played Hamza, one of his more fervent supporters. Above Johnny Sekka, as Bilal, reaches the top of Mecca's Kaaba in order to call the faithful to their prayers.

Brought into this year's releases under the convenient umbrella of 'Floating Releases', Fox's *Man Friday* has in fact had singularly few showings since its original short London run early in 1976. Up-ending Defoe's *Robinson Crusoe* story, it had Peter O'Toole as the weak white man who is eventually made the servant of the strong black man (Richard Roundtree), and it was all far too socially conscious to be wildly popular.

Bear on the rampage in Columbia's *Grizzly*, the story of a rogue bear who creates havoc in an American wild-life park before being finally tracked down and killed – from a helicopter.

To be commended for its brave attempt to be original on a small budget, Gala's *Eclipse* was made by two young men, Simon Perry (director-writer) and David I. Munro (producer), and was based on a subtle (and somewhat confusing) story about two identical twin brothers with a love–hate relationship that leads to a rather mysterious death. Tom Conti as the survivor (he played both roles) pays a Christmas visit to the deceased's alcoholic wife Gay Hamilton and small son Gavin Wallace, a visit which results in a good deal of tension.

Andy Warhol's contribution to the year's least memorable movies was *Bad*, in this scene from which Carroll Baker yells at her off-set hubbie to the amusement of her electrolysis patient Cyrinda Fox.

The already considerable number of American 'Road' films (films in which the principals involved motor-tramp their chequered ways across America) are always being added to – one of this year's contributions being Warner's *Rafferty and the Gold Dust Twins*, which was a cut above the average in its story of the relationship between three loners as they motor from Las Vegas to the parting of the ways at Tucson. Travellers included Alan Arkin (above) and Sally Kellerman.

L. Q. Jones, Raquel Welch and Bill Cosby attend to the wounded 'Speed' in Peter Yates's Fox film *Mother, Jugs and Speed*, a somewhat unusual story about a private ambulance company and their determination to stay in business in spite of all the attempts to put them out of it!

Warner's *Ode to Billy Joe* was based on the popular American folk-style song of the title about young romance in Mississippi which goes wrong and ends in the suicide of poor Billy! The stars were Robby Benson and Glynnis O'Connor and Bobbie Gentry, who composed the original song, sings it as a background.

Vaguely in the 'American Graffiti' category Columbia's *Drive-In* was the story of some of the local youngsters in a small Texas town, with the local Drive-In cinema the centre of their varied activities.

When Hollywood turns the eye inward it seldom comes up with a completely satisfactory film, and this year saw several examples of this, notably in CIC's screen version of *The Last Tycoon*, the last – and unfinished – F. Scott Fitzgerald novel about a Hollywood mogul (which many have seen as Irving Thalberg) whose impeccable taste eventually brings him into opposition with the 'front office' and the money-bags in New York, who seize the opportunity to sack him as ruthlessly as he in his time of power has summarily sacked others. Director Elia Kazan made it into a solid, somewhat stodgy and slow, if polished, film; starring Robert De Niro (left) as the tycoon (shown with Theresa Russell). Ray Milland and Robert Mitchum (above) played the purseholders.

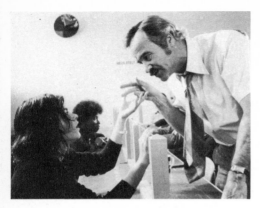

Jack Lemmon played that strange animal (in English eyes) a Bailbondsman in Fox's *Alex and the Gypsy*. He's at first reluctant but finally agrees to post a $30,000 bail for an ex-mistress (Genevieve Bujold) but to make certain she doesn't, as he fears, skip, takes her home and ties her to the bedpost!

Confrontation! Stacy Keach holds a trump card – the mobster Stephen Boyd's (left) daughter – in the final showdown between the alcoholic ex-cop and the man who has master-minded a plot which has included the kidnapping of Keach's ex-wife in this rough, brutal and four-letter word abounding British crime-thriller, *The Squeeze*, released by Warners.

Formerly a girlie/glamour stills photographer, George Harrison Marks branched out Director, Producer and Screenwriter with his own company's British sex comedy *Come Play With Me*. Here he's sandwiched between Nicola Austin and Mr Bergman's shapely daughter Anna.

Another example of Hollywood failing to bring Hollywood satisfactorily to the screen was to be seen in Peter Bogdanovich's *Nickelodeon*, which, quite obviously a work of love, attempted to recapture the joyfully haphazardness of the early days of silent movie-making and though funny in parts, and winningly enthusiastic always, never quite did it. Ryan O'Neal (with megaphone, right) played the accidental director, seen shooting a scene from one of his epics.

A sad-looking Twiggy singing her number in the Rank release *The Butterfly Ball*, which was a not completely successful attempt to make an original film based on a big Rock concert held in the Royal Albert Hall. Among the additional footage was a cartoon sequence from the Halas and Batchelor studios.

Roger Corman's UA release *Jackson County Jail* was yet another of these disturbing films which present the American provincial police as stupid or vicious or both, making life not only difficult but dangerous for anyone passing through their territory. In this superior if routine thriller Yvette Mimieux played the unfortunate lady traveller whose car and effects are stolen by a young thug and his girlfriend, is assaulted by the café owner she goes to for assistance, thrown into jail by the local sheriff for not having identity papers and raped by his assistant – whom she kills in self-defence! She then flees with an admitted killer (Tommy Lee Jones, with Sheriff Severn Larden and his deputy John Lawlor) and ends up in a pretty hopeless position as she is caught by the cops after killing her companion!

With the original *Virgin Soldiers* film the big commercial success that it was, a sequel was always on the cards and it turned up as an early 1977 Warner release, *Stand Up Virgin Soldiers*. Robin Askwith (centre) played the National Service soldier serving in Singapore who on the eve of demobilisation is told that, along with his fellow draftees, he'll have to serve a further six months in the Army, during which period his whoring and wooing is suddenly interrupted by a steadying glimpse of the real, shooting war.

A glimpse of the broad kind of humour which was the main ingredient of Terry Gilliam's crazy Columbia comedy *Jabberwocky*, which had something of a Monty Python air, along with echoes of *Alice in Wonderland* and the specialised fun of a Varsity revue. Cast of this medieval – often brutal! – farce included Max Wall as the King (right) with John Le Mesurier.

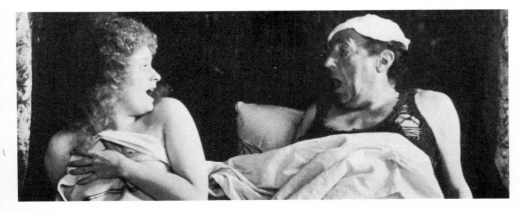

Tony Richardson was obviously hoping to repeat his considerable *Tom Jones* success with his UA release of another Henry Fielding novel, *Joseph Andrews*, which he made into a rather jolly, ribald romp beautifully photographed and stylishly framed. Michael Hordern played the parson as a cartoon comic sharing his bed with Natalie Ogle.

Michael Winner pulled out all the stops in his contribution to the 'Exorcist' cycle, *The Sentinel*, released by CIC. It was all about a weird old Brooklyn house which turns out to have the gateway to Hell in the attic, guarded by the blind resident Priest – John Carradine (above) with Arthur Kennedy.

Corrie ten Boom (Jeannette Clift, centre) tries to inspire her fellow inmates of Ravensbruck with her faith in GTO's *The Hiding Place*, the story of the ten Boom sisters who are discovered by the Germans to be smuggling Dutch Jews out of the country.

Fiona Richmond, the girl who writes and shows all about sex and whose story of erotic progress was followed in Oppidan's *Hardcore*.

Henry Brandon and the tiger who becomes a friend and inseparable companion in the remarkable Sun Classic film *When the North Wind Blows*, featuring the last of the Siberian tigers.

Bette Davis as one of the victims, and
Lee Montgomery (her grandson) who
just escapes, in UA's *Burnt Offerings*, the
story of a house with a murderous
atmosphere.

Barbara Harris – with 'daughter' Jodie Foster – who gave such a lovely, zany performance in Disney's *Freaky Friday*, a comedy about a mother and daughter magically changing bodies and each finding the other's life not quite what they had imagined it to be.

The impressive crash sequence in Universal–CIC's fine piece of familiar but quite brilliantly staged example of Hollywood hokum at its best, *Airport '77.*

The Continental Film

(You will find more detailed information about the films illustrated in 'The Releases of the Year in Detail' in between page 124 and 147.)

One of the most delightful surprises of the year, in the way of continental importations, was a most impressive comedy satire from Senegal, *Impotence – Xala* (Contemporary) which was made by Ousmane Sembene and based on one of his own novels. In relating the story of a crooked politician who comes unstuck when trying to raise the cash for a third wife, it made a serious comment on the opportunist blacks who when their country is freed take over from the whites. And it was made in a mixture of French and, considerably, the local Wolof tongue.

A left-wing-leaning Greek film, *The Travelling Players* (Artificial Eye Co.) used the story of a band of strolling players and their troubles to illuminate the history of the tumultuous years of Grecian history between 1939 and 1952 – and did it well enough to capture the Critics' Prize at the 1976 Cannes Film Festival. Extremely well directed, it was also enhanced by a remarkable performance from its leading star, Eva Kotamanidou. This scene shows Maria Vassiliou, playing her sister.

Even below his best, Roman Polanski is always fascinating and his somewhat rapidly made *The Tenant* (Paramount–CIC) was illustrative. Returning in this film to his favourite subject of paranoia, but working below his highest standard, he told a story about a timid young man who rents the Paris apartment of a girl who committed suicide by jumping from it – and is gradually driven by his imagination into doing the same thing. He wrote, directed and himself played the leading character (shown with concierge Shelley Winters) and did all with commendable imagination: showing, incidentally, that chills are not necessarily accompanied by revolting bloodiness in the current fashion.

Another memorable thriller, from France, was Robert Enrico's *The Secret* (Contemporary), a completely enthralling mystery about an escapee (Jean-Louis Trintignant) from a strange prison, where he is held for political crimes, who has a secret which he knows will result in his death if his pursuers ever catch up with him. Taking refuge with an artist and his mistress (Philippe Noiret and Marlène Jobert) he creates a growing tension between the trio which finally explodes into tragedy.

Continually reminiscent of *A Man and a Woman* (even to the catchy little theme music) *Cousin Cousine* was one of the best films of the year from any country. The theme: love that can become an entirely overriding force. The story: two cousins meet at a family party and begin a love affair which, increasingly openly displayed, causes ructions within the family. And the comedy, allied to witty observation of human nature, fine performances and general warmth made it a real vintage French movie.

Jacques Rivette's *Celine and Julie go Boating, or Phantom Ladies over Paris* (Contemporary) was one of the most infuriatingly – or endearingly, according to one's taste – 'different' films of the year; a very lengthy, individual, witty and crazily puzzling fantasy, quite impossible to outline, about the two Parisian girls of the title (Julie, left, played by Dominique Labourier and Celine, right, played by Juliet Berto) who by venturing into the 'other world', of their dreams, deny the baddies success with their plan to murder a small child – which they rescue from that 'other' world and bring into this as their final triumph! No matter if one loathed or loved it, it was a brilliant film not easy to forget.

France's extremely literate Eric Rohmer went to Germany to make *The Marquise Von O – Die Marquise Von O* (Gala), his beautifully realised adaptation of a German novel which in its Victorian melodramatic way told the sad story of the seduction, then wooing of the lovely Marquise (Edith Clever) by the Russian Count (Bruno Ganz) who saves her honour and then, perhaps, her life during the Russian invasion of Italy in 1799. Static and stylish, it was one of the year's most distinguished movies.

It is often difficult to see why certain films gain awards but there could be no argument about the movie which won Germany's best film of 1975 prize, Bernhard Sinkel's *Lina Braake* (Cinegate) which contained an outstanding performance by Lina Carstens (see with Fritz Rasp, as her artful old financial advisor) as the eighty-two-year-old who gets her own back on the bank which forces her into an old people's home, and it is all beautifully wrought and dryly amusing.

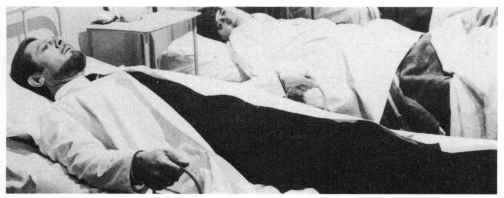

Set in the period that fascism was gaining ground rapidly in Italy, *Down the Ancient Stairs*, or *Per le Antiche Scale*, politics played a part in this story of a handsome doctor whose behaviour in charge of a psychiatric hospital hides his fear that he'll one day end up as one of the patients, like his unfortunate sister. And, when he realises that his medical methods are no good, breaks all his ties, throws off his responsibilities and goes out into an Italy increasingly madly in the grip of Fascism, *circa* 1930.

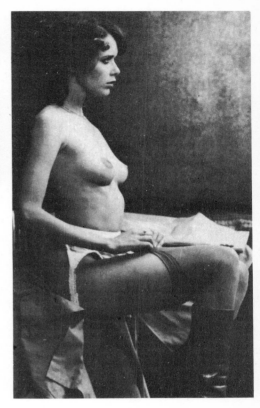

Alfredo, Alfredo (CIC) was a mild little Italian comedy, starring Dustin Hoffman, which was aimed – like so many of its kind before it – at love, marriage and divorce and the traps that lie in the path of the unwary sexual adventurer.

One of the most sexually explicit films from any country, certainly from Italy, *The Last Woman* (Columbia) was noteworthy for its almost constant full frontal nudity (male especially) and its presentation, in more detail than on the screen before, of love play and other sexual intimacies. Behind all this some sort of theme about woman's resentment of being regarded by the male as an object was occasionally apparent. Gérard Depardieu played the somewhat unattractive 'hero' and Ornella Muti played the girl who takes his departed wife's place.

A Fons Rademakers (Dutch) adaptation of the popular Nicholas Freeling novel *Because of the Cats, Rape* (Miracle) was a rather unsuccessful mixture of violence, political drama and detection mystery about a gang of unpleasant, wealthy youngsters persuaded by a degenerate, older character to carry out a campaign of destructive burglary and a gang rape – which leads to their final undoing.

With the original *Emmanuelle* still making box-office records all over the world it was inevitable that *Emmanuelle 2* (Intercontinental) should follow the same sexy lines. And indeed it did, with Sylvia Kristel carrying on with her considerable sexual education against finely photographed, exotic backgrounds and ending up in bed in a lewd trio tangle with her very understanding hubbie and their mutual girlfriend!

A sad and sobby little Italian film, *The Last Snows of Spring* was about a wealthy dad (Bekim Fehmiu) who only realises what his small son (Renato Cesti) means to him when he learns that the little chap has developed an incurable disease.

An impressive Norwegian contribution to the year's cinema was *Wives* (Contemporary), a somewhat long and untidy but shrewd and penetrating study of three young married women (two of them shown, Froydis Armand and Katja Medboe) who suddenly decide to revolt against their domestic responsibilities, but when they do so, find after some rather empty good fun that they really have no constructive ideas about what to do with their apparently rather boring lives.

Ingmar Bergman's *Face to Face* (Paramount–CIC) took on new depths because it was after this film that he himself suffered the same sort of traumatic mental breakdown which is portrayed in the film. Uncinematic in terms of movement, but endlessly fascinating and always offering philosophical food for thought, the film would have in any case been one to long remember for the performance of Liv Ullman as the woman psychiatrist who has to take time off from treating others in order to deal with her own case of mental disorder.

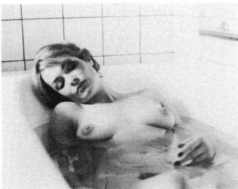

Elona Glenn was the attractive heroine of Sweden's *Private Pleasures* (New Realm), whose intimate sex life the camera's expert, greedy eye followed with intense concentration as it explored her outward and uninhibited inner or wishful thinking life.

Jan Nowicki and Maja Komorowska in the Polish *Family Life* (Contemporary), a rather heavily doom-laden story (which might well have been written by Ibsen) about a strange family living in a rotting house cage who even given the opportunity to break out cannot bring themselves to do it.

The Spoilers – Thong (Golden Harvest–Cathay) was a Thailand action melo starring Greg Morris as the foreign adventurer who is assigned to recapture the shipment of gold hijacked from the local police and taken into communist country.

From the more usual source, Hong Kong, *Stoner* (Golden Harvest–Cathay) was a typical mélange of criminals, cops, drugs and large-scale destruction.

The Wild Game (Contemporary) was a typical Rainer Werner Fassbinder (West German) film, a family piece about a fourteen-year-old daughter of a respectable German middle-class family who, willingly seduced, becomes hooked on sex so much that in order to continue seeing her boyfriend persuades him to murder her dad. Rolling in the hay, the girl Eva Mattes, and the boy Harry Baer.

The most remarkable thing about the French – very explicit, too explicit to get more than a special X (London) certificate and not likely to get a wide showing – sex film *Exhibition* was the investigation it made into the mind and morals of its star Claudine Beccarie (right) who, quite happy to take part in a pornographic film (such as the one we see in the making) and be seen copulating and enjoying her girlfriends, objects to four-letter, 'dirty' words and sexual aberration!

A major film made some years back by
Bernardo Bertolucci but only now
rescued for British screens by the
Artificial Eye Distributors, *The Spider's
Strategem* was a brilliant realisation of a
slight little sketch by Jorge Luis Borges,
which Bertolucci turned into a remarkable study of ambiguity as it told the
story of a young man who goes back to
the small town in which his father is
honoured as an anti-Fascist martyr but
soon finds there are flaws in the tale and
is eventually driven to wonder whether
his dad was the hero the statue in the
town square suggests, or the traitor some
of his friends think he was, or . . . Father
and son were both played by Giulio
Brogi.

Robert Hossein as the master crook in
Golden Era's *The Last Shot* who, forced
out of Paris by the cops, sets up business
in Nice, where his final escapade of
stealing an armoured truck with two
millions francs aboard leads to his
eventual demise.

Generally acknowledged as one of the best films of the year by any standard, Satyajit Ray's *The Middle Man* continued his examination of the less pleasing face of Indian commercial life by giving the story of a University student who, unfairly robbed of his honours degree, subsequently tries to make a living in the wheeling-dealing world of buying and selling. Made in black and white, technically below the most polished modern standards, it more than made up these shortcomings by the witty and acutely ironic observation and wonderful performances, including those of Bradip Mukerjee (left) as the young man and Robi Ghosh as his unmoral mentor.

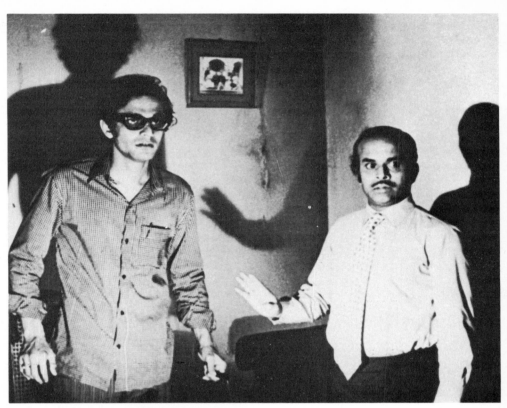

Some of the criminal Mastermind's robot assistants in Georges Franju's thriller (from Connoisseur) *Shadowman* or *L'Homme sans Visage* (also known as 'Nuits Rouges'), the story of the way that the crook plans to steal the jealously guarded gold of the old Knight Templars.

Costa-Gavras came up with another powerful political drama in his *Section Spéciale*, a relating of a particularly shameful chapter in French war history when the Vichy judiciary made a bargain with the Germans by which, in order to save the bunch of hostages taken when a Nazi officer is murdered, they agree to take three already sentenced (to jail) French prisoners, re-try and condemn them to be guillotined.

Though the story of Gala's *The Pink Telephone* was very familiar – that old one about the middle-aged man falling disastrously in love with a pretty young prostitute – it was given style and interest by lovely and ageless Mireille Darc's playing of the girl. Ruinously attached to her, Toulouse industrialist Pierre Mondi.

Typical Jean-Luc Godard contribution to the year's French output was his *Numero Deux*, a sort of illustrated lecture about his ideas concerning the place of male/female relationships in modern industrial society.

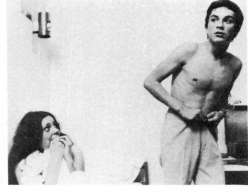

A practical joke typical of the group of French youngsters taking English lessons during a South Coast (Ramsgate) holiday in *A Nous les Petites Anglaises*, an often cruelly witty French film which included an uncomfortably true satirical impression of a 'typical' English family, with its cups of tea, brown ale and vulgarity! But the film was also honest enough to show the French teenagers as a pretty heartless bunch capable of petty crime, yet somehow it managed to retain an element of charm and romance in its story of young love. Above the young 'hero' Remi Laurent gets a shock when having seduced his girlfriend her parents arrive unexpectedly on the scene.

Though director/writer/actor Michel Drach chose to tell his *Les Violons du Bal* (Contemporary) in a needlessly complicated style, it was basically a simple and quite charming story (autobiographical apparently) about a small Jewish boy's, his mother's and grandma's adventures as they move, always one step ahead of the Vichy Police and the German deportation wagons, through France to safety in Switzerland. And it was quite a family film with Monsieur Drach's young son playing himself (as well as he playing himself!) and his wife playing his mother. And though a drama there was plenty of quiet humour in the film.

Quite a proportion of the Italian film imports to Great Britain during the year consisted of pretty minor, violent crime thrillers; like Miracle's *Death Dealers*, which was about a successful and ruthless crime-beating cop who is moved from his happy hunting-ground of Rome to Naples, where he soon begins to smash the local rackets, even if at fairly high human cost. Extreme right: John Saxon.

Happy ending, when Jean-Louis Trintignant (stepfather), Mireille Darc (mother) and Richard Constantini (son) are reunited after their shattering experiences in Serge Leroy's French chase film *Shattered*.

Penelope Lamour as the young wife whose sex suddenly takes on an uncontrollable and foul-mouthed, lustful life of its own in the French sex-comedy from Oppidan, *Pussy Talk*.

The Columbia–Warner release *Cry Onion* was a somewhat complicated Italian–West German–Spanish co-produced comedy about the struggle between farmers and the big oil combine which is intent on driving them off their farms so it can prospect for oil on their land. Franco Nero played the farmers' leader.

Though considerably less in number now, Hong Kong continued to export to us a proportion of its very considerable output of action films, such as Eagle's *Deadly China Doll*, in which athletic hero Carter Huang manages at the same time to smash a drug ring and revenge his brother's murder.

Variety's *Live Like a Cop, Die Like a Man* was another example of the same genre, with the Rome forces of law and order using the same kind of strong-arm methods as their criminal opponents. Marc Porel and Ray Lovelock emerged as a kind of Italian equivalent to America's Starsky and Hutch team, using the same kind of unconventional methods to achieve their aims.

Miracle's *Blue Belle* was a British–Italian sex film collaboration, set in Hong Kong and relating the erotic education of the shapely young Convent graduate of the title, with star Annie Belle supposedly re-living at least some of her real-life adventures.

Mona Mour played the title-role in the Cinecenta release of *The Gatekeeper's Daughter*, a minor piece of erotica about the daughter of a railway-crossing keeper who is raped, thrown out of her home and becomes a whore before she eventually finds happiness with her Prince!

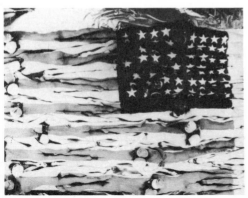

The eleventh 'The Banner' episode in Oppidan's *Dreams of Thirteen* (actually twelve, one episode contribution from a British director was scissored by our censor), which was the result of an offer by a rich German sponsor some years back to finance the filming of their most erotic fantasy by a number of international moviemakers. And it was a variable and not particularly elevating collection that resulted.

His first film to be made in France, *Mr Klein*, won for Joseph Losey the distinction of 'Cesars' (the French equivalent of the American 'Oscars', presented this year for only the second time) for both the film as a whole and for his direction. A beautifully subtle and stylish film which needed more than one viewing for full appreciation of its artistry, it told the story of a rich antiques dealer in Occupied Paris in 1942 who becomes involved with a Jewish namesake, who is using him as a cover for his work in the Resistance – an increasingly obsessive involvement which leads to final submissive disaster. Alain Delon, who also co-produced the film, gave one of his best performances in the title-role. Above he inspects the other Mr Klein's lodgings and left he takes tea, but gets little sympathy from Jeanne Moreau.

Comedian Pierre Richard (remember him in that wonderfully crazy French comedy 'The Tall Blond Man With One Black Shoe'?) makes a return to the screen in the Gala release of *French Mustard*, a comedy-satire from France in which he plays a shy professor who loses a lot of his reticence when he meets and falls in love with a visiting film-star (Jane Birkin, and not Danielle Minazolli who shares this scene with him).

The end of the story. The sniper, who has installed himself on the roof of a tall building and been picking off the police surrounding him, is finally shot and captured in Bo Widerberg's (Swedish) film *The Man on the Roof – Mannen Pa Taket*. Released by Connoisseur, it was a fascinating example of the way that a familiar story can be made to work brilliantly with original treatment.

Lili Monori as the young wife who while waiting for the return of her seafaring hubbie in Essential's Hungarian import, *When Joseph Returns – Ha Megjon Jozsef*, manages after some disturbing experiences to at last reach a mutual understanding with her mother, previously both a disliked and disapproving figure.

Jane Birkin in the Gala release of *I Love You, I Don't – Je T'Aime, Moi Non Plus*, which told a sad little love story about a homosexual and the girl – Miss Birkin – he meets at a wayside café.

Lina Wertmuller's Italian Warner release *Seven Beauties*, after garnering considerable critical and public success in America arrived in Britain to be generally frowned upon by the critics, who found this very deep black comedy about a Neopolitan 'survivor' (Giancarlo Giannini, front right) who eventually winds up in a German Concentration Camp, where to stay alive he makes love to the gross Commandant (left) and finally even picks out his fellow prisoners for death, not very amusing.

A pretty hefty looking Justine (Alice Arno) in the new French adaptation of the Marquis de Sade story of that title, now called *The Violation of Justine* and released by Tigon.

Angela Winkler as the press-persecuted, somewhat silly girl of the title with her on-the-run lover, Jürgen Prochnow, in West Germany's *The Lost Honour of Katharina Blum*, a scathing indictment of the country's press and police alike (Contemporary).

Honest cop Lino Ventura becomes aware that the killers of some of Italy's top judiciary may, instead of the revenge-seekers he initially suspected, be very highly placed politicians playing a power game in Francesco Rosi's gripping political thriller *Illustrious Corpses*, released by Cinegate.

Don't let that curly black wig fool you, the cigar-smoking fellow in the middle of trouble is Alain Delon, playing a successful gang-leading thief in Warner's French importation *Le Gang*.

The young people play their fated games (Pamela Villoresi, Theresa Ann Savoy, Lajos Balazsovits and Franco Branciaroli) in Miklos Jancso's Italian/Yugoslavian production *Private Vices and Public Virtues* (Eagle Films) which, somewhat ambiguously, seems based on the old 'Mayerling' story, with the story of a young Prince rejecting parental wishes for the sake of his own pleasures.

The bathed peasant virgins struggle to see into the Countess's bedchamber in Walerian Borowczyks highly erotic collection of diverse sexual essays in New Realm's *Immoral Tales*, which for all its poetic pretentions might be best described as another addition to the current posh-porn cycle!

Fantasies behind the Pearly Curtain

Hongkong Cinema
in Perspective
by Derek Elley

The breakthrough came at Cannes in 1972, where two Hongkong film companies, Shaw Brothers and Golden Harvest (through their distributor the Cathay Organisation), caused a minor stir by screening a selection of their product in the Market: interest was aroused and finally, after trying to attract Western distributors since the mid-sixties, Run-run Shaw succeeded in selling a costume-action drama called *The Invincible Boxer* to Warner Brothers. Retitled *5 Fingers of Death* in America and *King Boxer* in Britain, it had a sudden and amazing impact. In London at the Warner, Leicester Square, it took £42,000 in two months; Cathay soon responded with a modest fight picture called *Fist of Fury*, starring a certain Bruce Lee, which promptly broke every house record at the Rialto (less than 600 seats) and established the diminutive but spunky Lee as the first Oriental super-star. The words *kung-fu* (which only means 'skill' or 'technique') and 'martial arts' began to enter filmgoers' vocabulary, and the floodgates opened: *The Killer, The New One-Armed Swordsman,*
86

Hap ki do, The Big Boss, Enter the Dragon, Way of the Dragon, Chinese Vengeance, Intimate Confessions of a Chinese Courtesan . . . The boom continued through 1973, reached its climax in 1974 with the release of the rest of the Lee films, began to show signs of strain in 1975 as more and more rubbish was quickly sold to unsuspecting distributors, and petered out in 1976 in a wave of reissues and double-bills. The irony of the situation, as far as the West is concerned, is that only a couple of months after *Fist of Fury* established Bruce Lee as the major spearhead in the English-language market breakthrough, Lee himself was dead – in Hongkong, of acute cerebral oedema, on 20 July, 1973, at the age of thirty-two.
It is somehow typical of the whole situation that the West's appreciation of Hongkong's biggest star should be posthumous. There is an after-the-event strain running right through the saga which shows just how separate the European and South-East Asian industries are, and it is only now, after the popular box-office boom has died, that a

serious reassessment is taking place of the industry which provoked it. Largely thanks to the director King Hu, whose *A Touch of Zen* attracted the attention of critics who had sneered at other Hongkong products (at Cannes in 1975), the smug West has been forced to a certain extent to take notice of the vast repository of talent at work in Hongkong and Taiwan: even now, however, merely a handful of critics are prepared to consider the films in anything other than sub-Japanese terms, and one doubts whether the impetus provided by Hu's films (which are not typical of the mainstream) is strong enough to catapult other names to equal prominence.
The success story of Hongkong cinema is essentially the story of one family, the Shaws, owners of a Shanghai theatre and music-hall which staged plays and silent films during the early twenties. Shanghai at that time was the glamour and entertainment capital of mainland China, and when the family began to amass some capital, two of the four sons of father Shaw moved south to try their luck in Singapore – Run-run

Shih Chün and popular Mandarin actress Lin Ch'ing-hsia in Sung Ts'un-shou's lyrical *Ghost of the Mirror*.

Shaw (Shao Yi-fu) first, followed two years later by brother Run-me (Shao Jen-mei). Their prime objective was distribution and property rather than production, and by the late twenties they had built up an organisation which weathered the Depression of 1929 and went on to be the first to anticipate the success of talking pictures, *en route* producing the first Chinese talkie *The White Golden Dragon* in 1932. The Japanese invasion of South-East Asia and the Second World War dealt a heavy blow to the Shaw empire, although the brothers are reputed to have saved a considerable portion of their wealth by the simple expedient of burying it in the ground and digging it up years later when the coast was clear. Whatever the truth, the fifties saw the pair prosperous again with their cinema chain and property interests bigger than ever before, and in 1958 Run-run again instigated another decisive move – to Hongkong, where he found a vigorous but extremely localised film industry, churning out hundreds of black-and-white melodramas and comedies a year in the local dialect of Cantonese. (Written Chinese is the same everywhere; only its pronunciation differs from region to

Kuei Chih-hung's *The Tea House*, a typical example of the highly-characterised Cantonese comedies.

region – Mandarin, from the Peking region, being the 'standard' pronunciation, and Cantonese, from around Hongkong and Canton, being the most popular 'variant'; the two pronunciations sound completely different, and educated Chinese will generally learn Mandarin as an alternative to their own dialect so as to be able to speak to non-locals.) Run-run Shaw sized up the situation and decided to widen the industry's horizons: his films would all be dubbed into the more common currency of Mandarin, with simultaneous written Chinese and English subtitles; he would use the mass of talent which had moved to Hongkong and Taiwan when the Communists had taken over mainland China in the late forties; and he would film familiar historical subjects on a grand scale and in colour.

By the early sixties Shaw's policy had paid off and the now vast studio complex atop a hill in Kowloon had already taken shape. With Run-run masterminding production in Hongkong and Run-me handling distribution throughout South-

East Asia in Singapore, the Shaw Brothers formula was established. During the first half of the sixties the craze became musicals, and Shaws responded with product to feed the public's appetite. In 1964 Run-run, noticing the success of many Japanese swordplay pictures, experimented (in black and white) with a Chinese variety: entitled *Tiger Boy* (*Hu-hsia chien-ch'ou*), and starring a young contract actor called Wang Yü and directed by ex-scriptwriter Chang Ch'eh, it was to signal the trend for the next ten years, a fact also confirmed by the success of King Hu's *Come Drink with Me* (*Ta tsui hsia*) the following year. Hu then left Shaws to make the phenomenally successful *Dragon Gate Inn* (*Lung men k'o-chan*, 1966), while Chang Ch'eh stayed to become the studio's number one director in the *genre*, bringing to prominence a whole new generation of actors and actresses, most of whom are now in the superstar league, to replace the older generation who had seen the Shaws through their first years in the late fifties and early sixties.

The next change of direction, or rather new slant on a waning formula, came in the late sixties: a thoroughly Chinese equivalent of the martial arts film, based on the unarmed techniques developed in such secret societies and monasteries as Shaolin during the Middle Ages. It was Wang Yü again who paved the way, both directing and starring in *The Chinese Boxer* (*Lung hu tou*, 1969), and the cycle which the West was to dub *kung-fu* was born. At the same time, however, Shaw Brothers was dealt a body-blow which was to change the whole face of the

Yüeh Hua trapped in Ch'u Yüan's *Killer Clans*, a riveting study of betrayal and illusion in period China.

Li Han-hsiang's ornate *The Empress Dowager*, a splendid Shaw Brothers showpiece, with Lisa Lu as the Empress, Ti Lung the prone Emperor, and Hsiao Yao his sorrowing concubine.

Hongkong industry: Raymond Chow (Tsou Wen-huai), Hongkong-born and Shanghai-educated production manager who had joined the organisation in late 1958, left the company and started up his own production unit, Golden Harvest, in May 1970. He was to be joined later by other Shaws personnel, including Wang Yü.

Chow, after eleven and a half years of working alongside Run-run Shaw, had plenty of experience; all he lacked was sufficient money to realise his vision of a wider market for Chinese films, since the West was still unaware of this thriving corner of the film world (despite the fact that the Japanese industry had always enjoyed a cult following outside South-East Asia – something which rightly galls Hongkong film-makers). During 1970 Golden Harvest produced a number of pictures, none of them runaway successes; then in 1971 Chow, via a telephone call to Los Angeles, invited Bruce Lee, an overseas Chinese actor waiting for his big break to come in Hollywood, to star in a film called *The Big Boss* (*T'ang-shan ta hsiung*). Lee accepted Chow's terms – which represented something of a gamble at that stage of Golden Harvest's history – came to Hongkong, re-worked the script, and made the film in two months in Bangkok that same year. The job done, Lee returned to Los Angeles to appear in two more episodes of the TV series *Longstreet* (he had already done the pilot before leaving for Hongkong), convinced that his reputation would be made there rather than in his spiritual homeland. In South-East Asia *The Big Boss* caused a sensation at the box-office; but still

Hollywood took no notice. Lee, therefore, returned to Hongkong to shoot *Fist of Fury* (*Ching-wu men*, 1972), the film which confirmed his superstar status in that part of the world and which provided his first introduction to Western audiences. Golden Harvest was by now beginning to challenge the mighty Shaws, and Chow had a hot property on his hands; unable to equal any of the mighty offers being made to Lee, he came to an agreement to co-produce Lee's next film which he also directed, *The Way of the Dragon* (*Meng lung kuo chiang*, 1973), on a fifty–fifty basis with the star's own company, Concord Films.

By then even Hollywood was interested. The success of the TV series *Kung Fu*, starring David Carradine (derived from an idea in which Lee had desperately wanted to star in 1971), had proved there was a market for the fad in the US, and Warners, the company which had kept Lee dangling a few years earlier, now found themselves bidding for his services in *Enter the Dragon* (*Lung cheng hu tou*, 1973), a US/Hongkong co-production nominally directed by Robert Clouse. That over, Lee, between working on the dubbing of the film, started shooting the fight sequences for his fifth film, *The Game of Death* (*Szu-wang yu-hsi*). It remains uncompleted to this day, despite attempts by Golden Harvest to make something of the surviving footage using contract actor James T'ien (T'ien Chün).

Lee's sudden death in July 1973 stunned the whole of South-East Asia; elsewhere the world was just beginning to catch up on events of the past decade, and companies, from the smallest independent to Shaws and Golden Harvest, ransacked their archives for saleable product to cash in on the sudden worldwide popularity of Hongkong cinema. It is difficult to say how things would have turned out if Lee were still alive. At the time of his death there were rumours that he was thinking of joining the Shaws (who had made him a risible offer way back in the sixties when he was unknown); certainly Hongkong cinema would still have been on the map now, rather than in the indecisive position it currently holds. The simple fact is that, despite producing several stars of international fame (David Chiang, Angela Mao, Lo Wei, Wang Yü – the first and last of whom have made English-language co-productions), Hongkong has no one who has attracted mass attention in quite the same way as Lee. This should not really be a hurdle to international acceptance (Toshiro Mifune has never enjoyed Lee-status), but the film world does not tolerate empty voids.

In 1975 the Hongkong industry suffered a temporary recession, as much attributable to a lack of new directions as to financial causes. The martial arts boom had long since petered out by then (if Lee had not arrived it would have died even sooner), and producers tried every more fantastic variant in an effort to assess public taste. Golden Harvest's production (fifty-nine films in its first five years) has now been cut back to a token number, and the company is now more interested in distribution, in line with Cathay, the large Singapore-based distributor who handles GH product. If

anything, the last four years have seen a resurgence of the Cantonese film: in 1973 Shaws experimented with Cantonese soundtracks in Hongkong, and the next year Golden Harvest enjoyed a huge success with *Games Gamblers Play* (*Kuei ma shuang hsing*), a satire directed by ex-Shaws actor Michael Hui (Hsü Kuan-wen) and starring him and his pop-singer brother Samuel (Hsü Kuan-chieh). The team's subsequent efforts, *The Last Message* (*T'ien-ts'ai yü Pai-ch'ih*, 1975) and *The Private Eyes* (*Pan-chin pa-liang*, 1976) went on to become the biggest

grossers of their years, the latter taking HK$8·5 million in its first run alone. What are the general characteristics of this energetic film industry, and how does one set about fixing it in any sort of perspective? The general non-Chinese filmgoer, faced with an onslaught of unfamiliar names, faces, film titles and historical settings, is quite rightly confused, even though only a tiny proportion of Hongkong/Taiwan production (245 films in 1973/74; 182 in 1974/75; 142 in 1975/76) ever reaches foreign shores. For the researcher the language

Lo Lieh as *The Invincible Boxer* (GB: *King Boxer*), the film by Cheng Ch'ang-ho which marked Hongkong's break-through in the West; at right, Wang Chin-feng.

Director Li Han-hsiang at work at Shaws on *Moods of Love*, one of a recent spate of traditional erotic comedies; at his left, experienced actress Hu Chin and young starlet Shao Yin-yin.

(Angela) Mao Ying in Huang Feng's *Hap ki do*, which with its cleaner lines and ascetic heroine is in marked contrast to the Shaws studio style.

Whong In-sik and (Angela) Mao Ying in Huang Feng's *Hap ki do*, the most perfect of all the films she has made so far with the director.

barrier is considerable; there *is* plenty of information available (six regular monthlies wholly devoted to film, plus many others) but it is mostly in Chinese. Names are often difficult to distinguish, especially when printed in garbled transliterations, although many personalities adopt English Christian names to facilitate identification abroad: thus Mao Ying becomes Angela Mao, Li Hsiao-lung Bruce Lee, Chiang Ta-wei David Chiang, Miao K'o-hsiu Nora Miao, Hu Chin-ch'üan King Hu, Teng Kuang-jung Alan Teng. (Throughout this article I have transliterated all names and film titles into their Mandarin forms, from original Chinese sources.) As an extra wrinkle on the problem, even their Chinese names are frequently stage-names, along Hollywood lines: thus actor/producer Patrick Tse is known to Chinese audiences as Hsieh Hsien but in real life as Hsieh Chia-yü, and it is the name Li Yüan-chin which appears on Bruce Lee's gravestone.

If the names are not enough trouble, the film titles present an even greater problem. Most films are produced and released with an official English title as well as the Chinese one (though the former frequently has no connection in meaning with the latter, and, apart from changes during production, is sometimes different on the actual print to what appears on advertising and stills), but this was more often than not changed if a picture was sold abroad. *The Big Boss* (Chinese title: *T'ang-shan ta hsiung*, which means *Chinese Big Brother*) was released in the US as *Fists of Fury*; *Fist of Fury* (literally: *Ching Wu School*) became in the US *The Chinese*

Connection, which happened to be the British release title of Chang Ch'eh's *Duel of Fists* (*Ch'üan chi*, 1971; literally: *Fist Attack*). At its most extreme the problem can become: *The Invincible Boxer* (*T'ien-hsia ti-yi ch'üan*; literally: *The World's Number One Boxer*), known in Britain as *King Boxer* and America as *5 Fingers of Death*, the latter also being the British title of Chang Ch'eh's *Shaolin Martial Arts* (*Hung ch'üan yü yung ch'un*, 1974)! (Throughout this article I have referred to films under their original Hongkong English titles.)

There remains, also, a final hurdle in the films themselves. Most non-Chinese have become acquainted with them in versions which bear only token resemblance to the originals – a problem confronting the enthusiast of *any* foreign-language cinema, but exacerbated here. Appalling Anglo-American dubbing, miserable colour duping, illogical cutting by local distributors, plus censors' trims, and often a music track re-dubbed in Europe – these combined have produced films which bear scant relation to the originals and nurture the popular suspicion that Hongkong cinema lacks any sort of subtlety or technical polish. For example, the British print of Wang Yü's masterly *Beach of the War Gods* (*Chan-shen t'an*, 1972), cut by almost a quarter of an hour and featuring dark, milky colours and an array of baritone voices, gives no hint of the original's bright, clear-cut colour photography and far less portentous range of voices. Some of this butchery is almost a distorted parody of the Hongkong industry's own code of practice: even the original Chinese prints do not feature the actors' real voices (many do not speak Mandarin, and anyway all films are dubbed during post-synching by professional Mandarin dubbers) and the music tracks are often a compilation of uncredited excerpts from John Barry to Ennio Morricone, but at least the originals show a measure of appropriateness and genuine feel for dramatic form. Hongkong censorship can also be seen at work in moments of extreme violence, but is not half so sensitive as, for instance, the British censor, who fails to see that the fantastic effects are part and parcel of the flamboyant whole and not half as damaging as the morbidly realistic violence allowed to slip through in American product.

Thanks to the ability (equalled only by Indians) of Chinese abroad to set up self-contained societies, it is not difficult for interested parties to experience the original version of films; Britain alone has a late-night circuit encompassing London, Birmingham, Liverpool, Manchester, Glasgow, Edinburgh, Newcastle, Leeds, Bristol and Southampton. And the observant student will have noticed that signs of Asian activity *have* trickled through over the years: in 1962 Li Han-hsiang's *The Magnificent Concubine* (*Yang Kuei-fei*), one of Shaws' earliest successes and with a foreword by none other than Pearl S. Buck, was a Grand Prix winner at Cannes; another Shaw film, Lo Chen's *Vermilion Door* (*Hung ling lei*, 1964), starring Ling Po, Li Li-hua and Kuan Shan, was the Hongkong entry in the NFT's Commonwealth Film Festival in September 1965; films from Asia were shown at a special festival in Frankfurt in the spring of the same year; in 1970 the Edinburgh Festival even screened a South Korean melodrama, and by 1973 Derek Hill's enterprising New Cinema Club was showing programmes of Hongkong trailers and Hsü Tseng-hung and Yasuda Kimiyoshi's *Zatoichi and the One-Armed Swordsman* (*Tu-pi-tao ta chan mang-hsia*, 1971), the latter never publicly screened even in its dubbed version. And if the words *kung-fu* seemed new in 1973, it is worth remembering that a certain Malaysian company had run an advertisement in the Odeon circuit's *Showtime* magazine a full seven years earlier, exhorting patrons: 'Don't Be Bullied! You Too Can Become a Fearless Exponent of Chinese Kung-Fu Karato [*sic*] . . . the Authenic Chinese Self-Defence Art That Disables Instantaneously on Contact . . .' Stylistically – and from hereon I am concerned with the whole spectrum of Hongkong/Taiwan cinema, not just the martial arts films – the films draw on a variety of sources. The Italian industry is Europe's closest equivalent, and Hongkong cinema, with its inexhaustible energy, optimism, extrovert craftsmanship, and powers of adaptability and self-renewal, is tailor-made to appeal to anyone who mourns the passing of Italy's *peplum* genre and the era of 'spaghetti westerns' which followed it. The Chinese sword-hero unites the resonant Leone-spawned Italian gunfighter with the lone Japanese *samurai*, and comes up with its own unique invention. Since the mid-sixties almost all films have been shot in colour and scope (the latter process not using Panavision equipment, so some distor-

Shaws-actor-turned-independent-director Wang Yü in *One-Armed Boxer*; at left, T'ang Hsin.

Tall, highly athletic dancer-turned-actress Cheng P'ei-p'ei in Lo Wei's *None but the Brave* (GB: *The Kung Fu Girl*).

The charismatic Cheng P'ei-p'ei as *Golden Swallow* (GB: *The Girl with the Thunderbolt Kick*), one of the masterpieces of the costume swordplay *genre*, directed by Chang Ch'eh; at rear, Lo Lieh.

(David) Chiang Ta-wei, stuntman-turned-film-idol, and Ch'en Kuan-t'ai in Chang Ch'eh's *The Blood Brothers* (GB: *Chinese Vengeance*); both have been Chang *alumni* for the past decade.

tion results, but the demands of TV have not compromised directors into using wide-screen ratios instead), and film-makers have made the fullest use of their opportunities, tracking, zooming and changing set-ups with a frequency which rids the scope screen of the sense of cumbersomeness which afflicted many American productions. In general, Hongkong cinema disdains the traditional master-shot in favour of fresh camera set-ups for every cut; partly this reflects the rapid shooting-schedules demanded by the small budgets but equally reflects a tendency to identify the camera – and thus the audience – totally with the story-line – a thorough 'realisation' in cinematic terms rather than working the story to fit existing shooting manners.

In the martial arts films, most of the time is taken up with preparing and shooting the elaborate fight scenes, with minimal rehearsal and number of takes for dialogue passages. The resultant *brio* carries over, however, into other *genres*, notably the stream of glossy modern melodramas mostly shot in Taiwan (none of which, sadly, have ever been shown publicly in Britain), which show similar approaches to their subjects and often feature songs or song-montages in place of fight sequences. Between the two, stands the horror film *genre* which has produced some of Hongkong cinema's finest works: frequent use is made of China's vast literary legacy of ghost tales, and their realisation exploits to the full the possibilities of uniting the *fantastique* elements of the martial arts *genre* with a taste for true horror which shames Hammer Films into insignificance.

In the brief scope of this article it is possible only to sketch the personalities and themes at work, and one must perforce pass over the wide range of other *genres*: gangster films, Cantonese opera, comedies, period romances, thrillers, war films – in fact, as wide a range, if not wider (with the possibilities offered by the Asian equivalents), than Western cinema. The Hongkong industry is star-oriented and devoted to (in the words of Run-run Shaw) 'giving the public what it wants', though this does not preclude at all, just as it did not preclude Hollywood film-makers in the studio days, a degree of personal expression and individual style. Plots may be tied to a formula, and acting styles disconcertingly histrionic for Western tastes (particularly the much-used 'surprised reaction' shot), but one must accept these as normal characteristics of Hongkong cinema, rather than try to force the films ino Western moulds. Even working within the rigid Shaws set-up, directors have carved their own personal styles, and (in, for instance, the case of Li Han-hsiang) spells outside the studio system have not necessarily been beneficial. Chang Ch'eh, Shaws' foremost martial arts director, has since the early seventies set up his own company and worked with a regular repertory team of actors; but he is still linked with the studio in all but name. Run-run Shaw runs the Hongkong set-up with the precision and ruthlessness of a trained accountant: every year a certain number of trainee actors are accepted, put in an iron-clad contract on a token income, and housed, trained and used by the studio to the best of their ability. Aside from Golden

Harvest, which is run on substantially more modest lines, there is an impressive line-up of other production companies, who dip into the freelance acting pool for a star or two to headline a production. First Films and Goldig are the most enterprising, with production running at between six to a dozen pictures a year; Patrick Tse directs and produces his own films, generally glossy Taiwan melodramas featuring his (now ex-) wife Chen Chen; Kuo Nan-hung, an independent producer/director, has recently had

a string of successes revolving around a blatantly derivative re-working of the Shaolin cycle; and Great Wall Films, unofficially linked with mainland China, produce product half-way between the politically-oriented films of Peking and Shanghai, and the success-oriented mainstream of Hongkong.
How does one reach any point of reference in the array of unfamiliar faces? In fact, there are quite clear divisions, and once one has become used to recognising individual features, the per-

A Hu discovery, since matured into an exceptional actress: Hsü Feng in the leading role of *A Touch of Zen*.

Ch'iao Hung (centre) as the Buddhist high priest with amazing powers in King Hu's *A Touch of Zen*.

Erotic star Ch'en P'ing, with a nice line in female vigilante films, in Sun Chung's energetic *The Drug Connection*.

Ch'en Yao-ch'i's *Run Lover Run*, a beautiful and intelligent representative of the mass of glossy comic-romantic melodramas shot in Taiwan; here starring Lin Ch'ing-hsia and (Alan) Teng Kuang-jung (seen in top right picture).

sonalities also emerge. Of actors who are chiefly identified with martial arts films, the following are the most notable: Bruce Lee, of course, whose brand of panther-like intensity (like a coiled spring) was a physical expression of the intense Chinese nationalism which runs through his films; Wang Yü, an ex-Shaws trainee actor of uninspiring physique but steel-cold gaze, whose characters are marked by an obsessional interest in self-mutilation and physical constraint; David Chiang, ex-stuntman (who worked on *The Sand Pebbles*) turned Shaws contract artist, of diminutive boyish appearance but great agility, often teamed with the more impressive Ti Lung, who specialises in lone charismatic heroes dispensing ruthless personal justice; Fu Sheng, like the previous two, a Chang Ch'eh alumnus, who is used as a lightweight jokey balance which accords well with his thoroughly pop idol image; and the more stolid Ch'en Kuan-t'ai, Lo Lieh, Yüeh Hua, and (especially good at smooth villainy) Kou Feng. All these actors often appear in modern gangster or crime dramas, in similarly physical roles. On the distaff side, Hongkong boasts an impressive line-up of martial arts actresses, almost all of whom originally trained as dancers: Angela Mao, short, spunky Taiwanese ex-ballet star, specialising in restrained, morally ascetic characters (and generally under the measured direction of Huang Feng); Cheng P'ei-p'ei, a tall, extremely supple dancer (since retired from films and running a dance school in Los Angeles) of impressive stature and phenomenal toughness; Shih Szu, a Shaws actress of more conventional looks

but abrasive personality; Hsü Feng, a highly charismatic Taiwanese actress of no special agility but suggesting a remote, misty-eyed sexuality behind the ruthless exterior; and Chia Ling, a somewhat pert actress of noticeable flexibility, who also sports a nice line in comedy; and the fiery, tomboyish Shang-kuan Ling-feng.

On the other side of the coin are those personalities who mostly avoid historical or fighting heroics: Chen Chen, long-reigning Mandarin melodrama queen (now in her thirties) of impressive Audrey Hepburn-like range and character, from *gamine* to high society lady; Alan Teng, frequently her film partner, with more than a passing parallel to Alain Delon; Lin Ch'ing-hsia, slim, 'blue-jeaned' ex-teenage challenge to Chen Chen's position, who in four years has risen from obscurity to number 2 attraction and shown an affecting depth of characterisation; Ch'in Hsiang-lin, often teamed with her, who displays considerably more range than the wooden Alan Teng and who has a George Segal-like gift for light comedy which is too little used. One cannot possibly mention even a quarter of the remaining major personalities, but some will doubtless be familiar to readers: Nora Miao, who sadly was never allowed to fulfil the promise of her early GH roles (*viz.* the hopeless parts in Lee's films); Li Ching, the toast of South-East Asia during the sixties, but now having more success with her monthly agony-column and as a Shaws' ambassador, than in hard film roles; Ch'en P'ing, Hongkong's own sex queen, recently diversifying into a breathtaking series of

female vigilante pictures; Lisa Lu (Lu Yen), Hollywood-reared Chinese actress, who returned in triumph to make a large-scale Shaws costume picture; Li Li-hua and Ling Po, both representing the older generation of actresses who date from the fifties and early sixties; Miao T'ien, grizzled actor/producer of wide experience and erudition . . .
One may reasonably wonder whether the director's name can sell a picture at all in such an atmosphere, but certain personalities (for it is essentially around *personalities* that the cut-throat industry is organised) do have a public following. King Hu's small but painstaking *œuvre*, consciously striving after a more Western-style *mise en scène* while using thoroughly Chinese material, has so far peaked in *A Touch of Zen* (*Hsia nü*, 1968; reconstructed in its complete form in 1975) and the fluid *The Fate of Lee Khan* (*Ying-chun ko chih feng-po*, 1973), both emphasising the intangible qualities of the martial arts. Li Han-hsiang's dazzling collection of ornate costume dramas in imperial settings – *The Empress Dowager* (*Ch'ing kuo ch'ing ch'eng*, 1975), *The Last Tempest* (*Ying T'ai ch'i hsüeh*, 1976), both starring Lisa Lu, and *Empress Wu* (*Wu Tse-t'ien*, 1960) – and 'traditional' erotic comedies. Chang Ch'eh's systematic exploration of facets of heroism through the martial arts (fifty-plus films since 1964), currently floundering in an excess of technique and shortage of new ideas, but (especially his Shaws work during the late sixties like *Golden Swallow*/*Chin yen-tzu*, with Wang Yü and Cheng P'ei-p'ei, known in Britain as *The Girl with the Thunderbolt Kick*, and *Have Sword, Will Travel*/*Pao-piao*, with Ti Lung and David Chiang) formerly of appealing sensuousness and vigour. In the field of melodrama, Li Hsing has re-worked old models with tact and style: the classic *Execution in Autumn* (*Ch'iu chüeh*, 1971), a moving tale of spiritual re-birth set during the Han dynasty, *The Marriage* (*Hun-yin ta shih*, 1974), which escalates a formulary Taiwan-glossy plot through ludicrousy to ludicrousy, and the stridently anti-Japanese *Land of the Undaunted* (*Wu t'u wu min*, 1975). The young American-trained director Ch'en Yao-ch'i is also fulfilling the promise of his early pictures; the equally delightful *Run Lover Run* (*Ai-ch'ing ch'ang p'ao*, 1975) and *The Chasing Game* (*Chui ch'iu chui ch'iu*, 1976), both starring Lin Ch'ing-hsia and Ch'in Hsiang-lin, question the social and sexual ethics of modern Taiwanese melodramas with a Hawksian glee. Space prevents mention of myriad other talents – Pai Ching-jui, the temporarily eclipsed Lo Wei, Liu Chia-ch'ang, Sung Ts'un-shou, T'ang Shu-hsüan, Michael Hui . . . the list is endless and constantly renewing itself. And if, throughout this brief introduction to Hongkong cinema, I have concentrated more on facts than themes, on the hows rather than the whys, that is because ultimately the films speak for themselves, with a clarity and directness which curries to no pretensions other than entertainment and recognises no artificial division between that word and 'art'.

Bruce Lee (left) who acted in and also directed *Way of the Dragon*.

Made but not shown — The movies you may never see
by Michael Darvell

What have the following films in common: James Caan and Sammy Davis in *Man Without Mercy*; Elliott Gould in *Move*; Cliff Robertson in *Ace Eli and Rodger of the Skies*? Have you guessed the connection? Are the titles familiar? Maybe you read about them when they were in production. But if you live in Britain you certainly won't have seen them, either at the movies or even on television, for since those titles were made they have never been shown to a public audience at all in the United Kingdom. These are but three examples of an immense backlog of films that have failed to see the light of day, or a film projector! The horror of it all is that I could fill the whole of *Film Review* with hundreds upon hundreds of titles of films in a similar predicament. This represents a staggering amount of money spent on the making of films that nobody has seen. The situation in the United States is very different. There is such a demand for new products, and a wealth of outlets to exhibit films (e.g. more cinemas, drive-ins, extra TV networks with twenty-four-hour viewing) that virtually everything ever made crops up somewhere at some time or another on the cinema or home screen. In Britain, with its fluctuating number of cinemas and a reluctance on the part of distributors to experiment with difficult or out-of-the-ordinary films, anything that isn't recognisably, instantly promotable as an obvious money-spinner is relegated to the shelf – unseen – to await the day when it is sold to television, or buried for ever.

There are various categories of unseen films which broadly cover these areas:

1. Distributors just don't know what to do with them.
2. Censorship difficulties arise. Films are rejected by the Board and never re-submitted.
3. Product is acquired from another source, e.g. conglomerates that deal in more important and highly saleable commodities such as oil don't really know what to do with films, especially if they are inexperienced and have no cinemas of their own.
4. Films that are given limited 'try out' screenings and then shelved.

Most of the great unshown movies of our time fall into the first category. Whether these films are good, bad or indifferent is irrelevant, because there are so many that have never been given the chance to prove themselves one way or the other. And since, to a distributor, a successful film is one that makes money, then goodness (or badness) has nothing to do with it. What were, I wonder, the merits of *Billy Bright*, for instance? This 1969 Carl Reiner comedy starred Dick Van Dyke, Mickey Rooney and Cornel Wilde. Now we shall never know. Presumably Mr Van Dyke went out of favour when his TV show folded up, a fate that also happened to Rowan and Martin of *Laugh-In* fame. They made a film in the same year, *The Maltese Bippy*, but that, too, failed to appear over here. Where, oh where, is Roddy McDowall's picture *Tam Lin* (1968), starring Ava Gardner and Ian McShane? Admittedly it was involved in an unfortunate collapse of the company that was backing the picture, which stranded the production during filming. The company went into liquidation and *Tam Lin* never quite recovered. Eventually it was completed and released in the States four years after shooting began. Then it was sold straightaway to television. By the way, this is the film that is almost certainly known under two alternative titles: *The Devil's Widow* and *Toys*.

Some actors and actresses fare very badly when film after film seems to be dogged by misfortune and a whole procession of titles goes by, unseen by the public eye. Witness the work of Jon Voight whose first successful picture, *Midnight Cowboy*, was also his last. He has made several more films before and since *Midnight Cowboy*, but have you seen them? Has anyone? His last film, *Conrack*, received very poor handling by the distributors but at least it was shown. This is more than can be said for his *All American Boy* (1969), *Fearless Frank* (1967) and *Out of It*, directed by Paul Williams, the songwriter of *Bugsy Malone* and *Phantom of the Paradise* fame. Incidentally, whatever became of Paul's other opus, *Dealing*? Obviously misdealt – or mislaid – in 1971. Michael Douglas's film career has been none too hot to date. The only wide showing that any of his films received was for the Disney *Napoleon and Samantha* (1972).

Helmut Berger and Trevor Howard in Luchino Visconti's MGM film *Ludwig*. Originally shown to the press in 1973 and put immediately on the shelf (and briefly aired in public at the 1976 London Film Festival) it has never yet been given even a limited run in a British cinema.

Prior to that his *Summertree* a year earlier had a brief airing, but his film début in the 1970 *Hail Hero* still remains unshown, despite the starry cast of Peter Strauss, Melvyn Douglas, Arthur Kennedy and Teresa Wright. It took the television series *The Streets of San Francisco* to really put Michael (son of Kirk) Douglas on the public map. Television is in fact one of the few places where we are likely to see the films that were never shown in the cinema. This oft-maligned medium has provided a resting-place for many a lost movie. At the time of writing, BBC TV has just premièred the Goldie Hawn movie *The Girl from Petrovka* (1974) and repeated the Patricia Neal starrer *The Subject Was Roses* (1968) for which Jack Albertson was given an Oscar. It seems incredible that even an Academy Award winner

One Alice we've never seen through the looking-glass or anywhere else is Carol Marsh, who starred in a live-action and puppet feature film based on Lewis Carroll's story some years ago for the Rank Organisation, but which has never, so far as we know, had a single cinema showing, nor has it even been screened for TV. The director was Dallas Bower, the producer Lou Bunin and the screenplay of the 'Wonderland' book was by Henry Myers, Albert E. Lewin and Edward Eliscu. Alice, where art thou?

cannot find a place to be shown in a cinema. With such a recommendation from no less a body that the Academy of Motion Picture Arts and Sciences, you'd think that *The Subject Was Roses* would have rated at least a West End opening. Apparently not; all it gets is two TV screenings. Patricia Neal hasn't done too well with some of her other films: *The Road Builder* still remains unseen even in the country in which it was made. It has since suffered a change of title by becoming *The Night Digger*, but is still shelved. Maybe another change of title, to something like *Confessions of a Sexy Navvy*, would bring it out into the open! A London Film Festival entry, *Mother's Day* (also Patricia Neal, with Cloris Leachman) has at least been seen, albeit to a restricted audience at the National Film Theatre. But it's a virtual stranger to the general public.

Not even Elvis Presley is immune to the strange ways of film distribution. His *Change of Habit* lived up to its name and became another BBC TV première. We are still awaiting a screening, any sort of screening, for his *Live a Little, Love a Little* (with Rudy Vallee) which dates back to 1968. Jacqueline Bisset has had more than her unfair share of fantastic disappearing films. What became of *The Grasshopper*, in which she is said to have played her best role, or *The Secret World* (also known as *The White Ladder*)? Even her films that were shown (*The First Time, Believe in Me, Secrets, Stand Up and Be Counted*) all got very restricted releases. Poor Jacqueline.

Films you might have seen because they have been bought by television are becoming less rare nowadays. There is a film trade ruling in Britain that no film may be permitted a TV screening until at least five years after its initial release to cinemas. This rule is generally adhered to, although there have been exceptions. *The Ruling Class* was a test case and produced much ill-feeling within the industry, which felt it needed protection from being exploited by television. The ruling does not, however, apply to foreign-language films, which have been given, of late, concurrent cinema/TV premières. Moreover, the five-year embargo does not apply to films that were never released to British cinemas. So in these cases it is quite legitimate for distributors to sell their 'shelved' product direct to television, if they don't plan on a theatrical release. Sidney Lumet's *Bye Bye Braverman* (1969, George Segal) has been seen on TV, although never shown in a British cinema, except at the NFT. His other unreleased film *Blood Kin* (James Coburn, Lynn Redgrave) has only been seen at the NFT. *Pro*, the Charlton Heston 1969 starrer about a football hero, had a change of name – to *Number One* – and turned up on television. Gordon Parks' *Rain People*, another Lumet picture, *The Appointment* (Anouk Aimee, Omar Sharif), and the Albert Finney/Yvette Mimieux *Picasso Summer*, with a haunting score by Michel Legrand, all had British TV premières. Paul Mazursky, the director of *Bob and Carol and Ted and Alice*, *Blume in Love* and *Next Stop Greenwich Village*, has a favourite film of his own, which is *Alex in Wonderland* (with Donald Sutherland) made in 1971 but never widely seen. The film throws a nod in the direction of the

Lewis Carroll classic, but there the resemblance ends. Anyway, according to the director it has now become a favourite of student film societies, a veritable campus cult, which has made him happy; but since he actually made the film for a general audience he would be happier still if *Alex* had been given a better chance on general release. In Britain it cropped up on TV, and is now gone for good. Talking of *Alice in Wonderland*, apart from the famous Disney animated version of the 1950s, there have been several others: Jonathan Miller's very Freud-orientated TV film, the recent all-star British musical version, *Alice's Adventures in Wonderland* and Claude Chabrol's *Alice, or the Last Fugue* (1976) which takes off from a young woman's involvement in a car-crash, making it rather more of an *Alice Through the Windscreen*. But there does remain another and unseen version dating from 1947, which combined live action with puppets. Carol Marsh played Alice but the film has never, as far as we know, played anywhere.

All the Way Home (1963) was a very moving account of the James Agee story *A Death in the Family*, starring Jean Simmons and Robert Preston. Apart from a three-day run as a second feature at the Classic, Stockwell, in South London (which is where I saw it), its only other screening has been on television. *Act One*, Dore Schary's 1963 film of Moss Hart's famous autobiography, was scheduled for ITV one Sunday night, but cancelled. However, it has been seen at the National Film Theatre. George Segal, Jason Robards and George Hamilton were the stars.

Lunch Hour, also 1963, vanished so completely after it was made that even its director, James Hill, wrote to the magazine *Films and Filming* asking readers if they knew of its whereabouts! The only place it did go to was ITV, for a single Friday night screening in about 1965/66. It starred Shirley Ann Field and Robert Stephens as a couple who meet clandestinely in their lunch hour. An unusual film, it only lasted for an hour, which probably confused its distributors; hence the disappearing trick. But its pedigree was faultless: the script was by John Mortimer.

Other TV premières have been: Sal Mineo and Juliet Prowse in *Who Killed Teddy Bear?*, about a juvenile psychopath; Rupert Davies in *The Uncle* (1965), quite a famous unseen *cause célèbre* which was refused a general release by the two major circuits. I saw it *c*. 1966–67 at a charity film society show in Hampstead. Eventually (ten years later) it appeared on TV; *Shark* (1968) was Burt Reynolds in a Sam Fuller *Jaws*-type story. However, since the TV screening and since the success of *Jaws* it has finally been released to cinemas. Maybe it was a film made before its time, i.e. when sharks were not the hottest ticket at the cinema; *Going Home* (1972) starring Robert Mitchum, Jan-Michael Vincent, Brenda Vaccaro; *Star-Spangled Girl*, a Neil Simon comedy with Sandy Duncan (1971); *The Breaking of Bumbo* (Andrew Sinclair, 1971, based on his own novel) starring Richard Warwick was shown at the 1971 Cinema City Exhibition at the Roundhouse in London, and then five years later on television; *The Legend of Lylah Clare*,

Robert Aldrich's melodrama with Peter Finch and Kim Novak, was acquired by the ITV network, but why it was kept out of cinemas since 1969 is a total mystery.

Censorship is one of the major headaches of any film-maker, especially in Great Britain. It accounts for the holding up of several films and in some cases is responsible for their total disappearance. Every time a film is submitted to the British Board of Film Censors a very hefty fee is paid, and there is no guarantee that a film will receive a certificate. Once a film is refused a certificate the distributor may not think it is worth the time, or the cost, of re-submitting it. So he leaves it on the shelf. Many famous films hung fire like this and probably the most famous (not counting Howard Hughes' *The Outlaw*, which gained a reputation in spite of its total lack of controversial content) is *The Wild One*, which was made in 1953 but not released in Britain until 1968, when it was pushed out as a supporting feature to *A Dandy in Aspic*. The fifteen year wait did nothing but harm to the film, for

in the meantime it had totally lost the point that it was making about life in the 1950s. Of course it then seemed ludicrous that it should ever have been banned in the first place since it seemed so tame compared to the subjects and use of film in the late 1960s. Anyway its shelving did no damage to the film careers of Marlon Brando and Lee Marvin. *The Wild Angels* (1966) was another celebrated example of censorship holding up a film's distribution, although this Peter Fonda leather and drugs picture didn't take quite so long to be accepted by the censor. And of course when it did nobody noticed that it was slipped out quietly on release in harness with some other youth picture. Initially it had been taken up by Derek Hill's New Cinema Club, which put on a whole season of banned movies called Forbidden Film Festival. One that was not so lucky was Larry Peerce's *The Incident* with Jan Sterling, Jack Gilford, Beau Bridges and Thelma Ritter. It had a plot similar to *Dutchman* (which incidentally failed to obtain a BBFC certificate and finally won a Greater London

Council X-London rating): a violent confrontation on the New York underground railway. *Panic in Needle Park* (1971) was refused a certificate because it depicted the use and abuse of drugs; however, five years later the climate of opinion had changed (or the examiners at the BBFC had changed) and it was granted a pardon; maybe the fact that it starred Al Pacino had something to do with it, and so the distributors were able to cash in on his success in the two *Godfather* films.

Sometimes films just suddenly turn up after a long wait for no reason in particular. Such titles that finally made it are, like *Panic in Needle Park*, the result of another successful film, e.g. after *Blazing Saddles* made a big hit for director Mel Brooks in 1975, it was felt to be the right time to at last release his previously hidden comedy *The Twelve Chairs*, starring Ron Moody, after five years on the shelf. Likewise Woody Allen's *What's Up, Tiger Lily?* (1966) appeared ten years late, following the success of his more recent movies such as *Sleeper* and *Everything You Always Wanted to Know About Sex*. The ever-admirable Electric Cinema in London's Portobello Road revived *The Todd Killings* (1971) at a time when the Manson murders and similar crimes were current. They also rescued from obscurity the 1969 John Huston picture *A Walk With Love and Death* eight years after it was made. Going back a little further the John Wayne *Jet Pilot* took seven years to reach our screens; made in 1950 it actually turned up in 1957. Visconti's biography of the mad king of Bavaria *Ludwig* was almost shown to the press way back

Jacqueline Bisset (as Christine) is arrested after an escapade in which she has sky-written the first four-letter word in aerial advertising. And it is a scene in another film which few people have ever seen, National General's *The Grasshopper*.

in 1973, but was pulled out after bad notices on the Continent. It finally arrived at the 1976 London Film Festival and promptly disappeared again. Sidney Lumet's thriller *Hit!* did get as far as a press show but failed to open at the Ritz, Leicester Square. Topical note: whatever happened to *Gable and Lombard* which has been trade shown to the film magazines, fairly widely (and apathetically) reviewed but not yet screened?

Most of the titles I have quoted have only been from the late 1960s and early 1970s. There are still hundreds more to discover. Here are a few at random: *Happy Birthday Wanda June* (Rod Steiger, Susannah York), *Big Truck and Poor Clare* (Peter Ustinov, Francesca Annis), *Ghost in the Noonday Sun* (Peter Sellers), *Impossible Object* (Alan Bates, directed by John Frankenheimer, but left uncompleted), *Dirty Little Billy* (Michael J. Pollard), *The Hit Man* (Pam Grier), *First Love* (John Moulder Brown, Dominique Sanda, Richard Warwick, directed by Maximilian Schell), *Gangster Story* (directed by and starring Walter Matthau and made in 1960), *The Christian Licorice Store* (Beau Bridges, Jean Renoir), *The Comeback* (Miriam Hopkins, John Garfield, Jr, Gale Sondergaard), *The Yin and the Yang* (James Mason, Burgess Meredith), *Snowjob* (Gina Lollobrigida, Hugh O'Brian), *Madigan's Millions* (Dustin Hoffman), *Sleep is Lovely* (Peter McEnery), *The Last Movie* (Dennis Hopper), *Son of Dracula* (Ringo Starr), *Children of Rage* (Simon Ward), *Two People* (Peter Fonda and Lindsay Wagner), *The Promise* (John Castle, Ian McKellen), *The Gaunt Woman* (Rachel

Roberts, Anthony Quayle, Harry Andrews), *Welcome to Arrow Beach* (Laurence Harvey), *Two Gentlemen Sharing* (Robin Phillips), *RPM* and *Bless the Beasts and Children* (both Stanley Kramer), *A Talent for Loving* (Richard Widmark, Topol), *Operation Crosseagles* (Rory Calhoun), *Crossroads* (Dana Wynter, Ray Danton), *The Phynx* (an all-star cast of Hollywood favourites, 1969), *Brief Season* (Christopher Jones, Pia Degermark), *Run Shadow Run* (Robert Forster), *Questions* (Joseph Cotten), *Racing Scene* (James Garner), *Rabbit Run* (James Caan, Anjanette Comer), *Kill* (Jean Seberg, James Mason), *Help Stamp Out Fair Play* (Paul Michael Glaser), *The Beloved* (Raquel Welch, Richard Johnson, Jack Hawkins, Flora Robson), *Autumn Child* (Robert Shaw, Mary Ure, Sally Kellerman), *Scraping Bottom* (George Segal and Karen Black) and retitled *Born to Win*, *A Time for Dying* (Audie Murphy as Jesse James – was it ever finished?), and a clutch of Charlotte Rampling titles: *Going All Out, Looking Good, Corky, Nightmare Honeymoon*, which may or may not all be

the same film.

Finally we must award a trophy to the man who has acted in more unseen films than any other performer: Orson Welles, who apart from his uncompleted *Don Quixote* and the curiously vanishing (1942) *It's All True*, has made appearances in the non-appearing *Battle of Neretva* (1970), *Two Times Two* (Polanski) which became *Twelve Plus One*, Brian De Palma's *Get to Know Your Rabbit* (1970), *The Toy Factory* (with Pamela Franklin), *Malpertuis* (1972) and *Necromancy* (1972). His *Safe Place* (1971) with Tuesday Weld showed up at the Screen on the Green in London's Islington.

If you have seen any of the movies in the foregoing lists then you may count yourself as being very lucky, for you are almost certainly in the minority. The only advice I can give you if you spot them as being forthcoming attractions at your local ABC or Odeon Film Centre, is to go and see them as quickly as you can, for it is sure to be a case of 'now you see them, now you don't!'

And whatever happened to *The Bluebird*, the fantastically expensive Russian–American co-production with Elizabeth Taylor, made several years back and never shown – at least in Britain? (F.M.S.)

Oddly, it has taken ten years for Woody Allen's film *What's Up Tiger Lily* to reach us for a limited release and now only because his name has become worth something at the box-office!

Looking Back – When Croydon was the Film Capital of Britain

by John M. East

When the British film industry was in its infancy, several studios were built in Croydon, for although near London land was cheap and the surrounding hilly countryside was ideal for location work. Joe Rosenthal was a cameraman who came into prominence for his filmed coverage of the South African War and the Russo-Japanese War. He diced with death too frequently for his liking. In 1906 he settled in Croydon High Street and soon afterwards formed the Rosie Film Company. Rosenthal made a

number of 'art films' on an open air stage in his back garden. This was about twenty feet long and ten feet wide. It was mounted on a revolve to favour the sun, in those days the only means of lighting a set. There were braces supporting backcloths made of canvas on wooden frames. In 1909 Rosenthal released a factual film, *Life On A North Sea Trawler*.

Another pioneer called Hassan settled in Croydon and the producer, Bert Wynne, who ended his career making TV commercials, made his screen début in 1906 with him:

'When I left school I was articled to a surveyor in Croydon High Street. Nearby was an antique dealer called Hassan who had constructed a "stage" in the yard behind his shop.

'An actor called Batley was playing Dick Turpin in a sketch at the Croydon Empire. He was to be Hassan's star. However, the juvenile lead failed to turn up and they asked me to be his substitute. With a promise of a fee of five shillings, I managed to get the afternoon off from the surveyor.

'I was very happy to make love to Hassan's pretty daughter. However, in the middle of our embrace, a gust of wind totally wrecked the set, which crashed down, covering us with linen and broken timber. We finished the film the next day and in the following weeks I made several appearances for Mr Hassan. I decided to quit surveying and become an actor.'

The actor, Victor Lorraine, also played for Hassan:

'I was appearing at the Croydon Hippodrome in a drama in which I was a

'Got it in one take' says the triumphant cameraman on the set at the old Cricks and Martin Studio at Croydon – and note those 'prop' pebbles strewn around the floor.

policeman who disguised himself as a beggar to unmask the villain. Mr Hassan saw me in my dressing-room. He said he would write a film, using the plot of the drama, and it would be ready to start shooting at eight o'clock the next morning. He decided to call it *Harvey Corde, Detective*. I accepted £8 for three days' work.

'Soon after I arrived it started to rain. We were held up for two hours – the penalty of doing interiors *outside*! Incidentally, I had to be very careful in opening a door, the slightest jerk caused the set to wobble like a jelly.

'I saw this film in a cinema in Glasgow. It came to the scene where I confronted the villain dressed as a beggar. I turned round, removed my disguise and the subtitle read: "I am Harvey Corde the Detective!" The audience burst into applause – that seldom happens in cinemas today.

'I subsequently made a comic short at Croydon called *Larry, the Pig*. One scene showed me in a cart with a pig in the back. The animal suddenly went mad and jumped on my shoulders. What followed added up to a marvellous slapstick scene which would have been impossible to prepare. The director was delighted. I was bruised and frightened.'

By the early 1900s the commercial possibilities of the motion picture had been realised and the industry expanded at a prodigious rate. There were still penny gaffs on fairgrounds and short bioscopes on music-hall bills. However, purpose-built cinemas were opening, and because admission was cheap, and the films satisfied the lust of the eye, there was a big public for this new attraction. The Clarendon Film Company was founded in 1904 by Percy Stow and H. V. Lawley, a former partner of the pioneer producer, Cecil Hepworth. It was in an alley called Clarendon Road, off Limes Road, Croydon. They built a studio with a glass roof and a glass front to admit the maximum sunlight. There were two stages 60 × 25 ft. and 80 × 35 ft. There was a three-acre field nearby,

useful for exteriors, and an artificial lake in Boulogne Road (later bricked over and used as a children's playground). Clarendon made comic shorts, which were little more than fragments of life seen in an amusing way. A typical example, made in 1904, was called *Father's Hat, or, Guy Fawkes Day*. Children stole their father's hat for their guy. They arranged the guy to the best effect before running off to fetch some paraffin. The father arrived, spotted his hat, and decided to catch the children on the hop by wearing the mask and his hat and pretending to be the guy. The father was unperturbed when they returned and lit the straw, being unaware of the bucket of paraffin his daughter suddenly threw over him. The father scrambled out of the flames and chased the children.

By the mid-1900s things were bleak for British film-makers. With an uncontrolled flood of better productions coming from abroad, many went out of business. Clarendon, like other companies, made some factual films. They required little creative inspiration, and the Gaumont Company distributed many of them. One showed Edward VII and Queen Alexandra arriving in Dublin, walking down the quay, and the royal procession moving through the streets. With a length of 120 ft. it sold for £3 a print. *The Industrial Blind* was a rare example of a picture dealing with social welfare.

Fan postcard of Leah Marlborough, who could justly claim to have been one of Britain's first screen villainesses during her career at Cricks and Martin and Clarendon Studios, both at Croydon.

Intrepid heroes like *Sexton Blake* cropped up in dozens of cheap paperback novels. When H. V. Lawley left Clarendon in 1908, Percy Stow decided to invent a romantic figure who would star in a series of adventure pictures. The result was the fearless *Lieut Rose*, who immediately caught the public's fancy. Clarendon's artificial lake came in very useful and the anonymous actor who played *Lieut Rose* was quoted as saying: 'I won't meet my death by drowning – pneumonia is more likely to be the cause.'

The actress, Leah Marlborough, who played in a *Lieut Rose* production, said in an interview:

'I've often read about the invention of close-ups. I was called upon to depict horror, apprehension and remorse by standing behind a porthole, which was, in effect, a sort of picture frame inserted in a "flat". The camera was only a few feet away. When I saw the film only my face appeared and then the scene cut to the hero floundering in the depths. Again, although the studios were made of glass and constructed to catch the sun, I know they used electric light there to supplement the sun and the glare used to trouble my eyes.'

For Christmas 1907 Clarendon issued three comic shorts. *That's Not Right, Watch Me!* was about a silly man who mistakenly thought he could do other people's jobs, with comic results. *An Awkward Situation* concerned a man

A cold rehearsal – note the snow and icicles – outside the Cricks and Martin studios – *circa* 1910. Players unknown.

taking his bath when his lady friend was shown into his bathroom by an inefficient servant. *An Anxious Day for Mother* showed a doting mother as the victim of her two exceptionally mischievous children.

Clarendon made an ambitious version of Charles Kingsley's story, *The Water Babies* and billed 'magnificent and spectacular submarine effects' which were taken in the company's lake. Equally successful was a filmed adaptation of Browning's poem, *The Pied Piper*

of Hamelin and the company was not slow in singing its own praises: 'A masterpiece of absolute fidelity of detail. Costumes of the period – real rats – typical scenes. The most exquisite film production ever placed upon the market. Length 775 ft. Price: £19 7s. 6d.'

The final film offered for that Christmas is worthy of quoting in detail:

Clarendon's *The Soldier's Wedding* – Romantic! Exciting! Pathetic and Humorous!

Invalided home – aboard ship – a proposal – the wedding – a note saying the hero must leave for the front – a sad parting.

SOME MONTHS LATER: No news from the front – the young wife decides to go to the front as a nurse.

AT THE FRONT: Shells are falling in all directions. Our hero is seen helping the wounded to safety. Again he comes forward but this is for the last time. A troop of black men seize him and he is carried off. We discover him at the execution ground. In the delay, the wife, who has followed him, changes the cartridges. The hero fakes death when the executioner fires. The couple escape back to camp.

ONE YEAR LATER. Home again. Twins arrive for them.

LENGTH: 675 ft. PRICE: PRICE: £16 17s. 6d.

In 1908 Clarendon became more ambitious. They took a gamble in making a historical subject requiring expensive sets and special costumes. Called *The Cavalier's Wife*, it described the devotion of a Royalist lady of the Cromwellian period for her Lord, who was captured and imprisoned by the Roundheads. Clarendon made a determined effort to reach the front rank of film-makers. In 1913 they experimented with talking pictures, which depended on synchronisation with gramophone records. These were not successful. However, the company achieved wide publicity by engaging the Marchioness of Townshend as their screenwriter – hitherto writers were rarely billed – her titles included *The Convent Gate*, *The Family Solicitor*, *The Love of an Actress*, *Wreck and Ruin*, *When East Meets West*, *House of Mystery* and *A Strong Man's Love*.

Low Warren was brought in to write historical dramas for Clarendon and his *Saved by Fire* was well received. *The Bioscope*, the leading trade magazine of the time, wrote:

It was '. . . a chapter of real life . . . jealousy, weakness and desire, whirling in a mad game on the brink of a precipice.' The story of an actress, who was beautiful and unprincipled, who enticed the leading man from his 'poor, soft-eyed little wife, who, concealing herself among the curtains of the actress's boudoir . . . sees him about to succumb to this illicit love.' This was too much for the wife, who ran out, and in doing so, upset a lamp and the place caught fire. 'After a series of most exciting incidents, the actress dies, the couple are reconciled, and thus the story ends.'

Low Warren's screenplay, *King Charles*, an adaptation of Harrison Ainsworth's *Ovingdean Grange*, blended with actual historical records, was followed by the same author's *Old St Paul's*. Billed as 'Strong historical subjects' and given big

publicity, they employed hundreds of extras and special costumes were hired to lend authenticity. Sensational fire effects were achieved with the use of models. The films were box-office hits.

Mrs Grace Richards lived near the Clarendon's studio. She recalled the excitement its activities caused in the neighbourhood:

'We soon grew used to seeing actors going to and from the studio, often dressed in colourful costumes of a bygone age. Because of the shortcomings

of cinematography in those far-off days, they all had to wear bright yellow make-up.

'One day I was in our front garden peeling some potatoes for my mother when a big man stopped at the gate: "Finish those later on, my girl. I need you for a scene in the film."

'He explained that he wanted me to get on to the front of a milk cart at the invitation of the milkman and when he tried to kiss me, I had to pour a jug of milk over his head. He lost control of the horse which also got splashed and we disappeared up the street to cries of anguish from my screen father.

'I did as I was told and after an hour was rewarded with two shillings for my pains. Later on I was cast as a boy chimney-sweep and I had to climb out of the top of a soot-laden chimney built inside the studio. As a little girl, who kissed her father goodbye at East Croydon Railway Station, I was given five shillings. The subtitle read "Daddy goes to war." When I saw this picture, many women in the audience burst into tears.'

At the beginning of the First World War, Percy Stow was joined by H. M. Sharp – a former partner of G. H. Cricks, whose studio at Croydon will be described later. The company was as busy as ever, although the gallant *Lieut Rose* went off to do real active service. The company made a screen version of the historical novel, *Under the Red Robe*, comic shorts

Shooting on location on Shirley Hills, Croydon, Clarendon's *King Charles* (1913) which was to prove a big success.

and a series based upon the songs *On the Banks of Allen Water*, *The Lost Chord*, *Love's Old Sweet Song* and *If Thou Wert Blind*. With a view to catching the market for topical 'interest' films, they made *A Day With Our Territorials in the Field* and *Training Our Volunteer Constables*.

Soon, however, Clarendon was forced to close down. Films imported from the USA captured the imagination of the majority of British cinemagoers. The studio was eventually taken over by a renting company called Harma, and with a well-known American director, F. Martin Thornton, at the helm, several successful features were made there. The hero was invariably played by a robust new leading man, James Knight, and the villain by Bernard Dudley. Soon the public liked to see these two at loggerheads with each other. Harma made a film about the Wilde–Conn fight and a fictional boxing film, *The Happy Warrior* which was well received. It concerned an orphan, who was happier as a prize-fighter than claiming his rightful title.

By 1920 H. M. Jenks, who controlled Harma, was in financial trouble. The company was reorganised with the backing of some provincial exhibitors, who hoped to break the stranglehold of American films by going into production themselves. Despite capital of £150,000, the venture was unsuccessful and the studio closed within three years.

The premises have since been used for many purposes. When it was converted into a car maintenance shop, most of the glass of the roof and sides was removed. The pioneer, G. H. Cricks, formed a film

The popular though anonymous star of Clarendon's successful 'Lieut. Rose R.N.' series. Perhaps a reader could come up with his name?

Looking the part, James Knight played the hero of a number of Harma films: and also looking the part, Bernard Dudley (below) played the villain for them.

company with H. M. Sharp in 1901. They leased a site in London Road, Mitcham, consisting of a house, used as an office, a greenhouse which served as a laboratory and a field in which they built an open-air stage.

Leah Marlborough played for the company: 'An elderly actor insisted on keeping his overcoat near at hand and he would slip into it between shots. I can still see him on a particularly chilly September day, collar turned up, a scarf enveloping his face, with an umbrella in one hand and a vacuum-flask in the other. The cameraman had already adjourned to a neighbouring public-house and had forgotten to dismiss him for the lunch break.

'The actor was sitting on a bed in his "garret", while shining in the distance were the lights of London, all resplendent on a painted backcloth. A slight drizzle was falling, and, as his anguished face turned in my direction, he muttered: "Film acting, eh? More like a short cut to Hell, I'd say." '

Charles Beckley, who was born near the studio in 1894, often saw the Cricks and Sharp films being made on location: 'With a bit more money they might have beaten Mack Sennett in world popularity. I saw a laughable stunt where they had a boy riding his bike and reading a comic at the same time. He was so interested in that comic, he rode right up

Scene from a 1921 Harma Co. production called *Brenda of the Barge*.

the ramp of a removal van which drove off down the street.'

In 1908 the company was reconstructed and J. H. Martin replaced H. M. Sharp. They moved a few miles away and opened a studio in Waddon New Road, Croydon, having one stage, 65 × 30 ft. with a glass roof; an adjoining house was used for an office and dressing-rooms. Martin was already skilled in directing trick films and comic shorts. A typical example of the latter category was *She Would Wed* which described the frantic efforts of a lady of uncertain age to hook any man in sight, including a postman, a muffin man, a fat man, a cripple, a dude and eventually a blind beggar, whom she dragged to the registry office. *Father's Saturday Afternoon* showed a man's futile attempts to find a peaceful corner in his own home – he finally crawled into the dog's kennel.

By 1909 the market was flooded with films made in Britain and abroad, and Cricks and Martin were selling their efforts for as little as three old pence for a foot of film. They found factual pictures

cheap to make, and issued many including *The Birth of the Big Gun* and *Matches – Made in England*. In 1910 they released *Prison Reform*, which had on its advertising matter: 'With apologies to the Home Secretary, the Rt. Hon. Winston Churchill'. It made fun of proposals for better conditions in prisons.

Cricks and Martin, like Clarendon, used electric lighting to boost unpredictable sunlight, and the studio was technically in advance of its time. By 1911 they had

the largest staff of any film company in Britain. They tried valiantly to maintain a high standard of production, but they were soon overtaken by companies with larger capital resources.

Cricks and Martin produced the first British picture of feature length, *The Pirates of 1920*, released in 1911. This included a spectacular battle between an airship and a liner, involving the use of models. The heroic lieutenant dangled between the sea and the sky in a hair-raising way; the villain persecuted the heroine; it ended with a bomb, a last-minute rescue and the hero folded in the heroine's arms. Also in 1911, Cricks and Martin issued a spectacular military drama about a drummer boy, *The Mighty Atom*.

Cricks and Martin were jealous of Clarendon's success with their *Lieut Rose*

John East, the writer of this feature, nostalgically picks up the pieces when nine years later (1975) the old studio was reconstructed as a garage!

The old Clarendon Studios in Limes Road, Croydon, in 1966.

The way they used to 'sell' the movies in 1908!

series, and in 1911 they started their own series about the adventures of *Police Constable Sharpe*. Early in 1913 they launched another series featuring *Paul Sleuth, Crime Investigator*. When *Paul Sleuth* was involved with *The Mystic Seven*, there were many sensations, including a flight by a balloon, pursuit by an aeroplane and the automatic operation of a cinematograph camera hidden in a car to record its route.

Cricks and Martin were never slow to latch on to other firms' discoveries. By 1910 they were using the happy ending, with the hero embracing the heroine, a device which made American movies so popular. While many British companies were still content to film a stage play, Cricks and Martin, like Hepworth, favoured locations to add realism to their productions. For two dramas about smuggling, they went as far as the West Country to film seascapes and coastal scenes.

J. H. Martin was convinced the survival of the company depended on releasing low budget trick and comic films. He dissolved his partnership with G. H. Cricks and opened his own studio at Merton Park. Within a few years he had to give up, and to make a living turned to film processing.

G. H. Cricks remained in Croydon, and for the next two years still traded under the name Cricks and Martin. After the outbreak of war in 1914 he made two patriotic films. He issued a few comedy shorts and in 1915 a feature, *The Avenging Hand*, a study of the supernatural, in which a murder was committed by the stolen hand of an Egyptian mummy. Cricks was forced to cease production in 1916 and carried on a printing business in the laboratories of the Waddon New Road premises using the name of the Croydon Film Company. In 1916 the studio was taken by Maurice Sandground for a peppercorn rent of £65 a year. He was a film renter and he named his production company, the Gaiety Film Company. He made a few low budget comedies, and in 1919 two features, *Russia, Land of Tomorrow*, and *Kilties Three*. With capital of £5,750 Sandground financed films that nobody would book. He abandoned operations and by 1923 the studio and surrounding ground was being used as a garage.

For twenty years Croydon was called 'the pulse of the British film industry'. Production which started there overnight ceased, almost as quickly, never to be revived. Boreham Wood became the film capital of Britain. However, studios there, and in other places, owed much to the brave pioneers who put so much devotion and expertise into making films in Croydon.

The Female of the Species

by Peter Sasdy

One of the most important special features in next year's *Film Review* is to be a contribution by Anthony Slide on the history of the woman's place in the cinema – the other side of the cameras, a survey which will reveal that since the earliest days of the movies, when Alice Guy-Blaché in 1896 made the first fiction film in France (called *La Fée aux choux*) to the present day, when women directors and producers are working all over the world, women have played an important role in film production.
But what is it like for a male director to have a woman as his producer? I asked *Peter Sasdy*, who has just completed shooting *Welcome to Blood City* for EMI release and here is his reply.

At the time of legislative equality between the sexes, I am not quite sure that the question 'How does it feel working with women producers?' should be answered at all, just in case I am accused of sexual discrimination. My task is not so difficult once we establish my fundamental belief that there are only two kinds of producers – good ones and bad ones – regardless of their sexes. During the last few years I have directed three films involving lady producers, and my experiences were happy ones. First of all neither of the two producers I worked with – Aida Young in England and Marilyn Stonehouse in Canada – wanted to be treated differently from their male colleagues and, under the daily pressure of film-making, I soon forgot about their skirts – especially as one of them always wore trousers. . . . They both approached their work with enormous enthusiasm and had the lasting stamina of many well-known male producers. Also they had the added advantage as women to be 'Mums' of the unit – artists and technicians find it easier to confide in them than in their male counterparts.
On my last film *Welcome to Blood City* I found in Marilyn Stonehouse the best and most loyal partner I could hope for. Her tremendous local knowledge of the Canadian scene ironed out in advance so many of our difficulties, and the respect of the various unions for her made our lives much easier in comparison to other film companies from abroad.
Just in case I sound too biased in my brief 'confession' on women producers, let me mention the one and only negative side of the coin. In the moment of panic they become over-emotional and tend to take the shortcomings of others too personally. Or, when the fault is on their side, they seem to develop a rather **awkward stubbornness** – as a defensive mechanism – and this makes reasoning very difficult.
I believe this one negative aspect is due to the prejudices they have suffered from for so long, and they still feel the need to prove themselves as equals. As far as my own personal experiences are concerned, there is no need for further proof – cast and crew accept them and react to them in exactly the same way as to male producers. The time has arrived when the presence of women producers is a healthy and logical development within the international film industry.

Jack Palance and Keir Dullea in EMI's *Welcome to Blood City*, directed by Peter Sasdy.

IN MEMORIAM

EDDIE 'ROCHESTER' ANDERSON did not long survive Jack Benny, with whom he played, as his inseparable and outspoken black sidekick, for so many years in the latter's radio and TV series and also in his several films. Born in 1905, Eddie appeared in a number of films in the 30s, including *Gone With the Wind*, *Green Pastures*, *Jezebel* and many others, but it was with Benny that he sprang into prominence, becoming a great favourite, with his gravel-voiced comments and mobile features. He died in February, 1977, aged 72.

Sir **STANLEY BAKER**, who died at the early age of 48 while in Spain in the autumn of 1976, had been knighted only a few weeks prior to his death. Son of a Rhondda Valley miner, tough and ambitious, he appeared in his first film role at the age of 14 in *Undercover*. Thereafter he appeared in stage productions for several years, making a return to filming in the 1950s in a series of war/adventure films such as *The Cruel Sea*, *The Red Beret* and *A Hill in Korea*. Then came some equally arduous if less warlike parts in films like *Campbell's Kingdom*, *Violent Playground* and *Hell is a City*. But back to war he went in the very successful *The Guns of Navarone*. Then he began to show a greater sensibility and range with his performances in films like *Eve* and *Accident*. Not content with acting, Baker in the early 60s formed his own production company to make the spectacular and

highly successful film *Zulu*, going on to co-produce and star in several films, *Sands of Kalahari* and *Robbery* among them. More recently he had been devoting most of his attention to television (he was a director of Harlech Television), his last small-screen appearance being in a new serial based on Richard Llewellyn's book *How Green Was My Valley*.

With his wife, Ellen.

Better known for his stage work as actor and director, **ROMNEY BRENT** (real name Romulo Larrade, a diplomat's son) was also a playwright (among his credits the book for the musical adaptation of *Nymph Errant* in London in the 30s). But he did appear in a number of films including *Don't Go Near the Water* and *The Adventures of Don Juan*. He died aged 74 on 24 September 1976, in his native Mexico, to which he had returned a few years previously to teach.

STEPHEN BOYD, who died while playing a game of golf in California on 2 June 1977, at the early age of 49, had an Irish mother and a Canadian father. His real name was William Millar and he started his acting career as a child performer, joining the Ulster Group Theatre when he was only 16. In 1946 he went to Canada, where he appeared in repertory (as well as doing such jobs as a cinema commissionaire and café waiter). He returned to England and in 1952 was appearing at the Windsor Repertory Theatre and two years later began to get small parts on the West End stage. His film career was really launched with his performance in *The Man Who Never Was* in 1956, to be followed three years later by his outstanding work in *Ben Hur*. His other films included *Island in the Sun*, *Les Bijoutiers du Clair de Lune*, *The Caper of the Golden Bulls*, *A Man Called Noon*, *The Fall of the Roman Empire* and, most recently, in the British film, *The Squeeze*.

It was in 1953 that HENRI-GEORGES CLOUZOT made his classical suspense thriller *The Wages of Fear – Le Salaire de la Peur* (one of the few French films to have a successful general release in this country in its subtitled version) and so assured himself of a place in the history of the movies. Clouzot's output was relatively small, only about a dozen films in all, but this may be explained by his frequent bouts of ill-health and his many other activities, which included the writing of several plays, books and opera librettos. Refused entry into the French Navy, he originally studied law, then branched into journalism (he was one of the *Paris-Midi* writers for several years). He entered the movies as assistant director to Anatole Litvak, later becoming scriptwriter and it was not until 1942 that he directed his first film, *Le Corbeau – The Crow*. Among his best films were *Quai des Orfevres* (with Louis Jouvet) and *Les Diaboliques* (with his first wife as star). Born in 1907, Clouzot died in Paris, aged 69, in January 1977.

JOAN CRAWFORD, who died on 10 May 1977, in Hollywood, was one of the great stars of Hollywood's golden era – and one of its most durable products. Born in San Antonio, Texas, in 1904 (most sources; though given as 1908 in America's *Motion Picture Almanac*), she won a talent contest when she was 13. A professional dancer, she was seen by a talent-scout while appearing in a Broadway musical and made her screen début in a bit part in *Pretty Ladies* in 1925 – appearing in five other films that same year. Her first feature role was in

Sally, Irene and Mary in 1925, when she changed her real name of Lucille le Sueur to Joan Crawford (for a time she was also known as Billie Cassin). She went on to make something like one hundred films, of which *Our Dancing Daughters* (in 1928), *Dance, Fools, Dance, Grand Hotel* and *Rain* (in 1932), *The Women, The Last of Mrs Cheyney* and *Flamingo Road* are some of the best known. She won an Oscar for her performance in *Mildred Pierce* in 1945 and she gave a tremendous performance

opposite her old rival Bette Davis in *Whatever Happened to Baby Jane*. It was in another horror thriller, *Trog*, that she made one of her last appearances (in 1970). Seldom really outstanding, Miss Crawford was at least reliably good in whatever she did and she was brilliant in her adaptation to the necessity of changing her roles with the advancing years, switching from her earliest flapper-type career girl, and *femme fatale* roles, to the mature woman and finally to the highly specialised style of horror film acting. Perhaps her best epitaph would be that old familiar cry: 'They don't make stars like her anymore!'

The death of RICARDO CORTEZ, in a New York hospital on 28 April 1977, at the age of 77, takes yet another veteran from the screen. Cast largely as a Latin lover in his younger period, he was in fact Vienna born (real name Jack Krantz) of Austro-Hungarian parents. His first job in America was running errands for a Wall Street broking firm, during which time he took acting lessons in the evenings and eventually set off for Hollywood. Some of his many films include *The Torrent* (opposite Garbo), *Private Life of Helen of Troy, Shadow of a Doubt, Blackmail* and, his last in 1958, *The Last Hurrah*. More recently he returned to New York to join a Stockbrokers and also became agent for the purchase of film stories in both New York and Paris.

Although he did make occasional brief excursions into other kinds of movies (more notably in the Leslie Howard–Norma Shearer film of *Romeo and Juliet*, John Huston's Civil War classic *The Red Badge of Courage* and the original *A Star is Born*) ANDY DEVINE was kept busy all his life acting in Westerns. With the real name of Jeremiah Schwartz, born in Arizona in 1905, Devine started his film career as an extra in 1926 and though he often had straight or even dramatic roles (such as the man tragically hanged in the 1932 production of *Law and Order*), his bumbling appearance and gravel voice (sustained in a childhood accident which affected his vocal chords) soon brought him the comedy roles for which he became noted. He played the driver in John Ford's Western classic *Stagecoach* and did so well in the part that Ford used him in a number of his later films. In the 1940s Devine played Roy Rogers's sidekick in a series of ten films (performances which helped to bring his name twice into the *Motion Picture Herald*'s ten biggest money-making stars of the year lists in the late 40s) and did the same thing for Guy Madison in the television series about Wild Bill Hickok. Devine died in Hollywood on 18 February 1977 at the age of 71.

Though she made quite a considerable number of films, if she had never made more than one, *The Whisperers*, Dame EDITH EVANS would have earned her place in any film roll of honour and, indeed, the movie did bring her the best female performance of the year award at the 1967 Berlin Film Festival. Dame Edith made a remarkably impressive screen début in the 1948 film *Queen of Spades*, to be followed by more superb performances in *The Last Days of Dolwyn, The Importance of Being Earnest, Look Back in Anger, The Nun's Story, The Chalk Garden, David Copperfield, The Doll's House* and many other films. London born (8 February 1888), a milliner's apprentice at the age of 14, Dame Edith started attending dramatic classes when she was 16. It was here that she was seen by William Poel, who was so impressed with her he gave her the role of Cressida in his production of *Troilus and Cressida*. It was this that decided Dame Edith to cancel her apprenticeship and devote herself wholly to the theatre. So began a triumphant career that continued right up to her death, at the age of 88, in her sleep, at her Kentish home on 14 October 1976. With that wonderful voice and the vocal mannerisms (that she accentuated only in her later years) she will possibly be best recalled as a comedienne but she could when she wished easily call up great tragic reserves in classic drama and her approach to all her roles was endlessly subtle.

With Katharine Hepburn (left) in *The Madwoman of Chaillot*.

Peter Finch, centre, was the first deceased actor ever to be awarded an 'Oscar', winning it by his work in *Network*, his penultimate film before his death in 1977.

Born in London in 1916 (28 September), PETER FINCH was educated in Sydney, Australia, and made his stage début in that city in a production of the farce *While Parents Sleep*. In 1949 he made his first London stage appearance, but more than ten years before that, had started appearing in Australian films such as *Mr Chedworth Steps Out*. The long and highly successful international screen career that followed included fine performances in *The Wooden Horse, Elephant Walk, A Town Like Alice, The Shiralee, The Pumpkin Eater* and *Sunday, Bloody Sunday*, for which he won an 'Oscar' for the best actor's performance of 1971. Those who saw him in his last film, *Raid on Entebbe*, in which he played the Israeli Prime Minister, may have noticed that he looked a great deal older than his sixty years and it was while the film was having its première run in London that he died in Hollywood early in January 1977, after a heart attack.

WALTER FITZGERALD, who died a few days before Christmas 1976 at the age of 80, worked more in the theatre than in films, but following his screen début in 1930 in a British film, *Murder at Covent Garden*, he played a number of character roles in such popular features as *Squadron Leader X* in 1941, Disney's

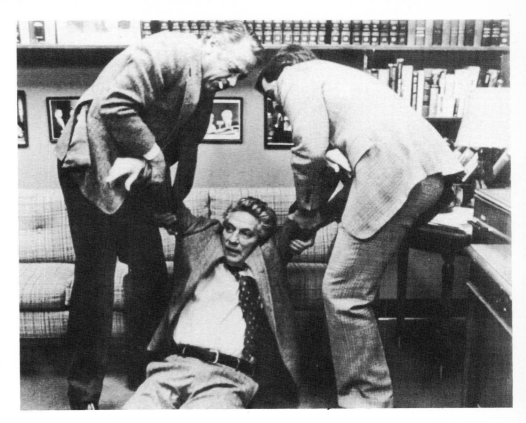

Treasure Island in 1949, *HMS Defiant* in 1962. Other film appearances were in *San Demetrio–London, The Cruel Sea* and *Cockleshell Heroes*. The son of a clergyman, born at Devonport, he began his acting career as an amateur while working at the Stock Exchange, his first professional appearance being in 1922.

A former amateur film critic (for Oxford's *Isis* magazine) CHARLES FREND began his career in films with

editing movies at the old B.I.P. studios at Elstree in 1931; moving over to Gaumont-British (and working on several Hitchcock pictures there) a couple of years later. He moved again, this time to Ealing Studios, in 1941 and it was there that he made his directorial début with the semi-documentary *The Big Blockade*. And it was this semi-documentary, realistic style that Frend continued to use for the greater part of his output: *San Demetrio–London; The Foreman Went to France; The Cruel Sea,* etc. He was less successful with his digressions, such as the rather pallid comedies *Barnacle Bill* and *A Run for Your Money*, or period pieces like *Johnny Frenchman*. It was Charles Frend, incidentally, who directed Ealing Studios's last film, a very ordinary cop melodrama called *The Long Arm*, made on the eve of the BBC taking over the studios in 1956. Arguably Frend's finest film was one of his less successful, commercially; his meticulously careful and detailed *Scott of the Antarctic*, with John Mills as the tragic explorer and with the haunting musical score by Vaughan Williams. After Ealing's closure Frend did little in the way of cinema movies, turning almost exclusively to television, for which he directed a number of series including *Danger Man*. He died on 8 January 1976, having been born in Pulborough, Sussex, sixty-seven years previously.

JEAN GABIN (real name Jean-Alexis Moncourge) who died in the city in which he was born, Paris, on 15 November 1976, was one of his country's most famous and respected film personalities, a fact proved by the almost nationwide homage paid to him at his funeral. Born of a theatrical family on 17 May 1904, his wide non-acting experience included working in an iron foundry and at other similar jobs for something like six years, three years as a Marine in the First World War and another three years in the French Navy, on a minesweeper, during the Second World War. Starting

his theatrical career as an extra at the *Folies Bergère*, he played on the music-halls, in cabaret and in operetta. Teamed with Mistinguett, he was soon topping the bills. His first film, made in 1930, was *Chacun Sa Chance* and so began a vast number of movies including many French screen classics, notably *La Belle Equipe*, *Pépé le Moko*, *Les Bas Fonds*, *La Grande Illusion*, *La Bête Humaine* and *Quai des Brumes*. In 1941 Gabin went to Hollywood and was soon busy on a film

entitled *Moontide*. Others followed but after the liberation in 1945 Gabin returned to France and continued to make a long series of films right up to his death (including a series in which he played the famous detective Maigret). His great quality was a rugged masculinity allied to sensitivity and in later years more especially his range became very wide, playing anything from a gangster to legal advocate and approaching all his roles with the same easy professionalism.

JAMES WONG HOWE who died of cancer at his home in Hollywood on 12 July 1976, at the age of 76, was one of the world's most outstanding motion picture cameramen. His real name was Wong Tung Jim and he was born in Canton, China, arriving with his parents in the United States in 1904, when he was five years old. In Washington, James's interest in photography started when he became the owner of a Brownie box camera while working on a number of jobs that included being an errand boy for a commercial photographer. Moving to Los Angeles, he obtained a job of salvaging rejected film stock in the cutting rooms, later becoming 'slate boy' to Cecil B. DeMille and assistant to several of his cameramen. But it was as a stills photographer of increasing reputation that he was asked to do some close-ups when a cameraman was taken ill. His reputation grew rapidly after his first film, *Drums of Fate* in 1922, and he went on to photograph hundreds of films. He won two Oscars (for *Rose Tattoo* and *Hud*) and was nominated for seven more.

But every film he made was photographically distinctive and of top class. He last appeared in public at a dinner given in his honour in February 1976.

JOHN HUBLEY, who died early in 1977, at the age of 62 during an operation for a heart condition, was the creator – with wife Faith – of that short-sighted cartoon character Mr Magoo. A former Walt Disney apprentice, he formed UPA in 1955 and began a flow of highly original, stylised and very un-Disney cartoons. He came to Britain last year to work on the feature cartoon of *Watership Down* and it was because of his heart trouble that he had to leave the unit and return to America.

NUNNALLY JOHNSON, who died from pneumonia in a Hollywood hospital on 24 March 1977, at the age of 79, was equally at home writing, directing or producing movies, though it was the first (*Grapes of Wrath* and *Holy Matrimony*) which brought him his Oscar nominations. In fact his credits include 79 screenplays (a few of them: *Three Faces of Eve, Woman in the Window, House of Rothschild, The Dirty Dozen*), some of which he himself produced, some directed. He was a reporter before he started writing for films and served in the First World War in the US Cavalry.

It was in the 1920s, as one of the leading figures in the German Expressionist group of moviemakers, that FRITZ LANG became famous for such classic films as *The Testament of Dr Mabuse*,

'*M*', *Metropolis, Siegfried* and *Liliom*. Turning down Hitler's offer of spearheading Nazi film production, Lang left Germany for America (in 1933) where after two idle years he made *Fury*. Thereafter he had a prolific output, most of his films being thrillers. Some of the best known of his American features include *You Only Live Once, Western Union, Scarlet Street, The Big Heat, Rancho Notorious, The Blue Gardenia* and *Beyond a Reasonable Doubt*. The last was made in 1956 and was followed by two years of inactivity and a return to Germany to produce a number of minor movies. After 1960 Lang's few professional activities were in the nature of lectures and festival appearances. He also played himself in Godard's *Le Mépris* in 1963. Increasingly stricken by blindness and other ills, Austrian-born Lang died at the age of 85, in his Hollywood home on 2 August 1976.

JACQUES PRÉVERT, who died at his Normandy home in April 1977, at the age of 77, was a poet and playwright best known in Britain for his screenplays of such screen classics as *Quai des Brumes, Les Enfants du Paradis* and *Le Jour se Lève*. For a period of ten years he worked closely with Marcel Carné. His last script, for which he received no credit, was *La Marie du Port*, made by Carné in 1950. Thereafter he concentrated on short films, radio and television and his poetry, of which he published several popular volumes.

ROBERTO ROSSELLINI – born Rome, 8 May 1906, died in that city on 3 June 1977 – earned his place in the cinema's roll of honour with his *Rome, Open City* (1945), the movie made while Italy was still occupied by the Nazis and the work which founded the Neo-Realism school of filming. Rossellini came from an artistic family: his father was an architect, his brother a composer. He entered the film business as a sound technician when he was 30. Given a documentary to make about a hospital ship, he used the sailors as his actors and the success of this novelty was to have an influence on all his later work. After *Open City* Rosselini made two other movies in similar style, *Paisa* and *Germany Year Zero*; and he continued to make a series of films on minute budgets using non-professional actors. His wholly fictional films were never quite so successful, though some of them (with stars like Anna Magnani and Ingrid Bergman – who he married in 1950 and was divorced from seven years later) all had considerable interest. In the late 50s

Rosselini turned increasingly to television and from 1961 onwards confined himself entirely to this medium (his last work was a telerecording of a concert in the Sistine Chapel for Italian TV). Though his own film work, on close examination, is on the thin side (he was capable of such mediocre films as *Stromboli*), his influence of other film directors has been immense and can often enough be seen in the films being made today.

Born in Connecticut, USA, on 4 June 1911 (or 1912; reference books vary between the two dates) ROSALIND RUSSELL, who died at the age of 65 (64?) in Los Angeles on 28 November 1976, was a product of the American Academy of Dramatic Art, which she joined after a tour of Europe undertaken when she left college. She started her career in provincial repertory (American Summer Theatre) and made her New York stage début in *Garrick Gaieties* in 1932. Her first movie was *Evelyn Prentice* in 1934, which started her on her long career on the screen, some of her more noteworthy appearances being in *China Seas, Craig's Wife, Night Must Fall, His Girl Friday* (an outstanding performance), *The Citadel, The Feminine Touch, The Women, Design for Scandal, My Sister Eileen, Mourning Becomes Electra* (a switch: though smart, sophisticated and even crazy comedy were her *forte*, she was capable of excellent straight dramatic performances), *Gypsy* and *Auntie Mame* (the role she created on Broadway and then so successfully transferred to the screen). So well proportioned that she always looked taller than she was (5 ft 5 in.), always beautifully and neatly dressed (for years she appeared in America's list of the ten best-dressed women) she was naturally elegant in her carriage, her voice and her acting.

Though as a stage actor Edinburgh-born ALASTAIR SIM played many classic roles, in the cinema he will always be recalled for some fine comedy performances, notably in the St Trinians farces. With his naturally lugubrious appearance and over-expressive face, and his remarkable voice, Sim always found it easy to win laughs from his audience. After his first film in 1934, *The Riverside Murder*, he appeared in more than thirty features including *The Squeaker, This Man is News, Waterloo Road, Captain Boycott, Laughter in Paradise, The Doctor's Dilemma* and *School for Scoundrels*. His last screen appearance was in Disney's *Escape from the Dark*, released in 1976. His more academic honours included being made Rector of Edinburgh University and Fulton Lecturer at New College, Edinburgh: and he was a Commander of the British Empire. He was 75 when he died of cancer in a London hospital on 19 August 1976.

PAULINE STARKE, who died on 3 February 1977, in Santa Monica at the age of 73, was a star of the silent screen, having started in the movies as an extra in D. W. Griffith's *Intolerance*. She went on to appear in more than fifty feature films, her last two being made in India (*Nine Hours to Rama* and *The Big Hunt*). She retired soon after she married stage producer George Sherwood in 1928 and subsequently resolutely stayed away from the limelight.

ONSLOW STEVENS, who died in California on 5 January 1977, at the age of 70, made more than half-a-hundred films during his career, which began in 1932 after his initial acting experience gained during four years in the theatre. Some of his more familiar roles include those in *Peg O' My Heart*, *Walk a Crooked Mile*, *The Night Has a Thousand Eyes*, *Sirocco* and *Lorna Doone*.

HERBERT WILCOX, who died during the weekend of 14–15 May 1977 at his Brighton home, did a great deal for the British film industry during the 30s and 40s, cheering a depressed British audience with a series of light, frothy and charming movies. Born in Cork, Ireland, in 1892, Wilcox entered the world of films – after serving with the Royal Flying Corps, 1914–18 – as a salesman. But within the year he had started his own distribution company, Astra Films (1919). In 1925 he founded the Elstree Studios with J. D. Williams and in 1928 began his series of films there under the British Dominions label. In 1932 he started the kind of film for which he became famous with *Goodnight Vienna* and *Carnival* (1932) and *Bitter Sweet* (1933). The following year he starred Anna Neagle (who was to become his wife and business associate until his death) in *Nell Gwynn*, later to make with her *Victoria the Queen* and *60 Glorious Years*. Between 1945 and 1948 he turned out the very successful light, musical comedies with Miss Neagle co-starring with Michael Wilding: *I Live in Grosvenor Square*, *The Courtneys of Curzon Street* and *Spring in Park Lane*. Latterly he was full of plans, none of them realised as film fashions changed.

There was something of a Sam Goldwyn flavour in ADOLPH ZUKOR's remark on the occasion of his 100th birthday: 'If I had known I was going to live to be a hundred I would have taken better care of myself!' In fact he was well enough preserved to retain the chairmanship of Paramount Pictures until the day he died, having only given up direct control of the company he had formed long ago, at the outbreak of the Second World War. A Hungarian who emigrated to the US when he was 16, Zukor was a successful furrier in Chicago when he became interested in the film business and in 1903 financed his first somewhat primitive arcade cinema, soon following this with a number of more conventional picture houses. Forming Famous Players he began first to import and then make the movies for his cinemas, later introducing to the screen such famous stars as Valentino, Gloria Swanson, W. C. Fields, Mae West and the Marx Brothers.

SOPHIE STEWART, the charming Scottish actress who died on 6 June 1977, at the age of 69, was best known for her considerable stage work rather than films, but she did appear with great credit in many of the British-made movies in the 30s and 40s as well as achieving solid celluloid success in America during the period. Her's was a warm and cosy personality, radiating unforced charm which probably came over the footlights even more forcefully than from the screen. Her first film was *Murder in the Red Barn* (1935) and one of her best film performances was as Lady Blakeney in *The Return of the Scarlet Pimpernel*. Other of her films included: *Marigold* (screen version of a great play success in which she appeared in the USA, Canada and Britain as well as on radio and TV), *Nurse Edith Cavell*, *My Son, My Son* (1940), *The Lamp Still Burns* (1943), *The Strawberry Roan* (1945) and *Uncle Silas* (1947). Originally intended for the ballet, she was about to make a world tour with the Anna Pavlova company when an accident forced her to change her career and she studied at RADA, making her stage début in 1925 in a production of *His Highness Below Stairs* at Oxford. Her last London play was *The Douglas Cause* in 1971, after which she kept north of the border and her home in Fife.

Awards and Festivals

With the proliferation of Festivals, Film 'Markets' and Awards of all kinds it is no longer possible to pretend that anything like a complete listing is practical. At the beginning of 1977 *Variety* issued a list of well over a hundred such events to be held during the year, some of which, of course, are of minor, local and highly specialised interest.

What has been done here is to record the major Festivals, and some others of possible wider interest. Some dates of Festivals to be held after this annual's press date are as follows:

San Sebastian September 10–21; *New York* September 23–October 9; *Thessalonika* September 24–October 2; *Arnhem* September 25–October 1; *Stratford, Ontario* September; *Pesaro* (New Cinema) September; *San Francisco* October 12–23; *Barcelona* (Colour) October; *Sitges* (Horror) October; *Nyon* (Shorts) October; *Cairo* November 7–20; *London* November 14–December 1; *Teheran* November 14–28; *Virgin Islands* November; *Paris* November; *Leipzig* November; *Istanbul* December; *Florence*, Festival dei Popoli December.

The Festival of Nations, Taormina – Italy, July 22–31

Best Film: PICNIC AT HANGING ROCK (Australia), directed by Peter Weir
Best Director: LEOPOLDO TORRE NILSSON for *Piedra Libre* (Argentina)
Best Actress: PRUNELLA RANSOME for *Quien Puede Matar A Un Nino* (Spain)
Best Actor: YVES MONTAND for *Police Python 357* (France)
Best Film by a New Director: THE BUS (Sweden) directed by Bay Okan
Certificate of Merit: SATURDAY NIGHT AT THE BATHS directed by David Buckley (USA)
First Annual Corrado Gagli Prize: LA HORA DE MARIA YEL PAJARO DE ORO

The Festival of New Perspectives at Locarno – Switzerland, August 5–15

Golden Leopard for Best Film: THE BIG NIGHT directed by Francis Reusserx (Switzerland)
The Silver Leopard: HARVEST 3000 YEARS directed by Haile Gerima (Ethiopia)
The Bronze Leopard: MARCO BELLOCHIO for his films in general
International Critics' Prize: JONAS – WHO WILL BE 25 YEARS OLD IN THE YEAR 2000 directed by Alain Tanner (Switzerland) and SHIRIN'S WEDDING directed by Helma Sanders (West Germany)

The San Sebastian Film Festival – Spain, September 11–22

Golden Shell Awards for Best Film: THE GYPSIES GO TO HEAVEN directed by Emile Lotianu (USSR)
Golden Shell Award for Shorts: OUVERTURE 2012 directed by Milan Blazekovic (Yugoslavia)
Special Jury Prize: CADDIE directed by Donald Crombie (Australia)
Best Actress: HELEN MORSE in *Caddie*
Best Actor: ZDZISLAW KOZIEN in *Skazany* (Poland)
Silver Shell Awards: COUSIN, COUSINE directed by Jean-Charles Tacchella (France) and VIEW OF A CLOWN directed by Vojtech Jasny (Germany)
Cantabrian Pearl Award for Best Spanish Language Film: LIBERTAD PROVISIONAL directed by Roberto Bodegas

The Cannes Film Festival – May 15–28, 1976

International Grand Prix: TAXI DRIVER (USA) directed by Martin Scorsese
Best Actor: JOSÉ-LUIS GOMEZ in *La Familia de Pascual Duarte* (Spain)
Best Actress: MARIA TÖRÖCSIK in *Deryné, hol van* (Hungary) and DOMINIQUE SANDA in *L'eredita Ferramonti* (Italy)
Special Jury Prizes: CRIA CUERVOS (Spain), directed by Saura, and DIE MARQUISE VON O (France–West Germany) directed by Eric Rohmer
Best Director: ETTORE SCOLA for *Brutti, Sporchi, Cattivi* (Italy)
Grand Prix for Shorts: METAMORPHOSIS, directed by Greenwald (Canada)
Fipresci Prize: IM LAUF DER ZEIT, directed by Wim Wenders (West Germany) and FERDINAND DER STARKE directed by Alexander Kluge (West Germany)

The Cork International Festival – Ireland, June 5–12 (Shorts)

General Interest and Documentary Prize: KANGAROO ISLAND directed by Ron Lowe (Australia)
Animated Film: POZAR directed by Witold Giersz (Poland)
Sport Film: SPEEDSAILORS directed by John Spencer (GB)
Fiction Short: ROMEO OF THE SPIRITS directed by Nicholas Janis (GB)
Irish Film Society Award: AGULANA directed by Frydman Gerald (Belgium)
Press Award for Best Irish Film: SUMMER SILVER directed by Neville Presho
European Commission Community Award: THE IMPRINT directed by Jacques Cardon (France)
National Film Studios of Ireland Award: TOM COOPER for pioneering sound film

production in Ireland with *The Dawn* made in 1936

The Berlin Festival – June 25–July 6
Gold Bear (Grand Prize): BUFFALO BILL AND THE INDIANS directed by Robert Altman (USA)
Silver Bears: CARO MICHELLE directed by Mario Monicelli (Italy) (Best Director); CANOA (Mexico) directed by Felipe Cazals (Jury Prize); AZONOSITAS (Hungary) directed by Laszlo Lugossy (Best First Film); BAGHE SANGUY (Iran) directed by Parviz Kimiavi
Silver Bears for Acting Performances: JADWIGA BARANSKA in *Noce I Dne* (Poland) and GERHARD OLSCHEWSKI in *Verlorenes Leben* (West Germany)
Golden Bear for Best Short Film: MUNAKATA, THE WOODCARVER by Yanagawa (Japan); Silver Bear: TRAINS by Daleb Deschanel (USA)
International Critics' Prize: LONG VACATIONS OF '36 (Spain)
Catholic and Protestant Award: LONELINESS OF CONRAD STEINER (Switzerland)

The Asian Film Festival – Pusan, South Korea, June 1976
Best Direction: BYUNG JANG HO for *The Common Woman* (S. Korea)
Best Scenario: CHANG YUN HSIANG for *Fragrant Flower v. Obnoxious Grass* (Taiwan)
Best Actor: CHOI MOO RYONG in *The Common Woman* (S. Korea) and KEN TAKAKURA for *Bullet Train* (Japan)
Best Actress: MARINI in *Love* (Indonesia) and AKIYOSHI KUMIKO in *Little Serpent* (Japan)

The Teheran Film Festival – November–December 1976
The Golden Ibex for Best Film: Martin Ritt's THE FRONT (USA). The Jury added a rider to the award: 'a superb script and outstanding performance by the star, Woody Allen'.
Best Director: NIKITA MIKHALKOV for *The Slave of Love*
Best Actor: ALAIN CUNY in *Irene, Irene*
Best Actress: LILY MONORI in *Nine Months*, with director Marta Meszaros getting a special diploma of honour
Special Jury Prize to FONS RADEMAKERS for his *Max Havelaar* (Dutch–Indonesian)
Best Short Film: SHADOW OF A DOUBT, by Rolf Orthel (Holland)

The Horror Film Festival, Sitges – October 1976
Gold Medal for Best Film: PROFONDO ROSSO, by Dario Argento (Italy)
Silver Medal for Best Script: DEATH WEEKEND by William Fruet (Canada)
Best Actor: PETER CUSHING in *The Ghoul* (GB)
Best Actress: BRENDA VACCARO in *Death Weekend* (Canada)
Best Photography: JEAN-JACQUES MATHY for *Le Nosferat* (Belgium)
Best Special Effects: PHIL CORY for *Bug* (USA)

The Canadian Film Festival, Toronto – October 1976
Best Film: LIES MY FATHER TOLD ME (plus Golden Reel award for earning the most money)
Best Actress: MARILYN LIGHTSTONE in *Lies My Father Told Me*
Best Actor: ANDRÉ MELANCON for *Partis*

Pour la Gloire
Best Director: HARVEY HUNT for *Golden Rod*
Special Jury Prizes to DENNIS ZAHORUK for *Brethren* and STEPHEN FRANKLIN and ALEX CRAMER for *The Last Cause*

Documentary and Shorts Films Festival, Leipzig – November 1976
Special Jury Prize: CITY AT DAWN (Vietnam)
Golden Dove for Best Film: THE PATH OF THE SOLDIER (USSR)
Silver Dove: CHILDREN OF UNDER-DEVELOPMENT (Columbia)
Special Animation Prize: BUFOSINCHRON-ISTI (Bulgaria) and RECONSTRUCTION OF A FAMOUS MURDER CASE (East Germany)

Festival of Animation Films, Ottawa, Canada – August 10–15, 1976
Grand Prix: THE STREET, by Caroline Leaf (Canada)
Special Jury Prize: LE PAYSAGISTE – MINDSCAPE by Jacques Drouin (Canada)
Special Homage mention of Jury: LOTTE REINIGER for *Aucassin et Nicolette* and for her outstanding contribution to the art of animation film

The 'Evening News' Awards for 1976
Best Film Comedy: THE RETURN OF THE PINK PANTHER, directed by Blake Edwards
Best Actor: PETER SELLERS for *The Return of the Pink Panther*
Best Actress: ANNETTE CROSBIE for *The Slipper and the Rose*
Best Film Drama: ACES HIGH, directed by Jack Gold
Best Film Newcomer: PETER FIRTH in *Aces High*

The International Festival of Cinema, Nyon, Switzerland – November 1976

Golden Sesterce Grand Prix for Best Film: Per Mannstaedt's NO MORE NUCLEAR PLANTS (Denmark)
Silver Sesterce Grand Prix: CHANTS DE LA BETE HUMAINE (Japan)
Silver Sesterce: Hillie Molenaar's ABORTION DOESN'T HAPPEN LIKE THAT (Belgium) and Georges Dufaux's AU BOUT DE MONAGE (Canada)
Special Jury Prizes: MORE THAN A MILLION YEARS (GB) and A DAY WITHOUT SUNSHINE (USA)

The Chicago International Film Festival, November 1976

Golden Hugo First Prize for Best Feature Film: Wim Wenders' KINGS OF THE ROAD (West Germany)
Silver Hugo for Best First Feature Film: Gregory Nava's THE CONFESSIONS OF AMANS (USA). Gold plaque to Bernhard Sinkel's LINA BRAAKE (Germany)
Special Jury Prize: Nagisa Oshima's REALM OF THE SENSES (Japan)
Gold Plaque for Best Animated Film: Bruno Bozzetto's ALLEGRO NON TROPPO
Silver Plaque to ALFRED SOLE for his thriller *Communion* (USA)
Jury Prizes: Anja Breien's WIVES (Norway); Zsolt Kezdi Kovacs' WHEN JOSEPH RETURNS (Hungary); Sohrab Shahid Saless's TIME OF MATURITY (Germany); Jiri Menzel's SECLUSION NEAR A FOREST (Czechoslovakia). And special commendation to FRED SCHEPISI for the photography in his *The Devil's Playground* (Australia)

The New York Film Critics' Circle Awards

Best Film of 1976: ALL THE PRESIDENT'S MEN
Best Director: ALAN J. PAKULA
Best Actor: ROBERT DE NIRO (for *Taxi Driver*)
Best Actress: LIV ULLMAN (for *Face to Face*)
Best Supporting Actor: JASON ROBARDS
Best Supporting Actress: TALIA SHIRE

For the second year the French Academy of Film Arts and Techniques presented their annual awards, called 'The Cesars', with more than 1,000 film 'creators and technicians' participating in the voting. Their choice, announced in Paris on 22 February 1977 was as follows:

The Cesars

Best French Film: MR KLEIN
Best Direction: JOSEPH LOSEY for *Mr Klein*
Best Foreign Film: Ettore Scola's WE LOVED SO MUCH (Italy)
Best Actor: MICHEL GALABRU in *The Judge and the Assassin*
Best Actress: ANNIE GIRARDOT in *Doctor Françoise Gailland*
Best Screenplay: THE JUDGE AND THE ASSASSIN by Jean Aurenche and Bertrand Tavernier
Best Supporting Actor: CLAUDE BRASSEUR in *An Elephant Can be Enormously Deceptive* and *The Big Operator*
Best Supporting Actress: MARIE-FRANCE PISIER in *Barocco*
Best Photography: BRUNO NUYTTEN for *Barocco*
Special Cesar: JACQUES TATI

The annual awards of the **British Academy of Film and Television Arts** for 1976 announced in March 1977:

Best Film: ONE FLEW OVER THE CUCKOO'S NEST (USA)
Best Direction: MILOS FORMAN for *One Flew Over the Cuckoo's Nest*
Best Actor: JACK NICHOLSON in *One Flew Over the Cuckoo's Nest*
Best Actress: LOUISE FLETCHER in *One Flew Over the Cuckoo's Nest*
Best Supporting Actor: BRAD DOURIF in *One Flew Over the Cuckoo's Nest*
Best Supporting Actress: JODIE FOSTER in *Bugsy Malone* (British)
Best Screenplay: ALAN PARKER for *Bugsy Malone*
Best Art Direction: GEOFFREY KIRKLAND for *Bugsy Malone*
Best Original Musical Score: BERNARD HERRMANN for *Taxi Driver* (USA)
Best Cinematography: RUSSELL BOYD for *Picnic at Hanging Rock* (Australia)
Best Feature Documentary: LOS CANADIENSES
Best Specialised Film: HYDRAULICS
Best Short Factual Film: THE END OF THE ROAD
Best Costume Design: MOIDELE BICKEL for *The Marquise of O*

As had been anticipated, *Network* won several of the **1976–77 Academy of Motion Picture Arts and Sciences Awards**, the famous 'Oscars', when they were announced at the annual prizegiving ceremony in Hollywood on 28 March. Here is the full list:

Best Film: ROCKY (USA)
Best Direction: JOHN AVILDSEN for *Rocky* (USA)

Best Actor: the late PETER FINCH for his role in *Network* (USA)
Best Actress: FAYE DUNAWAY for her performance in *Network* (USA)
Best Supporting Actor: JASON ROBARDS for his role in *All the President's Men* (USA)
Best Supporting Actress: BEATRICE STRAIGHT for her role in *Network* (USA)
Best Screenplay: PADDY CHAYEVSKY for *Network* (USA)
Best Cinematography: HASKELL WEXLER for *Bound for Glory* (USA)

Best Screenplay adapted from material from another medium: WILLIAM GOLDMAN for *All the President's Men* (USA)
Best Foreign Language Film: BLACK AND WHITE IN COLOUR (Ivory Coast)
Best Documentary Feature: HARLAN COUNTY (USA)
And as a suitable footnote to all these various lists of celluloid honours, the Bitter Apple Award given each year by the Women's Press Club (USA).
The 1976 Bitter Apple Award
TRUMAN CAPOTE, voted worst actor of the year for his performance in *Murder By Death*. Wise comment from Capote! 'I think I shall stick to my typewriter from now on.'

Rocky (Sylvester Stallone) and his girl (Talia Shire) are attacked by Paulie (Burt Young), her brother and Rocky's best friend, who has become jealous of their relationship, in *Rocky*, a United Artists film which won three of the 1976–77 Oscars.

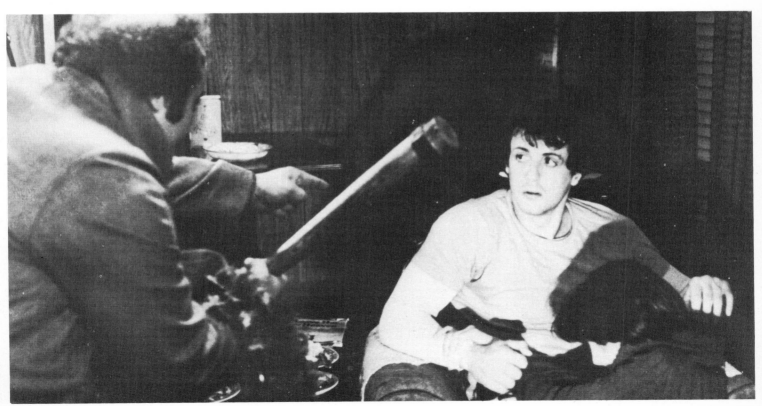

The Releases of the Year in Detail

Introductory Note: In this section will be found detailed notes on films generally released or otherwise shown in Great Britain during the period from the beginning of July 1976 to the end of June 1977. The situation of dating releases has become a little more tricky these days than in the past, when the pattern of film showing was far less flexible than now. Two good examples of the new system are *King Kong* and *The Return of the Pink Panther*, both of which after a quite wide initial release had a further circuit release at Easter. In all such cases the dates given here will be for the first release.

Where floating releases are concerned the endeavour is to give the first première showing for anyone who wants to track it down.

As there is inevitably a gap between the delivery of the manuscript and the appearance of the annual in the bookshops, and as these days release dates are often fixed at very short notice, it may be that one or two films released right at the end of the coverage of this annual may not be in this section. If this happens the chances are you'll find them in 'The In-Betweens' section and in this case they will be included in next year's volume in detail in this section.

As usual, certain abbreviations have been used in the following pages. For instance, Dir for Director, Pro for Producer, etc. As for the film companies, Fox stands for 20th Century-Fox, and UA for United Artists. Wherever known the producing company is given first and the distributor last: thus (Coleytown–First Artists–Warner) means that both the first named were associated with the production of the film and the last is the distributing company.

Lastly the matter of nationality. Wherever known this is given but with two, three and even four countries sometimes involved in a co-production it is not always easy to label precisely. Where no mention of nationality is made it can be taken as almost certain that the film in question is American in origin.

Abduction

A rather obvious fictional reconstruction of parts of the Patty Hearst case, with *Judith-Marie Bergman* as the student abducted and held prisoner by a group of white and black revolutionaries, who demand ransom from her parents, and her gradual involvement with her captors. Rest of cast: *David Pendleton, Gregory Rozakis, Leif Erickson, Dorothy Malone, Lawrence Tierney, Presley Caton, Catherine Lacey, Andrew Rohrer, Andrew Bloch, Pat Hernon, Dan Daniel, John Bartholomew Tucker, David Carroll.* Dir: Joseph Zito. Pro & Screenplay: Kent E. Carroll. (Hemdale.) Rel: Mar. 8. Colour. 94 Mins. Cert. X.

Aces High

Well-made story of the Royal Flying Corps at that point in the First World War, when the life of the sadly brave young fighter pilot replacements was reckoned to be about two weeks. 'Suggested' by R. C. Sherriff's *Journey's End* – a generous tribute in that the film is no more like it than many others in the past who have made no such nod to the famous play! Remarkably well handled aerial dog-fights and excellent performances by *Malcolm McDowell,*

Christopher Plummer and *Peter Firth.* Rest of cast: *Simon Ward, John Gielgud, Trevor Howard, Richard Johnson, Ray Milland, David Wood, David Daker, Barry Jackson, Ron Pember, Elliott Cooper, Tim Pigott-Smith, Christopher Blake, Jane Anthony, James Walsh, Pascale Christophe, Jacques Maury, Gilles Behat, Judy Buxton, Penny Irving, Trisha Newby, Imogen Claire, Jeanne Patou.* Dir: Jack Gold. Pro: S. Benjamin Fisz. Screenplay: Howard Barker. (S. Benjamin Fisz Productions/Les Productions Jacques Roitfield SARL–EMI.) Rel: Aug. 15. Colour. 114 Mins. Cert. A.

Adventures of a Private Eye

Broad, sex-slanted British comedy about a great detective's assistant who, left to mind the shop, does a little investigating on his own account. Cast: *Christopher Neil, Suzy Kendall, Harry H. Corbett, Fred Emney, Liz Fraser, Irene Handl, Ian Lavender, Julian Orchard, Jon Pertwee, Adrienne Posta, Anna Quayle, William Rushton, Robin Stewart, Diana Dors, Jonathan Adams, Richard Caldicot, Veronica Doran, Hilary Pritchard, Angela Scoular, Nicholas Young, Linda Regan, Linda Cunningham, Leon Greene, Ruth Kettlewell, Alan Wilson, Dave Carter, Graham Ashley, Peter Moran, Hot Toddy.* Dir: Stanley Long. Pro: Stanley and Peter Long. Screenplay: Michael Armstrong. (Salon–Alpha Films.) Rel: June 19. Colour. 90 Mins. Cert. AA.

Adventures of a Taxi Driver

Surely hardly representative of his mates in general, this cabbie spends most of his time avoiding the amorous advances of his fares, fleeing naked from their homes, or working – innocently – for crooks. Basic British comedy! Cast: *Barry Evans, Judy Geeson, Adrienne Posta, Diana Dors, Liz Fraser, Ian Lavender, Stephen Lewis, Robert Lindsay, Henry McGee, Angela Scoular, Brian Wilde, Rachel Dix, Natasha Staiteh-Masri, Marc Harrison, Jane Hayden, Graham Ashley, Dave Carter, Gloria Walker, Anna Bergman, Prudence Drage, Beatrice Shaw, Lee Crawford, David Auker, Andrew Secombe, Sue Vanner, Alan Wilson, Stephen Riddle, Desmond McNamara, Michael Worsley, Charles Pemberton, David Brierley.* Dir: Stanley Long. Pro: Peter and Stanley Long. Screenplay: Suzanne Mercer. (Salon – Alpha.) Rel: July 11. Colour. 90 Mins. Cert. X.

Aggression – L'Agression

A real curate's egg of a Franco-Italian film, the theme of which is the danger of vigilante action, shown through the story of a man and his family *en route* to the South of France for a holiday who are held up and assaulted by a gang of young motor-cycle thugs. During the fight that follows, the husband is knocked unconscious to find on recovery that his wife and child have been killed. But although the man comes to the obvious conclusion as to the murderers and acts accordingly it turns out that in fact the Hell's Angels, unconvincingly, were not the guilty ones. Cast: *Jean-Louis Trintignant, Catherine Deneuve, Claude Brasseur, Milena Vucotic, Jacques Rispal, Philippe Brigaud, Michelle Grellier, Robert Charlebois, Franco Fabrizi, Delphine Boffy, Leonora Fani, Jean Amos, Jacques*

Canselier, Jacques Chailleux, Etienne Chicot, Michel Delahaye, Daniel Duval, Tony Gatlif, Pierre Londiche, Claude Mercutio, Patrick Messe, Jean-Jacques Moreau, Mario Santini, Bernard Sury, Jacob Weizbluth, Philippe Welt, Pierre Davoust, Pierre Manciet, Edith Vergne, Jean Morin Diole, Gille Schneider, Angelo Rizzi, Alphonse Gola, Suzanne Pinoteau, Christiane Aumard, Martin Rousseau, Dominique Chassel, Danielle Mainard, Françoise Penzer, Renato Doria. Dir: Gérard Pirès. Pro: Alain Poire and Pierre Braunberger. Screenplay: Jean-Patrick Manchette; based on the novel by John Buell, *The Shrewsdale Exit*. (SNE Gaumont/Films du Jeudi/Films de la Seine, Paris–Primex Italiana, Rome–Antony Balch.) Rel: Floating. Colour. 99 Mins. Cert. X.

Airport '77
Highly entertaining and brilliantly managed piece of top-class Hollywood hokum which somehow manages to combine with style, and a tension that develops into seat-edging excitement, no less than three familiar plots: airplane hi-jacking, aerial disaster and undersea rescue! *Jack Lemmon* as the brave, resourceful pilot. Rest of cast: *Lee Grant, Brenda Vaccaro, Joseph Cotten, Olivia de Havilland, Darren McGavin, Christopher Lee, Robert Foxworth, Robert Hooks, Monte Markham, Kathleen Quinlan, Gil Gerard, James Booth, Monica Lewis, Maidie Norman, Pamela Bellwood, Arlene Golonka, Tom Sullivan, M. Emmett Walsh, Michael Richardson, Michael Pataki, George Furth, Richard Venture, Ross Bickell, Peter Fox, Beverly Gill, Charles Macaulay, Tom Rosqui, Arthur Adams, Anthony Battaglia, Elizabeth Cheshire, Charlotte Lord, Paul Tuerpe, Dan Robinson, Ted Chapman, Jim Arnett, Ron Burke, Chuck Hayward, Johana de Winter, George Whiteman, Jean Coulter, Chris Lemmon, John Clavin, John Kerry, James Ray Weeks, William Whitaker, Janet Brady, Mary Nancy Burnett, Bill Jelliffe, Rick Sorensen, Peter Greene, Asa Teeter, George Kennedy, James Stewart.* Dir: Jerry Jameson. Pro: William Frye. Screenplay: Michael Scheff and David Spector. (Jennings Lang–Universal–CIC.) Rel: May 21. Colour. 114 Mins. Cert. A.

Alex and the Gypsy
Jack Lemmon as that all-American figure, a bailbondsman, who puts up $30,000 bail for a former mistress but is determined she won't skip and leave him to foot the bill. Rest of cast: *Genevieve Bujold, James Woods, Gino Ardito, Robert Emhardt, Tito Vandis, Bill Cort, Todd Martin, Frank Doubleday, Joseph X. Flaherty, Robert Miano, Al Checco, Harold Sylvester, Clyde Kusatsu, Alan de Witt, Eddra Gale, Victor Pinheiro, Red Currie, Tamar Cooper, Georgie Paul, Renee Wedel, Chuy Franco, Charles Haid, Michael Blakely, Emanuel Kokonas, George Westcott, Ed Beagle, Irene Sale, Lupe Amaya.* Dir: John Korty. Pro: Richard Shepherd. Screenplay: Lawrence B. Marcus; based on the novel, *The Bailbondsman* by Stanley Elkin. (Richard Shepherd/John Korty–Fox.) Rel: Mar. 27. Colour. 99 Mins. Cert. AA.

Alfredo, Alfredo
English-dubbed Italian sex comedy with *Dustin Hoffman* as a husband whose attempts to win freedom from his wife leads him into becoming a campaigner for legal divorce in Italy – and then into the arms of an even more impossible second wife. Rest of cast: *Carla Gravina, Stefania Sandrelli, Clara Colosimo, Danielle Patella, Danika La Loggia, Saro Urzi, Luigi Baghetti, Duilio Del Prete, Renzo Marignano, Ettore Geri, Elisabetta Vito, Emanuela Fallini, Pier Anna Quaia.* Dir & Pro: Pietro Germi. Screenplay: Leo Benvenuti, Piero De Bernardi, Tulio Pinelli and Pietro Germi. (RPA/Rizzoli Films, Rome–Francoriz, Paris–CIC.) Rel: Floating. Colour. 110 Mins. Cert. AA.

All the Way Boys
Minor two-part adventure piece about a couple of pilot pals who carry out assignments in the Amazonian jungle country and end up with a fabulous emerald mine! Cast: *Terence Hill, Bud Spencer, Cyril Cusack, Michel Antoine, Rene Kolldehoff.* Dir & Written: Giuseppe Colizzi. (Avco Embassy–Seven Keys.) Rel: July 11. Colour. 92 Mins. Cert. A.

All This and World War II
Something of a mish-mash compilation effort which matches Beatle compositions to old newsreel and feature film extracts. (Fox.) Rel: Floating. Colour. 88 Mins. Cert. A.

At The Earth's Core
Excellent hokum based on Edgar Rice Burroughs' book about a brolly-clutching British professor – *Peter Cushing* inventor of the 'Iron Mole' – and his American financier/assistant (*Doug McClure*) and their adventures in the lost world at the centre of the earth, when taken there (by accident) by the professor's brain-child. Called Pellucidar, the 'Core' has lots of unpleasant things, with its beast-bird rulers, robotian assistants and unhappy, expendable, human slaves. Rest of cast: *Caroline Munro, Cy Grant, Godfrey James, Sean Lynch, Michael Crane, Bobby Parr, Keith Barron, Helen Gill, Anthony Verner, Andree Cromarty, Robert Gillespie, Laurie Davis.* Dir: Kevin Connor. Pro: John Dark. Screenplay: Milton Subotsky. (Amicus–British Lion.) Rel: Aug. 22. 90 Mins. Cert. A. Colour.

Baby Blue Marine
The title in America means 'Marine Reject' and *Jan-Michael Vincent* plays one who returns to his home town and poses as a hero from the South Pacific – until he owns up to the girl with whom he's fallen in love. Simple to the point of being naïve and struggling too hard to recapture the atmosphere of 1943. Rest of cast: *Glynnis O'Connor, Katherine Helmond, Dana Elcar, Bert Remsen, B. Kirby, Jr., Richard Gere, Art Lund, Michael Conrad, Allan Miller, Michael Le Clair, Will Seltzer, Ken Tobey, Lelia Goldoni, Marshall Efron, Barton Heyman, Adam Arkin, Damon Douglas, Barry Greenberg, Jim Blythe Barrymore, John Calvin, Richard Narita, Evan Kim, Keone Young, Phyllis Glick, William Martel, Abraham Alvarez, Warren Burton, Bill Sorrells, Carole Ita White, Duncan Gamble, Tita Bell, Lani O'Grady, Barbara Dodd, Tom Lee McFadden, James Lough.* Dir: John Hancock. Pro: Aaron Spelling and Leonard Goldberg. Screenplay: Stanford Whitmore. (Spelling/Goldberg–Columbia.) Rel: Sept. 11. Colour. 90 Mins. Cert. A.

Bad
Labelled as an Andy Warhol film though written, directed and produced – according to the credits – by other hands, this crazy, untidy and otherwise extremely unimpressive piece is about a housewife who runs a crime business, letting out girls to customers who haven't got the courage to do their own dirty business! Cast: *Carroll Baker, Gordon Oas-Heim, Cyrinda Fox, Matthew Anton, Perry King, Michael Forella, Kitty Bruce, Tere Tereba, Renee Paris, Stefania Casini, John Starke, Ruth Jaroslow, Geraldine Smith, Maria Smith, Michael Sullivan, Tito Goya, Charles McGregor, Brigid Polk, Lawrence Tierney, Charles Welch, Tom Quinn, Richard Cummings, Vasco Valladares, Barbara Hunt, Pat Way, Robert Hodges, Barbara Allen, Susan Blond, Jane Forth, Tamara Horax, Jerry Rosenberg, John Dunn, Joe Lambie.* Dir: Jed Johnson. Pro: Jeff Tornberg. Screenplay: Pat Hackett and George Abagnalo. (Andy Warhol/Jeff Tornberg–EMI.) Rel: Floating; first shown Feb. 1977. Colour. 104 Mins. Cert. X.

The Bad News Bears
Hilarious comedy about a kids' baseball team which is a hopeless failure until taken in hand by a boozy ex-professional (now a swimming bath cleaner-outer!) who, with the aid of a girl and a juvenile delinquent, takes them to the final of the league championship. During the game, fraught with minor drama, the coach learns from his charges that it is the game and not the winning that counts. And with lots of satirical allusions to the fanatical way that the Americans treat their favourite sport. Cast: *Walter Matthau, Tatum O'Neal, Vic Morrow, Joyce Van Patten, Ben Piazza, Jackie Earle Haley, Alfred W. Lutter, Brandon Cruz, Chris Barnes, Erin Blunt, Gary Lee Cavagnaro, Jaime Escobedo, Scott Firestone, George Gonzales, Brett Marx, David Pollock, Quinn Smith, David Stambaugh, Timothy Blake, Bill Sorrells, Shari Summers, Joe Brooks, George Wyner, David Lazarus, Charles Matthau, Maurice Marks.* Dir: Michael Ritchie. Pro: Stanley R. Jaffe. Screenplay: Bill Lancaster. (Jaffe/Ritchie–Paramount–EMI.) Rel: Jan. 23. Colour. 103 Mins. Cert. A.

Barry Lyndon
Stanley Kubrick's extremely long (187 mins plus interval), leisurely but often very lovely film of the William Makepeace Thackeray novel, about a young Irish lad with great ambitions and not too strong a moral sense. He climbs to the ownership of one of England's stately homes by way of Army service, desertion, double-espionage and the marrying of a milady widow with great wealth who he treats abominably, along with her son. But then he loses respect, his fortune and a useful piece of himself (his leg) and ends up by being banished to France. Glorious backgrounds, fine technical qualities, but slow paced and rather stiffly acted. Cast: *Ryan O'Neal, Marisa Berenson, Patrick Magee, Hardy Kruger, Steven Berkoff, Gay Hamilton, Marie Kean, Diana Koerner, Murray Melvin, Frank Middlemass, André Morell, Arthur O'Sullivan, Godfrey Quigley, Leonard Rossiter, Philip Stone, Leon Vitali, Michael Hordern.* Dir, Pro & Screenplay: Stanley Kubrick, based on the novel by Thackeray. (Warner.) Rel: Floating. Colour. 185 Mins. Cert. A.

The Battle of Chile, the fight of an unarmed people
Left-wing slanted documentary about the overthrow of the Allende government which gives a pretty comprehensive if biased account of the event. Dir & Screenplay: Patricio Guzman. (Equipo Tercer Ano with collaboration of Institutu Cubano del Arte e Industria Cinematograficos–The Other Cinema.) Rel: Floating; first shown London, Mar. 1977. Black and white. 205 Mins. On 16 mm. No cert.

Benji
Captivating, extremely simple story of, and starring, a cute mongrel dog and the way that he thwarts a plot of some teenage delinquents to kidnap and hold to ransom his two best young pals. Cast: *Peter Breck, Christopher Connelly, Patsy Garrett, Tom Lester, Mark Slade, Herb Vigran, Deborah Walley, Frances Bavier, Edgar Buchanan, Terry Carter, Ed DeLatte, Rene Marrou, Biff Painter, Victor Raider-Wexley, Charles Starkey, Larry Swartz.* And introducing *Cynthia Smith* and *Allen Fiuzat* as the two children. Dir, Pro & Written: Joe Camp. (Mulberry Square Productions–Columbia–Warner.) Rel: Aug. 22 (included in 1976–77 *Film Review* as a Floating Release). Colour. 86 Mins. Cert. X.

The Best of the New York Erotic Film Festival
In fact a collection of some nine short films from those American Festivals of 1972 and 1973, including two pornographic cartoons from about 1924, one highly artistic short and several other films of varying standards. (David Grant.) Rel: Specialised; Floating. Colour. 75 Mins. Cert. X.

The Big Bus
Consistently funny crazy satire comedy which takes the mickey not only out of the 'Big' films but lots of cinematic clichés as well as it follows the initial journey of the first atomic-powered long-distance coach from New York to Denver, a trip enlivened by a bomb placed on board by the international oil-producing cartel, a loss of brakes and a giddy balancing act over a chasm! Some nice performances and a remarkable, gimmicky bus creation. Cast: *Joseph Bologna, Stockard Channing, John Beck, Rene Auberjonois, Ned Beatty, Bob Dishy, Jose Ferrer, Ruth Gordon, Harold Gould, Larry Hagman, Sally Kellerman, Richard Mulligan, Lynn Redgrave, Richard B. Shull, Stuart Margolin, Howard Hesseman, Mary Wilcox, Walter Brooke, Vic Tayback, Murphy Dunne, Raymond Guth, Miriam Byrd-Nethery, Dennis Kort, James Jeter, Vito Scotti, Harry Holcombe, Morgan Upton, Dan Barrows, Della Thomas, Jess Nadelman, Michael W. Schwartz.* Dir: James Frawley. Written & Pro: Fred Freeman and Lawrence J. Cohen. (Cohen & Freeman/Phillips–Paramount–CIC.) Rel: Floating. Colour. 88 Mins. Cert. A.

The Bingo Long Travelling All-Stars and Motor Kings
The adventures of an all-blacks baseball team as they tour the backwoods of Georgia; a mixture of humour, insight and quiet, unforced racial innuendos. Excellent performances, lovely backgrounds. Cast: *Billy Dee Williams, James Earl Jones, Richard Pryor, Rico Dawson, Sam 'Birmingham' Brison, Jophery Brown, Leon Wagner, Tony Burton, John McCurry, Stan Shaw, De Wayne Jessie, Ted Ross, Mabel King, Sam Laws, Alvin Childress, Ken Foree, Carl Gordon, Anna Capri, Joel Fluellen, Sarina C. Grant, Jester Hairston, Emmett Ashford, Ted Lehmann, Fred Covington, Greg Oliver, John R. McKee, Brooks Clift, Morgan Roberts, Marcia McBroom, Lidia Kristen, Steve Anderson, Dero Austion.* Dir: John Badham. Pro: Rob Cohen. Screenplay: Tom Joyner, L. Andrew Stone and Richard Wells. (Motown/Pan Arts Enterprises–CIC.) Rel: Floating. Colour. 111 Mins. Cert. A.

Blondy
The complicated and frightening situation that the wife of a United Nations disarmament expert finds herself in when tempted into an affair with a young man: a situation that develops into mystery and murder. Somewhat confused and confusing political drama with lots of loose ends. Cast: *Bibi Andersson, Rod Taylor, Catherine Jourdan, Mathieu Carrière, Hens Meyer, Paul Guers, Christian Barbier.* Dir: Sergio Gobbi. Pro: Armand Tabuteau. Screenplay: Lucio Attinelli, Catherine Arley and Sergio Gobbi, based on the novel by Catherine Arley. (Paris/Cannes Productions–TIT, Munich–Alpha.) Rel: July 11. Colour. 105 Mins. Cert. X.

Bloody Hands of the Law
English-dubbed, Italian crime thriller about a dedicated cop who shrugs off beatings and even the murder of his beloved as he slowly but surely brings to justice the Italian branch of a ruthless international crime ring. Cast: *Philippe Leroy, Silvia Monti, Tony Norton, Cyril Cusack, Sergio Fantoni.* Dir & Screenplay: Mario Gariazzo. Pro: not named. (Difnei Cinematografica–Eagle Films). Rel: Floating. Colour. 97 Mins. Cert. X.

Blue Belle
British–Italian film about the sexual education of Annie in Hong Kong, where she is taken by her 'father'/lover when she comes out of convent school. Based on 'part of' the adventures of the film's blonde star *Annie Belle*. Rest of cast: *Charles Fawcett, Felicity Devonshire, Ciro Ippolito, Maria Rohm, Tim Street, Linda Ho, Ted Thomas, Linda Slade, Al Cliver, Chan Yiu Lan, Inez Pellegrini.* Dir: Massimo Dallamano. Pro: Harry Alan Towers. Screenplay: Peter Welbeck, Massimo Dallamano and Marcello Koscia. (Miracle.) Rel: Floating; first shown London, Feb. 1977. Colour. 86 Mins. Cert. X.

Breaking Point
Canadian film about a judo school manager who comes into opposition with the local mafia when he confirms the identity of a couple of muggers and eventually, the cops having been unable to protect him, confronts the gang boss on his own territory and excitingly eliminates him and all the baddies in a pitched battle. Cast: *Bo Svenson, Robert Culp, Belinda J. Montgomery, Stephen Young, John Colicos, Linda Sorenson, Jeffrey Lynas, Gerry Salsberg, Richard M. Davidson, Jonathan White, Alan McRae, Dwayne McLean, Doug Lennox, Jim Hunter, Bud Cardos, Joanna Noyes, Ken Camroux, Ken James, Bill Kemp, David Mann.* Dir: Bob Clark. Pro: Claude Heroux and Bob Clark. Screenplay: Roger E. Swaybill and Stanley Mann. (Breaking Point Productions, with assistance of Canadian Film Development Corp. and Famous Players–Fox–Rank.) Rel: Jan. 30. Colour. 92 Mins. Cert. X.

Buffalo Bill and the Indians or Sitting Bull's History Lesson
Robert Altman's stylised, original Western which, set within the confines of the Buffalo Bill Wild West Show, has, while it tells the amusing story of Sitting Bull's confrontation with William F. Cody, something to say about America's shabby treatment of her Indians and allied subjects; in fact, another piece of Altman Americana. Cast: *Paul Newman, Burt Lancaster, Joel Grey, Kevin McCarthy, Harvey Keitel, Allan Nicholls, Geraldine Chaplin, John Considine, Robert Doqui, Mike Kaplan, Bert Remsen, Bonnie Leaders, Noelle Rogers, Evelyn Lear, Denver Pyle, Frank Kaquitts, Will Sampson, Ken Krossa, Fred N. Larsen, Jerri and Joy Duce, Alex Green, Gary MacKenzie, Humphrey Gratz.* Dir & Pro: Robert Altman. Screenplay: Alan Rudolph and Robert Altman. (Dino de Laurentiis–EMI.) Rel: July 23. Colour. 123 Mins. Cert. A.

Bugsy Malone
Original, witty musical which takes the gangster movie formula of the 1920s and 1930s, with all the old clichés, laughs at it, deletes the violence, gives it a series of modern musical numbers and then hands it over to a cast of children for interpretation. What emerges is good, clean and happy fun. Cast: *Scott Baio, Florence Dugger, Jodie Foster, John Cassisi, Martin Lev, 'Humpty' Albin Jenkins, Paul Murphy, Davidson Knight, Sheridan Earl Russell, Paul Chirelstein, Dexter Fletcher, Vivienne McKonne, Helen Corran, Andrew Paul, Michael Jackson, Jeffrey Stevens, Peter Holder, Donald Waugh, Michael Kirby, Jon Zebrowski, Jorge Valdez, John Lee, Ron Meleleu, Paul Besterman, Kevin Reul, Brian Hardy, Bonita Langford, Mark Curry, Kathryn Apanowicz, Lynn Aulbaugh, Nick Amend, John Williams, Herbert Norville, Louise English, Kathy Spaulding, Fifi Marchese, Romana Kyriakou, Jonna Garbutt, Melanie Kelly, Beverley Horn, Susan Baker, Geraldine Cobb, Caren Lumsdale.* Dir & Screenplay: Alan Parker. Pro: Alan Marshall. (Fox–Rank.) Rel: Sept. 26. Colour. 93 Mins. Cert. U.

Burnt Offering
Long, leisurely, old-fashioned, highly incredible (and confusing) thriller about a strange and malevolent presence in the attic of the large and lovely old mansion which is rented by a family of father, mother, son and old Auntie for their summer holidays. And soon the father tries to kill the boy, the old Aunt dies horribly, and mother spends a lot of her time in the attic until the day that dad bursts open to door to see what's goin on in there . . . Cast: *Karen Black, Oliver Reed, Burgess Meredith, Eileen Heckart, Lee Montgomery, Dub Taylor, Bette Davis, Anthony James, Orin Cannon, James T. Myers, Todd Turquand, Joseph Riley.* Dir & Pro: Dan Curtis. Screenplay: William Nolan and Dan Curtis; based on the novel by Robert Morasco. (P. E. A. Films–Dan Curtis Production Services–Casa Co.–U.A.) Rel: June 12. Colour. 115 Mins. Cert. AA.

The Butterfly Ball

Film of a Rock concert in the Royal Albert Hall given a fairy-tale atmosphere by the introduction of some Halas and Batchelor cartoon sequences, dressing up players in animal costume and adding a commentary by *Vincent Price*. And there are some other, oddly chosen inserts of war scenes which hardly help the package. Cast: *James Anderson, Simon Beal, Mark Bishop, Stephanie Charles, Adam Clark, Deborah Cliff, Juliet Cox, Alphonso Dilieto, Amanda Dobbs, Julie Griffiths, Simon Henderson, Catrina Hilton, Ian Heare, Michael James, Sally Lamb, Michael Portman*. And *Twiggy* contributes a song, Roger Glover's 'Homeward'. Dir & Pro: Tony Klinger. Screenplay: Tony Klinger; based on the book *The Butterfly Ball and Grasshopper's Feast* by William Plomer and Alan Aldridge. (Oyster Films–Rank.) Rel: Floating; first shown London, Mar. 1977. Colour. 87 Mins. Cert. U.

Car Wash

Noisy, pop-music-splashed, considerably black movie about a day in a Los Angeles Car Wash, where too many people appear to do too little work as they concentrate on their own personal problems and have fun at the cost of their fat and futile white boss. Cast: *Franklyn Ajaye, Sully Boyar, Richard Brestoff, George Carlin, Prof. Irwin Corey, Ivan Dixon, Bill Duke, Antonio Fargas, Michael Fennell, Arthur French, Lorraine Gary, Darrow Igus, Leonard Jackson, DeWayne Jessie, Lauren Jones, Jack Kehoe, Henry Kingi, Melanie Mayron, Garrett Morris, Clarence Muse, Leon Pinkey, The Pointer Sisters, Richard Pryor, Tracy Reed, Pepe Serna, James Spinks, Ray Vitte, Ren Woods, Carmine Caridi, Antonie Beckler, Erin Blunt, Reginald Farmer, Ricky Fellen, Ben Fromer, Cynthia Hamowy, John Linson, Ed Metzger, Antar Mubarak, Derek Schultz, Mike Slaney, Al Stellone, Jackie Toles, Janine Williams, Otis Sistrunk, Timothy Thomserson, Jason Bernard, Jay Butler, Rod McGrew, J. J. Jackson, Sarina C. Grant, Billy Bass*. Dir: Michael Schultz. Pro: Art Linson and Gary Stromberg. Screenplay: Joel Schumacher. (Art Linson–Universal–CIC.) Rel: May 28. 97 Mins. Colour. Cert. AA.

Carquake

American/Hong Kong production which looks suspiciously like another, if different, working of the *Death Race 2000* plot, with various entrants having various fortunes in a ruthless car race across America from coast to coast; with plenty of violence, some satire and an amusingly hokumish ending. Cast: *David Carradine, Bill McKinney, Veronica Hamel, Gerrit Grahame, Robert Carradine, Belinda Balaski, Judy Canova, Carl Gottlieb, Archie Hahn, David Arkin, John Herzfeld, James Keach, Dick Miller, Louisa Moritz, Mary Woronov, Patrick Wright, Stanley Clay, John Alderman, Deidre and Gretchen Ardell, Allan Arkush, Gary Austin, Linda Civitello, Jim Conners, Roger Corman, Peter Cornberg, Joe Dante, Miller Drake, Wendy Bartell, Joe McBride, Todd McCarthy, Mike Finnell, S. W. Gelfman, Paul Glickler, David Gottlieb, Lea Gould, Diane Lee Hart, George Wagner, Glen Johnson, Jonathan Kaplan, Aron Kincaid, Saul Krugman, James Lashly, Keith Michel, Read Morgan, Mary-Robin*

Redd, Glynn Rubin, Martin Scorsese, Donald C. Simpson, Joe Wong, Paul Bartel. Dir: Paul Bartel. Pro: Sam W. Gelfman. Screenplay: Paul Bartl and D. C. Simpson. (Harbor Productions, Los Angeles/Shaw Bros., Hong Kong–Cross Country Productions–Hemdale.) Rel: May 21. Colour. 93 Mins. Cert. A.

Carrie

Grisly Grand Guignol piece about an abused schoolgirl – bullied by her classmates at school and by her religious fanatic mother at home – who finds she has strange psychic powers and when her moment of triumph (being chosen Queen of the school Prom Dance) is exploded by a bitchy practical joke on her, uses these powers to bring about a horrifying holocaust both in the hall and her home – where at her command knives, axes and other implements impale themselves in her mother's body! Impressive performances by *Sissy Spacek* as the girl and *Piper Laurie* as her Ma. Rest of cast: *Amy Irving, William Katt, John Travolta, Nancy Allen, Betty Buckley, P. J. Soles, Sydney Lassick, Stefan Gierasch, Priscilla Pointer, Michael Talbot, Doug Cox, Harry Gold, Noelle North, Cindy Daly, Dierdre Berthrong, Anson Downes, Rory Stevens, Edie McGlurg, Cameron De Palma*. Dir: Brian De Palma. Pro: Paul Monash. Screenplay: Lawrence D. Cohen; from the novel by Stephen King. (Monash/Palma–UA.) Rel: Feb. 20. Colour. 97 Mins. Cert. X.

Carry On England

The twenty-eighth 'Carry On' differs mainly from the previous twenty-seven of these famous British, broad and blue-veined comedies in that it is the first to get an AA cert. Otherwise the humour is predictable in a story about a mixed anti-aircraft Battery during World War II whose main exercises are sexual until Captain *Kenneth Connor* arrives on the scene with the task of maintaining some sort of discipline, an effort which quickly lands him in the – literally – four-letter word. Rest of cast: *Windsor Davies, Patrick Mower, Judy Geeson, Jack Douglas, Diane Langton, Melvyn Hayes, Joan Sims, Peter Jones, Peter Butterworth, David Lodge, Julian Holloway, Linda Hooks, Patricia Franklin, Vivienne Johnson, Barbara Rosenblat, Johnny Briggs, Brian Osborne, Larry Dann, Jeremy Connor, Barbara Hampshire, Tricia Newby, Jeannie Collings, Louise Burton, Linda Regan, Billy J. Mitchell, Paul Toothill, Richard Bartlett, Peter Banks, Peter Quince, Richard Olley*. Dir: Gerald Thomas. Pro: Peter Rogers. Screenplay: Jack Seddon and David Pursall. (Peter Rogers–Fox–Rank.) Rel: Oct. 31. Colour. 89 Mins. Cert. AA.

C.A.S.H.

Occasionally funny comedy about a military human guinea-pig who, after being subjected to endless poison gas and other tests, is thrown out of the US Army because he no longer functions as a normal human being. So he turns to crime, immobilising a whole town and robbing the banks there, only to be chased by his old unit and brought to bay in the hills . . . Cast: *Elliott Gould, Eddie Albert, Harry Guardino, Godfrey Cambridge, Jennifer O'Neill, Alan Manson, Donald Barry, Richard Masur, Howard Hesseman, Matt Greene, James Brown*. Dir: Ted Post. Pro: George Barrie. Screenplay: Malcolm Marmorstein.

(George Barrie/Brut–Scotia–Barber). Rel: Mar. 20. Colour. 92 Mins. Cert. AA.

Céline and Julie Go Boating, or Phantom Ladies Over Paris – Céline et Julie vont en Bateau

Very long, occasionally self-indulgent, quite crazy, puzzling, beautifully acted, witty, highly individual and thoroughly fascinating Jacques Rivette film which uses all the magic of the screen to put across a story impossible to outline: other than to say that it is about two girls in Paris who join forces to try and rescue a small child under a murder threat in the world of their dreams, and how they do eventually carry off what must be the greatest 'trick' of the year! Lots will love it, lots more won't understand a single celluloid foot of it! Cast: *Juliet Berto, Dominique Labourier, Bulle Ogier, Marie-France Pisier, Barbet Schroeder, Philippe Clevenot, Nathalie Asnar, Marie-Thérèse Saussure, Jean Douchet, Adèle Taffetas, Anne Zamire, Monique Clément, Jerome Richard, Michael Graham, Jean-Marie Senia, Jean-Claude Biette, Jean Eustache, Jean-Claude Romer, Michel Caen, Jean Eustache, Jacques Bontemps*. Dir: Jacques Rivette. Pro: Barbet Schroeder. Screenplay: Jacques Rivette, Eduardo di Gregorio, Juliet Berto and Dominique Labourier. (Contemporary.) Rel: Floating; first shown Sept. 1976. Colour. 192 Mins. Cert. AA.

Clockwork Nympho

Amusing title for a sex film about a somewhat precocious young lady who, arriving to spend three weeks with her mother's married friends Paul and Gabby, determinedly seduces both of them in turn, but then has the grace to bring the two together again before leaving! Cast: *Beatrice Harnois, Jean Roche, Roland Charbauy*. Dir, Pro & Screenplay: Max Pecas. (Border Films.) Rel: Floating. Colour. 86 Mins. Cert. X.

Come Play With Me

British sex film about a couple of crooks who take refuge in a Highlands health farm suddenly beset by a bevy of beautiful belles from a chorus line who undertake to nurse and give every satisfaction to the male patients! Cast: *Irene Handl, Alfie Bass, George Harrison Marks, Ronald Fraser, Ken Parry, Tommy Godfrey, Bob Todd, Rita Webb, Cardew Robinson, Sue Longhurst, Jerry Lorden, Mary Millington, Henry McGee, Michael Locan, Dennis Ramsden, Norman Vaughan, Queenie Watts, Valentine Dyall, Derek Aylward, Michael Balfour, Bunty Garland, Thick Wilson, Toni Harrison Marks, John Denny, Milton Reed, Isabella Rye, Billy Maxim, Suzy Mandell, Suzette Sangallo Bond, Penny Chisholm, Mireille Alonville, Suzette St Clare, Sonia, Nicole Austine, Marta Gillot, Pat Ashley, Anna Bergman*. Dir, Screenplay & Co-Pro (with David Sullivan): George Harrison Marks. (Rolevale–Tigon.) Rel: Floating; first shown, April 1977. Colour. 90 Mins. Cert. X.

Confessions of a Driving Instructor

Robin Askwith once again, for the third time (and third film) changes his occupation but not his free-wheeling life-style, spending most of his time in trying to keep his customers from driving him into bed. All very British basic sex stuff! Rest of cast: *Anthony Booth, Sheila White, Doris Hare, Bill Maynard, Windsor Davies, Liz Fraser, Irene Handl, George Layton, Lynda Bellingham, Avril Angers, Maxine Casson, Chrissy Iddon, Ballard Berkeley, Suzy Mandel, Sally Faulkner, Peter Godfrey, Mamaris Hayman, John Junkin, Anthony Morton, Geoffrey Hughes, Sally Adez, Donald Hewlett, Daniel Chamberlain.* Dir: Norman Cohen. Pro: Greg Smith. Screenplay: Christopher Wood, based on the novel by Timothy Lea. (Swiftdown–Columbia.) Rel: 12 Sept. Colour. 90 Mins. Cert. X.

The Confessions of Winifred Wagner
Pruned (from five hours) large-screen version of television feature which is almost entirely an interview with Hastings-born Mrs Wagner, in which she defends her long friendship with Hitler ('a purely human, personal and private bond . . . he was absolutely sweet with children . . . if Hitler walked through that door today I should be just as pleased and happy to see him here as I ever was') and her even longer involvement with the Bayreuth Festival. Dir: Hans Jürgen Syberberg. Edited: Agape Dorstewitz. German dialogue with English sub-titles. (Contemporary.) Rel: Floating; first shown Nov. 1976. Black and white. 104 Mins. Cert. A.

Cousin, Cousine
Delightful French film, reminiscent at times of *Un Homme et une Femme* because of its theme: of love becoming such a powerful force between a man and a woman that it can override all family and moral considerations (also reminiscent of the catchy little theme tune). A film which in its ironic observation of human nature, its integral comedy and its overall charm and beautiful performances is something of a throwback to the vintage years of the French cinema. Cast: *Marie-Christine Barrault, Victor Lanoux, Marie-France Pisier, Guy Marchand, Ginette Garcin, Sybil Maas, Jean Herbert, Pierre Plessis, Catherine Verlor, Hubert Gigoux.* Dir & Screenplay: Jean-Charles Tacchella. Pro: Bertrand Javal. (Curzon Film Dist.) Rel: Floating; first shown London, Oct. 1975. Colour. 95 Mins. Cert. AA.

Cross of Iron
Sam Peckinpah presents the violence and horrors of modern warfare in his adaptation of the book by Willi Heinrich about a personal confrontation between the professional survivor soldier Sergeant Steiner (a particularly gritty performance by *James Coburn*) and the Prussian officer whose ruthless and single objective is to win the Iron Cross. The scene is the beginnings of the big retreat on the Russian front in 1943. Peckinpah revels in the explosions, the bombardments, the pathetic infantry charges but in the end makes it all slightly, if explosively, unreal. Rest of cast: *Maximilian Schell, James Mason, David Warner, Klaus Lowitsch, Roger Fritz, Vadim Glowna, Fred Stillkraut, Burkhardt Driest, Dieter Schidor, Michael Nowka, Veronique Vendell, Arthur Brauss, Senta Berger.* Dir: Sam Peckinpah. Pro: Wolf C. Hartwig. Screenplay: Julius J. Epstein and Herbert Asmodi; based on the book of the same title by Willi Heinrich. (Arlene Sellers and Alex Winitsky–Rapid Film, Munich–Terra

Filmkunst, W. Berlin–Anglo EMI.) Rel: Mar. 8. Colour. 100 Mins. Cert. X.

Cry Onion – Cipolla Colt
Complicated, pretty crazy Italian–Spanish–West German comedy about the struggle between the ruthless oil company and farmer Onion and his supporters, who are being bulldozed out of their land. Cast: *Franco Nero, Martin Balsam, Sterling Hayden, Emma Cohen, Duilio Cruciani, Fernando Castro, Leo Anchoriz, Helmut Brasch, Romano Puppo, Neno Zamperla, Massimo Vanni, Daniel Martin, Alejandro de Enciso, Manuel Zarzo, Charly Bravo, Dick Butkus, Wal Davis, Dan Van Husen, Xan Das Bolas, Lucy Tiller, Leopoldo Frances, Vidal Molina, Antonio Pica.* Dir: Enzo Castellari. Pro: Carlo Ponti. Screenplay: Luciano Vincenzoni and Sergio Donati. (Compagnia Cinematografica Champion, Rome–CIPA, Madrid–TIT, Munich–Columbia-Warner.) Rel: Floating. Colour. 91 Mins. Cert. A.

Deadly China Doll
Carter Huang as the athletic hero (in a Hong Kong melodrama) who is on a double-pronged mission: for the Government to intercept an illegal consignment of drugs and for himself, personally, to kill his brother's murderer! And in both he is finally successful, after plenty of the usual slam-bang action. Rest of cast: *Angela Mao, Nang Kung Hsun, Ke Hsiang Ting.* Dir: Huang Feng. Pro: Andrew G. Vajna. Screenplay: Ho Jen. (Eagle Films.) Rel: Floating. Colour. 90 Mins. Cert. X.

Death Dealers – Napoli Violenta
Italian cops and robbers piece, with Inspector Betti moved from Rome to Naples to carry on his ruthless war against crime, clearing up quite a number of rackets – at a cost! Cast: *Maurizio Merli, John Saxon, Barry Sullivan, Guido Alberti, Elio Zamuto, Maria Grazia Spina, Silvano Tranquilli, Attilio Duse, Pino Ferrara, Tommaso Palladino, Enrico Maisto, Carlo Gaddi, Massimo Deda, Paolo Bonetti, Domenico Do Contanzo, Giovanni Cianfriglia, Fulvio Mingozzi, Pierangelo Civera, Ivano Silveri, Marzio Onorato, Gennaro Coumo, Domenico Messina, Carlos De Carvallo, Vittorio Sancisi, Nino Vingelli, Luciano Rossi, Ricardo Petrazzi, Invana Novak, Franco Odoardi, Gabriella Lepori.* Dir: Umberto Lenzi. Pro: Sergio Borelli. Screenplay: Vincenzo Mannino. (Pan-European Productions–Miracle.) Rel: Mar. 6. Colour. 93 Mins. Cert. X.

Death Weekend
Gory, brutal and flesh-creeping account of the way a girl kills the four morons who invade the house to which she has been invited for the weekend and murder her hosts. Rape, throat-cutting and burning alive are just some of the incidents in a horribly sadistic movie. Cast: *Brenda Vaccaro, Don Stroud, Chuck Shamata, Richard Ayres, Kyle Edwards, Don Granbery.* Dir & Screenplay: William Fruet. Pro: Ivan Reitman. (Reitman/Dunning/Link–Brent Walker.) Rel: Nov. 28. Colour. 84 Mins. Cert. X.

The Devil's Rain
Bridging three centuries with cloven hoof, devil

worshipper Corbis returns to his old desert country haunts to start recruiting his devilish band . . . and that's when the real horror starts! – and it is all a bit too confused to be successful. Cast: *Ernest Borgnine, Eddie Albert, Ida Lupino, William Shatner, Keenan Wynn, Tom Skerritt, Joan Prather, Woodrow Chambliss, John Travolta, Claudio Brook, Lisa Todd, George Sawaya, Erika Carlson, Tony Cortez, Anton La Vey, Diane La Vey, Robert Wallace.* Dir: Robert Fuest. Pro: James V. Cullen and Michael S. Glick. Screenplay: Gabe Essoe, James Ashton and Gerald Hopman. (Sandy Howard–Rank.) Rel: Sept. 29. Colour. 86 Mins. Cert. X.

The Diamond Mercenaries
Telly Savalas as a ruthless Chief Security Officer investigating the theft of diamonds from a South African mine is suddenly faced by the situation that his assistant is leading the gang of mercenaries who stage the big raid. Rest of cast: *Peter Fonda, Christopher Lee, O. J. Simpson, Maud Adams, Hugh O'Brian, Ian Yule, Michael Mayer, Victor Melleney, Richard Loring, Stuart Brown, Marina Christelis, Frank Shelley, Peter Van Dissell, Cocky Thlothlalemaje, Ian Hamilton, Dale Cutts, Don McCorkindale, Marigold Russell, Frank Douglas.* Dir: Val Guest. Pro: Nat and Patrick Wachsberger. Screenplay: Michael Winder, Val Guest and Gerald Sanford. (Seven Keys.) Rel: July 4. Colour. 105 Mins. Cert. AA.

Die Marquise von O . . .
Eric Rohmer's stylised, static and highly successful adaptation of the German novel by Heinrich von Kleist, which he made in Germany (in German) in order to capture the right nuances of this highly melodramatic, Victorian-style drama about an incident in the Russian invasion of Italy in 1799; more particularly and essentially the love story of the Russian Count who saves the Marquise from rape at the hands of some of his soldiers, seduces her during her subsequent drugged sleep, and only after much travail on her – pregnant – part is finally accepted as a fit husband. Cast: *Edith Clever, Bruno Ganz, Peter Lühr, Edda Seippel, Otto Sander, Hezzo Huber, Ruth Drexel, Eduard Linkers, Eric Schachinger, Richard Rogner, Volker Prachtel, Marion Muller, Heidi Moller, Petra Meier, Manuela Mayer.* Dir & Screenplay: Eric Rohmer. Pro: Klaus Helvig and Barbet Schroeder (Les Films du Losange, Paris–Janus Film, Frankfurt/Main–Gala.) Rel: Floating; first shown London, 6 Oct. 1976. Colour. 102 Mins. Cert. A. (Winner of the Special Jury Prize at Cannes Festival 1976.)

Double Exposure
Minor British thriller about jealousy, abduction, and the girl who wavers between the magnate whose mistress she is and the photographer who steals her from him. Cast: *Anouska Hempel, David Baron, Alan Brown, Robert Russell, Julia Vidler, Dean Harris, Alan Hay, Declan Mulholland, Grahame Mallard, Hugh Martin, Roy Sampon, Mary Maude, Trevor Ainsley, Ishaq Bux, Ali Baba, John Lee, Bob Babenia, James Giles, Hazel O'Connor.* Dir, Pro & Screenplay: William Webb. (Westwind–Columbia/Warner.) Rel: May 31. Colour. 81 Mins. Cert. AA.

Down the Ancient Stairs – Per le Antiche Scale
A sort of Italian spin-off from *One Flew Over the Cuckoo's Nest*, except it is the doctor rather than the patients who is spotlighted. It is the story of a handsome Tuscan medico in charge of a psychiatric hospital whose extrovertism hides his basic fear that he'll end up like his sister, a vegetable hidden away in a small cell in the place. The discovery – by a woman doctor who unlike all the others cannot be won over by his charm – that his curative methods are based on a false premise, brings about his decision to sever his personal and professional ties and go out into the world – which he finds in the increasing grip of the madness of Facism, *circa* 1930. Cast: *Marcello Mastroianni, Françoise Fabian, Marthe Keller, Barbara Bouchet, Pierre Blaise, Lucia Bose, Adrianna Asti, Silvano Tranquilli, Charles Fawcett.* Dir: Mauro Bolognini. Pro: Alvaro Mancori. Screenplay: Raffaele Andreassi, Mario Arosio, Tullio Pinelli, Bernardino Zapponi and Sinko Solleville Marie; based on the novel by Mario Tobino. (Italian International, Rome–Les Productions Fox Europa, Paris–Fox–Rank.) Rel: Floating; first shown Aug. 1976. Colour. 102 Mins. Cert. X.

Dreams of Thirteen
An erotic portmanteau, made some years back when a German millionaire offered thirteen international moviemakers the money to film their most erotic fantasy – not all of whom obliged. In Great Britain it emerged minus one of the episodes (Britain's Falcon Stuart's episode about two women raping a man) and adds up to a not too savoury collection of variable standard. 1. 'Janitor – Father' by Nicholas Ray (USA) with *Nicholas Ray, Melvin Miracle, Armeke Spierenburg, Dawn Cumming, Marvelle Williams, Mary Moore, Kees Koedood, Falcon Stuart, Barbara, Burnie Taylor.* 2. 'Contrasts' by Max Fischer (Germany) with *Max Kraft, Lee Kraft, Barbara, Maureen Gray, Marvelle Williams, Dawn Cumming, Jack Monkall, José Tapia-Esqullyn, Johnny Lamerse, Jerry Abnes.* 3. 'Flames' by Heathcote Williams (GB) with *Heathcote Williams.* 4. 'Deep Skin' by and with *Max Fischer* (Germany). 5. 'Another Wet Dream' by Jens Joergen Thorsen (Denmark), with *Saskia Holleman and Bent Weed.* 6. 'Dragirama' by Oscar Gigard (Yugoslavia). 7. 'A Face' by Max Fischer (Germany) with *Manushka.* 8. 'On a Sunday Afternoon' by Gert Koolman (Holland) with *Dawn Cumming* and *Bent Weed.* 9. 'Politfuck' by Sam Rotterdam (Yugoslavia) with *Melvin Miracle, Manuschka.* 10. 'The Private World of Hans Kanters' (Holland). 11. 'The Banner' by Lee Kraft (USA). 12. 'The Plumber' by Lee Kraft (USA). (Oppidan, UK Films). Rel: Floating; first shown London, Feb. 1977. Colour. 98 Mins. Cert. X.

Drive-In
Youthful follies, fun and fury centred on a drive-in cinema in a small Texas town and reminiscent of previous, better movies in the same 'graffiti' vein. Cast: *Lisa Lemole, Glenn Morshower, Gary Cavagnaro, Billy Milliken, Lee Newsom, Regan Kee, Andy Parks, Trey Wilson, Gordon Hurst, Kent Perkins, Ashley Cox, Louis Zito, Linda Larimer, Barry Gremillion, David Roberts, Phil Ferrell, Joe Flower, Carla Palmer, Carrie Jessup, Bill McGhee, Gloria Shaw, Jessie Lee Fulton, Robert Valgova, Michelle Franks, Jack Isbell,* *Dejah Moore, Curtis Posey, Billy Vance White, Hank Stohl.* Dir: Rod Amateau. Pro: Alex Rose and Tamara Asseyev. Screenplay: Bob Peete. (Columbia.) Rel: Jan. 23. Colour. 96 Mins. Cert. A.

Drum
Another venture into the deep, dark and very nasty Deep South of America of *Mandingo*, with lots of sex, brutality and violence in its story of the horrors of slavery. Cast: *Ken Norton, Lillian Hayman, Brenda Sykes, Warren Oates, Isela Vega, Pam Grier, Yaphet Kotto, John Colicos, Fiona Lewis, Paula Kelly, Royal Dano, Rainbeaux Smith, Alain Patrick, Clay Tanner, Lila Finn, Henry Wills, Donna Garrett, Harvey Parry, May R. Boss, Ilona Wilson, Monique Madnes, Eddie Smith, S. A. Lewis, Harold Jones, Maurice Emanuel, Larry Williams, Julie Ann Johnston, Jean Epper, Bob Minor.* Dir: Steve Carver. Pro: Ralph Serpe. Screenplay: Norman Wexley; based on the novel by Kyle Onstott. (De Laurentiis–EMI.) Rel: Sept. 18. Colour. 100 Mins. Cert. X.

The Duchess and the Dirtwater Fox
Western comedy with *George Segal* as the not very successful wanderer who lives on his wits, and *Goldie Hawn* as the dancehall girl with social ambitions, and what came of their meeting and subsequent association. Rest of cast: *Roy Jenson, Bob Hoy, Jerry Gatlin, Walter Scott, Bennie Dobbins, Thayer David, Pat Ast, E. J. Andre.* Dir & Pro: Melvin Frank. Screenplay: Melvin Frank, Barry Sandler and Jack Rose. (Frank–Fox.) Rel: Sept.19 (included in 1976–77 *Film Review* as a Floating Release). Colour. 104 Mins. Cert. AA.

e' Lollipop
Simple South African film about the deep friendship between a coloured boy and a white orphan which ends with the first sacrificing his life for the second; a film with some excellent performances (notably from *José Ferrer* as the Catholic Father in charge of the mission where the boys are raised and *Bess Finney* as his Sister assistant) and a few pertinent comments. Rest of cast: *Karen Valentine, Norman Knox, Muntu Ben Louis Ndebele, Ken Gampu, Bingo Mbonjeni, Simon Sabela, Naomi Van Niekerk, Fanie Bekker, Phoebe Bhengu, Henry Sidumo, Maurel Msimang, Roberta Durrant, May Dlamini, Andrew Molelekeng, Cynthia Moledi, Stanley Greene, Jon Richards, Don Burns, Alice Webb, John Byrd, Larry Silvestri, Al Nesor, John Ridge, P. J. Sidney, Arthur French, Doug Stark, Joe Hanrahan, Al Fann, Josip Elic, Victor Shangee.* Dir & Screenplay: Ashley Lazarus. Pro: André and Philo Pieterse. (Columbia–Warner.) Rel: Aug. 22. Colour. 93 Mins. Cert. U. (Included in 1976–77 *Film Review* as a Floating Release.)

The Eagle Has Landed
Nicely tense thriller about a Nazi plot to abduct Churchill while he is supposedly enjoying a quiet week-end on the Norfolk coast. With *Michael Caine* as the high-principled, cool and jaunty leader of a small band of German paratroopers sent, disguised as Poles on an Exercise, for the job. But a heroic gesture by one of the Germans in saving a small girl from drowning, at the cost of his own life, leads the vicar to glimpse the truth and as a result he and his flock are taken to the church where the Germans are besieged by Americans. And then the violent twist in the tail when *Caine*, having decided on a suicide mission as an alternative to the original plan, finally confronts and shoots the surprised man smoking the big cigar . . .! Rest of cast: *Donald Sutherland, Robert Duvall, Jenny Agutter, Donald Pleasence, Anthony Quayle, Jean Marsh, Sven-Bertil Taube, John Standing, Judy Geeson, Treat Williams, Larry Hagman, Siegfried Rauch, Alexei Jawdokimov, Richard Wren, Michael Byrne, Joachim Hansen, Denis Lill, Rick Parse, Leonie Thelen, Keith Buckley, Terry Plummer, Tim Barlow, John Barrett, Kate Binchy, Maurice Roeves, David Gilliam, Jeff Conaway, Asa Teeter, Robert G. Reece, Jack McCulloch.* Dir: John Sturges. Pro: Jack Wiener and David Niven, Jr. Screenplay: Tom Mankiewicz; based on the novel by Jack Higgins. (Lew Grade/Associated General Films–CIC.) Rel: April 17. Colour. 132 Mins. Cert. A.

Echoes of the Road
Minor piece about rootless trio on the road; girl and boy and old-timer who is attempting to make it back to his old farm to die. A mixture of youthful passion, confused social comment, rock music and pallid satire. Cast: *Jack Albertson, Lesley Warren, Martin Sheen, Michael Ontkean, Hal Baylor, George Chandler, Mike Road, Eddie Firestone, William Mims, Robert Donner, Kathleen Harper, Harold J. Stone.* Dir: John Florea. Pro: Chris Whittaker and Ed Garner. Screenplay: Anthony Blake. (Whittaker–Brent Walker.) Rel: Floating. Colour. 88 Mins. Cert. A.

Eclipse
Interesting, obtuse, but commendable first feature from two young British moviemakers, made on location on the west coast of Scotland with a small budget and a four-week shooting schedule. Basically difficult to translate into visual terms, it is about two identical twin brothers between whom is a love–hate relationship, so that when the dominating elder (by minutes) is drowned in a boating accident the question – did he fall overboard or was he pushed? – remains under the surface and adds tension to the survivor's Christmas holiday stay with the dipsomanic and frustrated widow and her small son. A quietly, leisurely fascinating little collector's piece with one needlessly disturbing sequence when the younger brother sadistically kills a cat by shutting it in the oven. Cast: *Tom Conti, Gay Hamilton, Gavin Wallace, Paul Kermack, David Stuart, Jennie Paul, Patrick Cadell.* Dir & Screenplay: Simon Perry. Pro: David I. Munro. Based on a novel by Nicholas Wallaston. (Celandine–Gala.) Rel: Floating; first shown London, Mar. 1977. Colour. 85 Mins. Cert. AA.

Emily
British period (*circa* 1920's) posh porn! The story of the young lady of the title who after flirting with both male and female friends decides to lose her innocence to her friend's husband, which she does by luring him into the ferns and stripping naked. Good production qualities, nice English rural backgrounds and a script which, perhaps understandably, is not credited! Cast: *Koo Stark, Sarah*

129

Brackett, Victor Spinetti, Jane Hayden, Constantin de Goguel, Ina Skriver, Richard Oldfield, David Auker, Jeremy Childs, Jeannie Collings, Jack Haig, Pamela Kundell. Dir: Henry Herbert. Pro: Christopher Neame. Screenplay: Anthony Morris. (Brent Walker Dist.). Rel: Floating. Colour. 87 Mins. Cert. X.

Emmanuelle 2
Sequel to the highly successful, erotic Emmanuelle No. 1! Continuing the sexual experiences of that very 'free' married couple Emmanuelle and Jean, who copulate and tell and finally, to make things more exciting, persuade a young girl to go off with them on a sensually liberated triangle holiday to Bali . . . and all tangled up in bed together we leave them . . .! Pretty backgrounds, lovely photography, attractive players, incredibly bad dubbed dialogue. Upper-drawer titillation, based on the book by Emmanuelle Arsan. Cast: Sylvia Kristel, Umberto Orsini, Catherine Rivet, Frederic Lagache, Caroline Laurence, Florence Lafuma, Venantino Venantini, Henri Czarniac, Tom Clark, Christiane Gibelin, Eva Hamel, Laura Gemser. Dir & Screenplay: Francis Giacobetti. Pro: Yves Rousset-Rouard. (Intercontinental Film Distributors.) Rel: Nov. 7. Colour. 80 Mins. Cert. X.

The Enforcer
'Dirty Harry' – alias tough New York cop Harry Callahan, alias star Clint Eastwood – gets demoted, and finally suspended for his refusal to depart from his own brave and brutal way of dealing with crooks and murderers. But it is he and his rough ways which rescue and free the kidnapped mayor, even though the accomplishing of his unofficial mission brings about the death of yet another of his partners, this time (to his initial disgust but eventual regard) a woman cop – Tyne Daly. Rest of cast: Harry Guardino, Bradford Dillman, John Mitchum, DeVeren Bookwalter, John Crawford. Dir: James Fargo. Pro: Robert Daley. Screenplay: Stirling Silliphant and Dean Reisner. (Columbia–Warner.) Rel: Jan. 9. Colour. 96 Mins. Cert. X.

Escape from the Dark
A somewhat more serious than usual Disney family charmer about three children – two miner's boys and the pit manager's daughter – who when they hear that the pit ponies are being made redundant and likely to go to the knackers, hatch a plot to snatch them to the surface and hide them . . . a plan that fails but, because of a mine disaster, in fact brings them almost total success in the end. Amusing, moving and thrilling by turns. Cast: Alastair Sim, Peter Barkworth, Maurice Colbourne, Susan Tebbs, Geraldine McEwan, Prunella Scales, Leslie Sands, Joe Gladwin, Chloe Franks, Andrew Harrison, Benjie Bolgar, Jeremy Bulloch. Dir: Charles Jarrott. Pro: Ron Miller. Screenplay: Rosemary Anne Sisson, from a story by her and Burt Kennedy. (Disney.) Rel: Aug. 1. Colour. 104 Mins. Cert. U.

Everybodys
Erotic French film about a deserted wife who finds unexpected solace just at the moment she prepares to commit suicide. Cast: Karine, Pierre Dany, Richard Darbois. Dir: Max Pecas. Pro: Roger Michel. Screenplay:

Barbera Sommers. (Rebel Films.) Rel: Floating; first shown London, May 1977. Colour. 67 Mins. Cert. X. (No other details available.)

Exhibition
French sex film about the making of a pornographic film, with lots of graphical sequences from the film itself – including close-ups of bi-sexual love-making and lots of full frontals! Faced with the label 'documentary' the GLC decided that a film about a pornographic film was not pornographic, a decision that reversed the official censor's refusal of a certificate and let it be seen in London. What emerges from the considerable and fascinating interview sequences with the film's star (France's foremost sex film actress) was an intriguing portrait of a girl quite happy to be filmed in any kind of sexual situation but refusing to allow four-letter, 'dirty' words, and otherwise revealing all kinds of crazy contradictions. Cast: Claudine Beccarie, Benoit Archenoul, Frédérique Barral, Béatrice Harnois, Michel Dauba, Patrick Segalas, Ellen Coupey, Mandarine, Didier. Dir: Jean-François Davy. Pro: Leavell. Screenplay: Jean-François Davy. (Contrechamp, Paris–Oppidan, (UK) Ltd.) Rel: Floating; first shown London, Dec. 1976. Colour. 96 Mins. Cert. X (London).

F for Fake
A masterly documentary from Orson Welles which beginning with an examination of famous painter-forger Elmyr de Hory (whose post-Impressionist studies in the styles of the masters fooled private and public art galleries all over the world) and his biographer Clifford Irving (who became famous in his turn for faking Howard Hughes's autobiography), wittily and wonderfully digresses – with all the art of the true magician – to pose all kinds of questions and throw in all sorts of fecund ideas about deception, reality, art and life: and while maintaining continually that the film is fact, takes time out to introduce a fictional (?) tale about twenty-two Picasso paintings. A truly brilliant example of the art of Welles; philosopher, magician, tale-teller and great movie-maker. Leading players: Orson Welles, Oja Kodar, Elmyr de Hory, Clifford Irving, Edith Irving, François Reichenbach, Joseph Cotten, Laurence Harvey. Dir: Orson Welles. Pro: François Reichenbach. Screenplay: Orson Welles and Oja Palinkas. (Essential Cinema.) Rel: Floating. Colour. 85 Mins. Cert. U.

The Face of Darkness
A short feature about a politician who uses occult ritual as an instrument to further his extreme personal ambitions but is finally enslaved by the evil he has created! Described by the producers as 'a chilling exploration of the constant conflict within society between the potential for good and evil!' Cast: Lennard Pearce, John Bennett, Roger Bizley, David Allister, Gwyneth Powell, Jonathan Elsom, Susan Banahan. Dir & Screenplay: Ian F. H. Lloyd. Pro: Not credited. (Cromdale Films–Brent Walker.) Rel: Nov. 18. Colour. 54 Mins. Cert. X.

Face to Face
Ingmar Bergman's remarkable 'chamber' film about the mental breakdown of a woman psychiatrist/psychologist, her descent into the consequent mental hell and her

emergence – permanent or temporary nobody can say; a theme made more poignant and disturbing by the fact that some time after this film Bergman himself suffered the same kind of collapse. A film full of philosophical and psychological threads acted with magnificence by Liv Ullmann, who gives the role the perfection it needs for this film to work. Rest of cast: Erland Josephson, Gunnar Bjornstrand, Aino Taube-Henrikson, Kari Sylwan, Sif Ruud, Sven Lindberg, Tore Segelcke, Ulf Johanson, Kristina Adolphson, Gosta Ekman, Kabi Laretei, Birger Malmsten, Goran Stangertz, Marianne Aminoff, Gosta Pruzelius, Rebecca Pawlo, Lena Ohlin. Dir, Pro & Screenplay: Ingmar Bergman. (Dino de Laurentiis–Cinematograph–Paramount–CIC.) Rel: Floating; first shown London, Oct. 1976. Colour. 136 Mins. Cert. X.

Family Life
Dialogue-weighted Polish film with a very Scandinavian atmosphere about a doomed family living in a rotting mansion to which the successful young designer son is called from Warsaw when his father has an accident. There he finds his dad suffering from the after-effects of the explosion of his illicit still in the basement (and also from drinking too much of his merchandise), the aunt running the household with sour resignation and then his sister apparently steadily going off her trolley. When they refuse all offers of help to break out of the web they have woven around themselves the son goes back to the city and cuts himself completely off from them. Cast: Daniel Olbrychski, Jan Norwicki, Jan Kreczmar, Maja Komorowska, Halina Mikolajska, A. Milewska, B. Soltysik, B. Kobrzynska, W. Kornak, J. Binczycki, K. Strassburger. Dir & Screenplay: Krysztof Zanussi. Pro: Janina Krassowska. (Contemporary.) Rel: Floating; first shown Aug. 1976. Colour. 93 Mins. Cert. AA.

Family Plot
In his seventy-seventh year Alfred Hitchcock produces one of his most polished suspense thrillers; exciting, technically brilliant and, for all the coincidences and occasional implausibilities, one of the most satisfyingly credible and logical stories yet. A deft mixture of chills and chortles, typical wit and impish references to past successes, it's about a couple of couples: a young professional medium and her taxi-driver boyfriend who are searching for a vanished heir for the large reward that has been offered, and a villainous jeweller who with his mistress makes kidnapping and ransoms a highly profitable sideline. And how their two paths converge, meet and cross each other with murder the motive. Cast: Bruce Dern, Karen Black, Barbara Harris, William Devane, Ed Lauter, Cathleen Nesbitt, Katherine Helmond, Wareen J. Kemmerling, Edith Atwater, William Prince, Nicholas Colasanto, Marge Redmond, John Lehne, Charles Tyner, Alexander Lockwood, Martin West. Dir & Pro: Alfred Hitchcock. Screenplay: Ernest Lehman; based on the novel by Victor Canning, The Rainbird Pattern. (Universal–CIC.) Rel: Sept. 12. Colour. 121 Mins. Cert. A.

Feelings
British film about the legal position of families in which the mother has had a child by artificial insemination or natural

donor: illustrated by a case in which the donor, when he reads some years later that the child has inherited a fortune, sues the woman for custody of the child. A tale told with some apparent seriousness, plenty of nude couplings and with some pleasant performances. Cast: *Kate O'Mara, Paul Freeman, Edward Judd, Bob Sherman, David Markham, Beth Ann Porter.* Dir: Laurence Britten. Pro: Basil Appleby. Screenplay: James Stevens. (Miracle.) Rel: Floating. Colour. 90 Mins. Cert. X.

Fighting Mad

Routine, sometimes repellingly violent Roger Corman film about the Little Man v. the Giant Corporation. *Peter Fonda* in familiar role as the returned son who takes up his father's struggle to stay put on his horse ranch which the local open-cast mining organisation want to take over. Rest of cast: *Lyn Lowry, John Doucette, Philip Carey, Scott Glen, Kathleen Miller, Harry Northup, Ted Markland, Gino Franco, Noble Willingham, Peter Fain, Allan Wyatt, Laura Wetherford, Gerry Wetherford.* Dir: Jonathan Demme. Pro: Roger Corman. Screenplay: Jonathan Demme. (Corman–Fox.) Rel: Floating. Colour. 88 Mins. Cert. X.

Fire

Thriller about a forest fire started by a convict which spreads danger to life and devastation to property as it sweeps towards the small lumber town of Silverton. Cast: *Ernest Borgnine, Vera Miles, Patty Duke Astin, Alex Cord, Donna Mills, Lloyd Nolan, Neville Brand, Ty Hardin, Gene Evans, Erik Estrelda, Michele Stacy, Patrick Culliton, James W. Gavin.* Dir: Earl Bellamy. Pro: Arthur Weiss. Screenplay: Norman Katkov and Arthur Weiss. (Warner.) Rel: June 12. Colour. 97 Mins. Cert. A.

Flood

Thriller about a small town threatened and finally inundated when the earth dam which holds back the lake above it is breached and the waters sweep down to bring death and destruction. Cast: *Robert Culp, Martin Milner, Barbara Hershey, Richard Basehart, Carol Lynley, Roddy McDowall, Cameron Mitchell, Eric Olson, Teresa Wright, Francine York, Whit Bissell, Leif Garrett, Ann Doran, Elizabeth Rogers, James Griffith, Edna Helton, Gloria Stuart, Jack Collins.* Dir: Earl Bellamy. Pro: Arthur Weiss. Screenplay: Arthur Weiss & Don Ingalls. (Warner.) Rel: June 5. Colour. 97 Min. Cert. U.

The Food of the Gods

Sensational SF thriller based on the H. G. Wells story about a mysterious 'food' which appears on some farmland and which, eaten by the local rats, turns them into ravaging monsters which attack any unfortunate human that comes into their orbit! And the effects, the film's mainstay, are pretty impressive. Cast: *Marjoe Gortner, Pamela Franklin, Ralph Meeker, Ida Lupino, Jon Cypher, Belinda Balaski, Tom Stovall, Chuck Courtney, Reg Tunnicliffe, John McLiam.* Dir, Pro & Screenplay: Bert I. Gordon. (Samuel Z. Arkoff–American International.) Rel: May 14. Colour. 88 Mins. Cert. X.

Freaky Friday

Disney comedy about a mother and her young daughter who each thinks the other is the lucky one – and then magically change places, with the humour inherent in such a freaky situation! Two good performances in the leading roles by *Jodie Foster* and *Barbara Harris.* Rest of cast: *John Astin, Patsy Kelly, Dick Van Patten, Vicki Schreck, Sorrell Booke, Alan Oppenheimer, Ruth Buzzi, Kaye Ballard, Marc McClure, Marie Windsor, Sparky Marcus, Ceil Cabot, Brooke Mills, Karen Smith, Marvin Kaplan, Al Molinaro, Iris Adrian, Barbara Walden, Shelly Jutner, Charlene Tilton, Lori Rutherford, Jack Sheldon, Laurie Main, Don Carter, Fuddle Bagley, Fritz Feld, Dermott Downs, Jimmy Van Patten.* Dir: Gary Nelson. Pro: Tom Leetch. Screenplay: Mary Rodgers; based on her own novel. (Disney.) Rel: June 5. Colour. 100 Mins. Cert. U.

French Mustard

French small-town crazy comedy which pokes fun at politics, press and the cinema as the local worm – a staid maths professor at the local girls' school – turns when he meets the lovely film-star! Cast: *Pierre Richard, Jane Birkin, Claude Piéplu, Jean Martin, Danou Minazzoli, Vittorio Caprioli, Henri Guybet, Julien Guiomar, Bruno Balp, Clément Harrari.* Dir: Claude Zidi. Pro: Henri Brichetti. Screenplay: Claude Zidi, Pierre Richard and Michel Fabre. (Gala.) Rel: Floating. Colour. 98 Mins. Cert. AA.

From Noon Till Three

Comedy Western about lucky outlaw Dorsey and the pretty widow who after saving him from a bank raid failure (and the noose) suffers for their love and builds a legend on it and then kills herself to perpetuate the story! Cast: *Charles Bronson, Jill Ireland, D. V. Fowley, Stan Haze, Dan Douglas, Hector Morales, Bert Williams, William Lanteau, Betty Cole, Davis Roberts, Fred Franklyn, Sonny Jones, Hoke Howell, Howard Brunner.* Dir & Screenplay: Frank D. Gilroy; based on his own novel of that title. Pro: M. J. Frankovich and William Self. (Frankovich–Self– UA.) Rel: Oct. 17. Colour. 99 Mins. Cert. AA.

The Front

A comedy, with tragic trimmings, about a horribly serious subject: the Senator McCarthy political witch-hunts in America in the late 40s and early 50s, when anyone suspected of left-wing (communist) sympathies could be publicly examined and then put on a black-list, which meant they could obtain no radio, television or film-work. *Woody Allen* as the almost illiterate restaurant cashier and part-time bookie's runner who volunteers to 'front' (banned writers submitted material under other names – and were paid less than when they wrote under their own!) for one, two and then three black-listed pals; becoming well-off on his 10% rake-off, then big-headed about his 'success', but, finally, when himself called in front of the Un-American Activities Senatorial Committee, coming good; an explicit pay-off line that, however richly deserved, is hardly likely to endear him to the senators! Plenty of laughs but with the tragedy always implicit and sometimes pretty stark. And the writer, director and co-star (*Zero Mostel*) of the film were all themselves on the list

at the time! Rest of cast: *Herschel Bernardi, Michael Murphy, Andrea Marcovicci, Remak Ramsay, Marvin Lichterman, Lloyd Gough, David Margulies, Joshua Shelley, Norman Rose, Charles Kimbrough, M. Josef Sommer, Danny Aiello, Georgann Johnson, Scott McKay, David Clarke, I. W. Klein, John Bentley, Julie Garfield, Murray Moston, McIntyre Dixon, Rudrich Wilrich, Burt Britton, Albert M. Ottenheimer, William Bogert, Joey Faye, Marilyn Sokol, John J. Slater, Renee Paris, Gino Gennaro, Joan Porter, Andrew Bernstein, Jacob Bernstein, Matthew Tobin, Marilyn Persky, Sam McMurray, Joe Jamrog, Michael Miller, Lucy Lee Flippin, Jack Davidson, Donald Symington, Patrick McNamara.* Dir & Pro: Martin Ritt. Screenplay: Walter Bernstein. (Columbia.) Rel: Mar. 8. Colour. 95 Mins. Cert. AA.

Futureworld

Begins where *Westworld* left off: years after the robot uprising and decimation of the guests at the fabulous pleasure resort of Delos, which has been refurbished, re-roboted with more fail-safe methods and re-opened. But two curious reporters (*Peter Fonda* and *Blythe Danner*), invited to trumpet its delights, discover the secret in the cupboard – the manufacture by the new director of perfect robot doubles of his illustrious guests so that he can replace them and through his replacements eventually control the world! All pretty dotty but with some impressive pseudo-scientific backgrounds. Rest of cast: *Arthur Hill, Yul Brynner, John Ryan, Stuart Margolin, Jim Antonio, Allen Ludden, Robert Cornthwaite, Angela Greene, Darrell Larson, Nancy Bell, John Fujioka, Dana Lee, Burt Conroy, Dorothy Konrad, Alex Rodine, Joanna Hall.* Dir: Richard T. Heffron. Pro: Paul N. Lazarus III and James T. Aubrey. Screenplay: Mayo Simon and George Schenck. (Samuel Z. Arkoff–American International–Brent Walker.) Rel: Oct. 24. Colour. 108 Mins. Cert. A.

The Gatekeeper's Daughter – Fille du Gardier-Barrière

Silent, black-and-white film in the style of the old screen melodramas but far more erotic/pornographic than was ever likely to be seen in its period! The story of pretty little Mona, the daughter of the level-crossing keeper, who is raped, thrown out of home, meets her Prince – and only after many men and many adventures later finds happiness with him. Cast: *Mona Mour, Michel Dussarat, Annick Berger, Maritin, Guy Gallardo, Jean-Paul Farré, Valérie Kling, Pablo Vigil, Jean-Paul Muel, Gérard Boucaron, Bouboule, Geronimo Savarini, Marcel Yonnet, Roland Topor, Carlos Pavlidis, Jacques Jourdan, Frédérique Noiret, Innocentia Sorsy, Sarah Sterling, Celia Booth, Lydie Pruvot, Françoise Diago, Brigitte Pujol, Anita Langelnsaan, Dominique Grousset, Philippe Corteyn, Mario Lima, François Borysse, Henri Bevillon.* Dir: Jérôme Savary. Pro: André Barret, Bernard Bolzinger, Christian Dansas, Eric Simon and Claude Bazerolle. Screenplay: Roland Topor and Jérôme Savary. (Alliance de Production Cinématographique/Fatty's Productions–Cinecenta.) Rel: Floating; first shown London, Mar. 1977. Black and white. 85 Mins. Cert. X (London).

Genesis – A Band in Concert
Film largely centred on the Group's concert at Bingley Hall, Stafford, in the summer of 1976. The musicians: *Michael Rutherford, Phillip Collins, Tony Banks, Steve Hackett, Bill Bruford.* Dir & Pro: Tony Maylam. (Worldmark/Samuelson International and Tony Smith–EMI.) Rel: Feb. 27. Colour. 45 Mins. Cert. U.

The Giant Spider Invasion
SF thriller about the discovery of some diamond-plated eggs near a small town in Wisconsin from which emerge strange spiders, one of which grows to vast size and goes on the rampage: a webby sort of King Kong! Cast: *Barbara Hale, Steve Brodie, Leslie Parrish, Alan Hale, Robert Easton, Kevin Brodie, Christiane Schmidtmer, Bill Williams, Tain Bodkin, Paul Bentzen, William W. Gillett, Diane Lee Hart, J. Stewart Taylor, David B. Hoff.* Dir: Bill Rebane. Pro: Bill Rebane and Richard L. Huff. Screenplay: Robert Easton and Richard L. Huff, from the latter's story. (Cinema Group 75–Transcentury Pictures–Hemdale.) Rel: May 21. Colour. 76 Mins. Cert. A.

Goodbye Norma Jean
Somewhat cheap and nasty biopic about the early life of Marilyn Monroe, suggesting she was little better than a prostitute as she single-mindedly sought cinematic stardom. With *Misty Rowe* suggesting her looks but none of her talent, vitality and sense of fun. Rest of cast: *Terence Locke, Patch MacKenzie, Preston Hanson, Marty Zagon, André Philippe.* Dir, Pro & Screenplay (last with Lynn Shubert): Larry Buchanan. (GTO Films.) Rel: Oct. 17. Colour. 95 Mins. Cert. X.

The Great Ecstasy of Woodcarver Steiner
Werner Hertzog, German, documentary about the young woodcarving artist who is also one of the world's great ski-jumping champions; his practice, fears, falls and final triumph. Dir, Pro & Written: Werner Hertzog. (Contemporary.) Rel: Floating. Colour. 47 Mins. Cert. U.

The Great Scout and Cathouse Thursday
Broad, bawdy comedy Western with plenty of knockabout, dubious story lines (such as the Indian who plans to get his own back on the whites by personally spreading VD through the local whorehouse) and cardboard characters. Cast: *Lee Marvin, Oliver Reed, Robert Culp, Elizabeth Ashley, Strother Martin, Sylvia Miles, Kay Lenz, Howard Platt, Jac Zacha, Phaedra, Leticia Robles, Luz Maria Pena, Erika Carlson, C. C. Charity, Ana Verdugo.* Dir: Don Taylor. Pro: Jules Buck and David Korda. Screenplay: Richard Shapiro. (Samuel Z. Arkoff–Jules Buck Productions–American International–Brent Walker.) Rel: March 13. Colour. 100 Mins. Cert. AA.

Grizzly
About the killer bear loose in an American national park which takes a toll of casual visitors, the naturalist who sets out to bring it back alive (with a tranquilliser gun) and a forest ranger before being finally hunted down from the air with a rocket launcher! Cast: *Christopher George, Andrew Prine, Richard Jaeckel, Joan McCall, Joe Dorsey, Kermit Echols, Charles Kissinger, Tom Arcuragi, Vicki Johnson,* *Harvey Flaxman, Catherine Rickman, Maryann Hearn, Mike Clifford, David Newton, David Holt, Susan Orpin, Brian Robinson, Sandra Dorsey, Gene Witham.* Dir: William Girdler. Pro & Screenplay: David Sheldman and Harvey Flaxman. (Columbia.) Rel: Jan. 16. Colour. 89 Mins. Cert. A.

The Gumball Rally
Routine story of an American coast-to-coast Rally/Race and the assortment of characters who take part, including the bumbling cop who does his best to stop the (illegal) contest. Cast: *Michael Sarrazin, Norman Burton, Gary Busey, John Durren, Susan Flannery, Harvey Jason, Steven Keats, Tim McIntire, Joanne Nail, J. Pat O'Malley, Tricia O'Neil, Lazaro Perez, Nicholas Pryor, Raul Julia.* Dir & Pro: Chuck Bail. Screenplay: Leon Capetanos. (First Artist Productions–Warner.) Rel: Oct. 17. Colour. 107 Mins. Cert. A.

Hang Up
A black-and-white Los Angeles narcotics squad cop team bring a dope pusher to a violent end after the coloured cop has fallen in love with and seen murdered his girl 'lead'. Cast: *William Elliott, Marki Bey, Cliff Potts, Michael Lerner, Wally Taylor, Timothy Blake, Fredd Wayne, Midori, David A. Renard, Pepe Serna, Rafael Campos, Lynn Hamilton, William Bramley, Bob Delegall, Barbara Baldavin, Morris Buchanan, Danny 'Big' Black, Herbert Jefferson Junr., Jerry Ayres, Joe Renteria, Sy Prescott, George Murdock.* Dir: Henry Hathaway. Pro: T. W. Sewell. Screenplay: John B. Sherry and Lee Lazich; based on the book *The Face of the Night* by Bernard Brunner. (Brut Productions–Scotia–Barber.) Rel: Mar. 20. Colour. 93 Mins. Cert. X.

Hardcore
British sex film with the shapely and show-all *Fiona Richmond* reminiscing to *Anthony Steel* about her many and varied copulatory adventures. Rest of cast: *Victor Spinetti, Graham Stark, John Clive, Graham Crowden, Jeremy Childs, Percy Herbert, John Hamill, Joan Benham, Heather Deeley, Trevor Thomas, Arthur Howard, Roland Curram, Donald Sumpter, Neil Cunningham, Ronald Fraser, Linda Regan, Patricia Bourdin.* Dir: James Kenelm Clarke. Pro: Brian Smedley-Aston. Screenplay: Michael Robson. (Target–Norfolk International.) Rel: Floating; first shown London, April 1977. Colour. 82 Mins. Cert. X.

Harry and Walter Go To New York
Rather slim comedy, with efforts to reach the Laurel and Hardy, Mack Sennett and Marx Brothers styles and standards, about a couple of second-rate vaudevillians at the turn of the century who, in jail for picking their audience's pockets, break out with the stolen plans of a bank robbery, planning to do the job before the planner can get out of jail to do the job himself! And in spite of some frantic hard work it isn't as funny as it might have been. Cast: *James Caan, Elliott Gould, Michael Caine, Diane Keaton, Charles Durning, Lesley Ann Warren, Val Avery, Jack Gilford, Dennis Dugan, Carol Kane, Kathryn Grody, David Proval, Michael Conrad, Burt Young, Bert* *Remsen, Ted Cassidy, Michael Greene, James De Closs, Nicky Blair, George Greif, John Hackett, Phil Kenneally, Jack Brodsky, Karlene Galegly, Colin Hamilton, Roger Til, Tom Lawrence, Ben Davidson.* Dir: Mark Rydell. Pro: Tony Bill. Screenplay: John Byrum and Robert Kaufman. (Columbia.) Rel: Floating. Colour. 112 Mins. Cert. U.

Hedda
Screen version of the Henrik Ibsen play in which *Glenda Jackson* in the title-role successfully toured GB. Rest of cast: *Peter Eyre, Timothy West, Jennie Linden, Patrick Stewart, Constance Chapman, Pam St Clement.* Dir. & Screenplay: Trevor Nunn. Pro: Roberts Enders. (Brut Productions–George Barrie/Robert Enders–Scotia–Barber.) Rel: Floating; first shown London, Feb. 1977. Colour. 102 Mins. Cert. A.

Helter Skelter
Remarkably authentic and otherwise impressive reconstruction of the infamous Charles Manson 'Family' case: the horrible murder and mutilation of pregnant film-star Sharon Tate, her friends and some of her neighbours in their Hollywood homes by Charles Manson and his hippy followers – mostly girls – in August 1969, a motiveless series of horrifying killings (the boasted number was 35) which led to the court case after which Manson and four of his female followers were condemned to death, a fate they avoided because the case was complex and lasted so long the death penalty was abolished while it was proceeding. With the result, the film intones in a startling footnote, all the killers come up for parole in 1978! Good performances by an unfamiliar cast, a magnetic one by *Steve Railsback* as Manson. Rest of cast: *George Dicenzo, Nancy Wolfe, Marilyn Burns, Christina Hart, Cathey Paine, Allan Oppenheimer, Rudy Ramos, Sondra Black, George Garro, Vic Werber, Howard Caine, Jason Ronard, Skip Homeier, Marc Alaimo, Bill Durkin, P. R. Allen, David Clennon, Adam Williams, Jonathon Lippe, James E. Brodhead, Anne Newman Mantee, Joyce Easton, Wright King, Jon Gries, Edward Bell, Roy Jenson, Paul Mantee, Ray Middleton, Anthony Herrera, Al Checco, Robert Hoy, Stanley Ralph Ross, Bart Burns, Jerry Dunphy, George Pitnam, Linda Chiles, Mary Kay Pass, Laura Ash, Carol Ita White, Martha Evens, Dorothy Meyer, Norman Bartold, Tracy Morgan, Raphael Baker, Bert Williams, Ralph Montgomery, Richard Venture, Douglas McGrath, Louise Claire Clark, Bert Conway, Larry Pennell, John Fain, Tony Moss, Jim Boles, Paul Kent, Robert Rothwell, Jack Miller, Alan Dexter, Will Brodhead, Josh Albee, John Evans, Ronald Gold, Sidney Clute, Steve Gries, Blair Aaronson, Bruce French, Foy Martin, Phil Montgomery, Joe Roman, Lionel Decker, Bill Sorrells, John Furlong, Robert Ito, Rod Arrants, Buy Remsen, Read Morgan, Cal Haynes, Barbara Mallory, Asta Hansen, Deborah Parsons, Melody Hinkle, Deanne Gwinn, Leila Davis, Sondra Lowell, Kathleen Delvin, Mary Jo Thacher, Tracy Tracton, Eileen Dietz Elber, Patricia Post, Lindsay V. Jones.* Dir & Pro: Tom Gries. Screenplay: J. P. Miller, based on the book by Vincent Bugliosi (the Special Prosecutor in the case) with Curt Gentry. (Lorimar–Hemdale.) Rel: March 8. Colour. 92 Mins. Cert. X.

The Hiding Place
The story of the ten Boom sisters in Holland and Ravensbruck Concentration Camp, where they are all sent – one to die, another to be released in error, the others to survive – after the Nazis have discovered that they are helping Dutch Jews to escape deportation. Cast: *Julie Harris, Eileen Heckart, Arthur O'Connell, Jeannette Clift, Robert Rietty, Pamela Sholto, Paul Henley, Richard Wren, Broes Hartman, Lex Van Delden, Tom Van Beek, Nigel Hawthorne, John Gabriel, David De Keyser, Carol Gillies, Lillias Walker, Irene Prador, Janette Legge.* Dir: James F. Collier. Pro: Frank R. Jacobson. Screenplay: Allan Sloane and Lawrence Holben; based on the book by Corrie ten Boom and John and Elizabeth Sherrill. (William F. Brown–World Wide–GTO Films.) Rel: Floating. Colour. 147 Mins. Cert. A.

Hollywood Cowboy
Highly hilarious comedy about the Iowan farm boy who fancies himself as a Western scriptwriter, almost by accident finds himself in Hollywood and equally unexpectedly himself a sagebrush star! And the lovingly but amusingly created background is that of the 'B' Western of the 30s. Cast: *Jeff Bridges, Andy Griffith, Donald Pleasence, Blythe Danner, Alan Arkin, Richard B. Shull, Herbert Edelman, Alex Rocco, Frank Cady, Anthony James, Burton Gilliam, Matt Clark, Candy Azzara, Thayer David, Wayne Storm, Marie Windsor, Anthony Holland, Dub Taylor, Raymond Guth, Herman Poppe, William Christopher, Jane Dulo, Dave Morick, Jacques Foti, Stuart Nisbet, Tucker Smith, Richard Stahl, Linda Borgeson, Titus Napoleon, Barbara Brownell, Granville Van Dusen.* Dir: Howard Zieff. Pro: Tony Bill. Screenplay: Rob Thompson. (Bill/Zieff–MGM–CIC.) Rel: Floating. Colour. 103 Mins. Cert. A.

Homebodies
Rather tasteless but inarguably amusing American (1973) black comedy about the inhabitants of an old people's home who set out to remove by murder those they consider responsible for trying to get them evicted and have the place pulled down for future redevelopment! Cast: *Peter Brocco, Frances Fuller, William Hansen, Ruth McDevitt, Paula Trueman, Ian Wolfe, Linda Marsh, Douglas Fowley, Kenneth Tobey, Wesley Lau, Norman Gottschalk, Irene Webster, Nicholas Lewis, John Craig, Joe de Meo, Michael Johnson, Alma Du Bus, Eldon Quick, William Benedict.* Dir.: Larry Yust. Pro: Marshall Backlar. Screenplay: Larry Yust, Howard Kaminsky and Bennett Sims. (Cinema Entertainment Corp–Essential.) Rel: Floating; first shown London, March 1977. Colour. 96 Mins. Cert. X.

How Yukong Moved the Mountains
Monumental French documentary about modern China which in five parts and twelve hours of film (!) assembled and presented by Joris Ivens and Marceline Lorinan, gives a friendly and detailed picture of life as lived by some Chinese in modern China. The sections are as follows: Part 1: *A Woman and a Family*, and *Rehearsal at the Pekin Opera* (105 & 32 Mins.); Part 2: *The Fishing Village, The Football Incident* and *Behind the Scenes at the Peking Circus*

(102, 51 & 16 Mins.); Part 3: *The Drug Store, The Army Camp* and *Traditional Handicrafts* (81, 57 & 15 Mins.); Part 4: *The Generator Factory* and *Professor Tsien* (129 & 13 Mins.); Part 5: *The Oilfields* and *Impressions of a City – Shanghai* (87 & 6 Mins.). Dir: Joris Ivens and Marceline Lorinan. (Capi Films–The Other Cinema.) Rel: Floating; first shown at The Other Cinema, Jan. 1977. Colour. 763 Mins. Cert. (not fixed).

The Human Factor
Decreasingly credible, but always exciting, often violent and brutal thriller from Edward Dmytryk about an American NATO worker in Naples who, after his wife and family are brutally assassinated for no apparent reason, persuades his computer expert pal to use all available technical resources to lead to the killers so that he can take revenge on them. Cast: *George Kennedy, John Mills, Raf Vallone, Arthur Franz, Rita Tushingham, Frank Avianca, Haydee Politoff, Tom Hunter, Barry Sullivan, Fiamma Verges, Danny Houston, Michael Mandeville, Ricky Harrison, Hillary Lief, Robert Lowell, Mrs. Robert Lowell, Shane Rimmer, Anne Ferguson, Lewis Charles, Corinne Dunne, Sharon Kellogg, Eugene Wade, West Buchanan, Conchita Airoldi, Joe Jenkins, Vincenzo Crocitti.* Dir: Edward Dymtryk. Pro: Frank Avianca. Screenplay: Peter Powell and Thomas Hunter. (Avianca–Rank.) Rel: July 4. Colour. 96 Mins. Cert. X.

I Love You, I Don't – Je T'Aime, Moi Non Plus
Sad little French film about a sad little love affair between a homosexual and the girl he meets in a sad little snack-bar! And the background is a sort of no-man's land on the edge of the city and on the edge of the public refuse dump. Cast: *Jane Birkin, Joe Dallesandro, Hugues Quester, René Kolldehoff, Jimmy Lover Man Davis.* Dir & Screenplay: Serge Gainsbourg. Pro: Jacques-Eric Strauss. (President Films/Renn Productions–Gala.) Rel: Floating; first shown April, 1977. Colour. 88 Mins. Cert. X.

I Will, I Will . . . for Now
Rather flat sex comedy which is basically concerned with the humours of sexual incompatibility in its story about an ex-husband and wife who find, however much they fight when together, they cannot really live happily apart. But the bubbles are too few and far between; the sparkle too intermittent. Cast: *Elliott Gould, Diane Keaton, Paul Sorvino, Victoria Principal, Warren Berlinger, Candy Clark, Robert Alda, Madge Sinclair, Carmen Zapata, George Tyne, Helen Funai, Sheila Rogers, Michele Clinton, Lou Tiano, Alvin Lum, Charles Herbert, James Brown, Ron Cummins, David Bowman, Andy Murphy, Sel Skolnik, Renata Vanni, Catherine Jacoby.* Dir: Norman Panama. Pro: George Barrie. Screenplay: Norman Panama and Albert E. Lewin. (George Barrie–Brut Productions–Scotia Barber.) Rel: Feb. 6. Colour. 103 Mins. Cert. X.

I Will If You Will – L'Infermiera
Minor Italian sex comedy about a rich wine-grower who, stricken down with heart disease when making illicit love, recovers – to the annoyance of his relatives, who then organise a lovely nurse for him and hope for the best! In fact the vintner marries her, to the family's fury, and then

suffers a further, fatal attack while consummating the marriage. Cast: *Ursula Andress, Duilio Del Prete, Lino Toffolo, Mario Pisu, Luciana Paluzzi, Jack Palance, Daniele Vargas, Carla Romanelli, Marina Confalone, Stefano Sabelli, Attilio Duse.* Dir: Nello Rossati. Pro: Carlo Ponti. Screenplay: Paolo Vidali, Claudia Florio, Nello Rossati and Roberto Gianviti. (Compagnia Cinematografica Champion–Intercontinental.) Rel: Nov. 7. Colour. 106 Mins. Cert. X.

Illustrious Corpses
Complicated – and sometimes confusing – but always gripping Italian political thriller in which an honest cop, investigating the murder of several of the country's top judiciary, finds his own somewhat logical theories disproved as his enquiries bring him closer and ever more dangerously closer to a solution involving the political parties themselves – and finally suffers for his dogged perseverance. Cast: *Lino Ventura, Fernando Rey, Max vor Sydow, Charles Vanel, Tino Carraro, Marcel Bozzuffi, Paolo Bonacelli, Alain Cuny, Maria Carta, Luigi Pistilli, Tina Aumont, Renato Salvatori, Paolo Graziosi, Anna Proclemer, Carlo Tamberlani, Enrico Ragusa, Corr do Gaipa.* Dir: Francesco Rosi. Pro: Alberto Grimaldi. Screenplay: Francesco Rosi, Tonino Guerra and Lini Januzzi; based on the novel *Il Contesto* by Leonardo Sciascia. (Cinegate.) Rel: Floating; first shown London, May 1977. Colour. 120 Mins. Cert. A.

Immoral Tales
Walerian Borowczyk's basically unpleasant, if superficially poetic, collection of several tales with sex – mostly deviationist sex at that – as the entire motivation. 'The Tide' is about a 16-year-old girl's initiation into oral sex; 'Therese the Philosopher' is about a girl who finds solace with a cucumber; In 'Lucretia Borgia' Lucretia enjoys group sex with her father and brother! And all the time the camera's salacious affair with the female genitalia continues unceasingly. Casts: 'The Tide'; *Lise Danvers, Fabrice Luchini.* 'Therese': *Charlotte Alexandra.* 'Lucretia': *Florence Bellamy, Jacopo Berinizi, Lorenzo Berinizi.* Dir & Screenplay: Walerian Borowczyk. Pro: Anatole Dauman. (New Realm.) Rel: Floating; first shown London, May 1977. Colour. 103 Mins. Cert. X (London).

Impotence – Xala
Quite delightful social satire from Senegal which in telling the personal story of the rise and fall of an ambitious importer who sells a hundred tons of rice under the counter to fund the marrying of his third, young wife, is found out by his crooked Chamber of Commerce colleagues and replaced with an even more blatant crook. And beneath the fun an acid comment on the black man who takes the sacked white man's place when his country has become 'freed'. Made in French and Wolof dialogue. Cast: *Tierno Leye, Seune Samb, Miriam Niang, Younouss Seye, Dieynaba Niang, Fatim Diagne, Ilimane Sagna, Douta Seck, Makhouredia Gueye, Abdoulaye Seck, Doudou Gueye, Farba Sarr, Moustapha Toure, Martin Sow, and the beggars of Dakar.* Dir. & Screenplay: Ousmane Sembene; based on his own novel of the same title. (Contemporary.) Rel:

Floating; first shown London, Nov. 1976. Colour. 123 Mins. Cert. AA.

The Incredible Sarah
Glenda Jackson giving a quite memorable performance as Sarah Bernhardt in this otherwise routine and flawed biopic about the great actress. Rest of cast: *Daniel Massey, Yvonne Mitchell, Douglas Wilmer, David Langton, Simon Williams, John Castle, Edward Judd, Rosemarie Dunham, Peter Sallis, Bridget Armstrong, Margaret Courtenay, Maxwell Shaw, Patrick Newell, Gawn Grainger, Lawrence Douglas, Neil McCarthy, Peter Davidson, Stephan Chase, David Muldowney.* Dir: Richard Fleischer. Pro: Helen M. Strauss. Screenplay: Ruth Wolff. (Readers Digest–CIC.) Rel: Floating. Colour. 106 Mins. Cert. A.

Inserts
Another Hollywood fim about Hollywood, this time set in the 1930s and concerning a story about a 'Boy Wonder' director of the silents (*Richard Dreyfuss*, a remarkable performance) who is now reduced to making pornograhic films in his own house, drinking endless bottles of brandy as he tries to inject some sort of art into his skinflicks. And, indeed, among all the porn and the vulgarity in the film there is an occasional glimpse of art or something very much like it. Rest of cast: *Jessica Harper, Stephen Davies, Veronica Cartwright, Bob Hoskins.* Dir & Screenplay: John Byrum. Pro: Davina Belling and Clive Parsons. (UA.) Rel: Floating; first shown London, Mar. 1977. Colour. 117 Mins. Cert. X.

Jabberwocky
Crazy comedy which has reflections of Monty Python humour, Lewis Carroll and a Varsity revue in its broad and bawdy relation of a medieval story of a dragon and its slaying by the young cooper's apprentice. Cast: *Michael Palin, Max Wall, Deborah Fallender, John Le Mesurier, Annette Badland, Warren Mitchell, Brenda Cowling, Harry H. Corbett, Rodney Bewes, Dave Prowse, Bernard Bresslaw, Alexandra Dane, Derek Francis, Peter Cellier, Frank Williams, Anthony Carrick, Kenneth Thornett, John Bird, Neil Innes, Paul Curran, Graham Crowden, Kenneth Colley, Christopher Logue, Janine Duvitski, Tony Aitkin, Peggyann Clifford, John Blain, Ted Milton, John Hughman, John Gorman, Glenn Williams, Bryan Pringle, Terry Jones, Anne Way, Brian Glover, Desmond Jones, Eric Chitty, Julian Hough, Harold Goodwin, Tony Sympson, Bill Gavin, Willoughby Goddard, Sarah Grazebrook, Bob Raymond, Anita Sharp-Bolster, George Silver, Peter Casillas, Simon Williams, John Sharp, Jerrold Wells, Gordon Rollings, Mollie Maureen, Peter Salmon.* Dir: Terry Gilliam. Pro: Sandy Lieberson. Screenplay: Charles Alverson and Terry Gilliam. (Michael White–Umbrella Entertainment Productions–Columbia.) Rel: April 3. Colour. 101 Mins. Cert. A.

Jackson County Jail
Roger Corman thriller with a story about a young woman who decides to drive from Los Angeles to her new job in New York. *En route* a young thug and his hippy girlfriend steal her car and everything in it and throw her into the road; when she goes to a wayside café for help the owner assaults her; thrown into jail by the local sheriff for not

having anything to identify her, she is brutally raped by his assistant, whom she kills with a chair; escaping with a convicted murderer, the two flee until the Law catches up with them, killing the man and apprehending her . . . Another disturbing look at America's rural law-keepers, who appear to be little if any better than the criminals they are supposed to be confronting; all adding up to what might be used as anti-American propaganda. Exciting, well-directed and terrifying, if possible! Cast: *Yvette Mimieux, Tommy Lee Jones, Robert Carradine, Frederic Cook, Severn Darden, Howard Hesseman, John Lawlor, Britt Leach, Nan Martin, Nancy Noble, Lisa Copeland, Clifford Emmich, Michael Ashe, Edward Marshall, Marcie Drake, Betty Thomas, Ken Lawrence, Arthur Wong, Marci Barkin, Michael Hilkene, Roy David Hagle, William Molloy, Ira Miller, Jackie Robin, Gus Peters, Patrice Rohmer, Amparo Mimieux, Mary Woronov, Richard Lockmiller, Jack O'Leary, Duffy Hambleton, Mark Carlton, Don Hinz, James Arnett, Norma Moye, Hal Needham.* Dir: Michael Miller. Pro: Jeff Begun. Screenplay: Donald Stewart. (Roger Corman–New World Pictures–UA.) Rel: May 14. Colour. 84 Mins. Cert. X.

James Dean – First American Teenager
Documentary about this young rebel/actor, with interviews with friends and colleagues and extracts from his three feature films. Also incorporating sequences from the previous documentary, *The James Dean Story* (1957). Dir & Screenplay: Ray Connolly. Pro: David Puttnam and Sandy Lieberson. (Visual Programmes Systems.) Rel: Floating; first shown London, Mar. 1977. Colour. 80 Mins. Cert. AA.

John and the Magic Music Man
A delightful twenty-minute film by Anthony Hopkins (he wrote the dialogue, delivers it and composed the music) which uses a slight little fantasy story to present to the audience the shapes, sounds and names of the instruments of the orchestra, played by the Young Musicians' Symphony Orchestra. Especially intended for children but a most agreeable film for adults, too. Dir & Co-Pro: Carin Scott. Pro: Talal Kanafani. Composed, written and narrated: Anthony Hopkins. (RSTC–Rosc Ltd.) Rel: Jan. 2. Colour. 20 Mins. Cert. U.

Joseph Andrews
Tony Richardson returns to his *Tom Jones* triumph in this adaptation of another Henry Fielding novel, which he broadens and simplifies and otherwise construes into a happy, bawdy, fast-moving tale decorated by bottoms and bosoms and some gorgeous, stylish colour photography. Cast: *Ann-Margret, Peter Firth, Michael Hordern, Beryl Reid, Jim Dale, Natalie Ogle, Peter Bull, Sir John Gielgud, Hugh Griffith, Timothy West, Wendy Craig, James Villiers, Karen Dotrice, Ronald Pickup, Penelope Wilton, Norman Rossington, Patsy Rowlands, Vanessa Millard, Jenny Runacre, Bernard Bresslaw, Kenneth Cranham, Murray Melvin, Willoughby Goddard, Stefan Gates, Pauline Jameson, Dame Peggy Ashcroft.* Dir: Tony Richardson. Pro: Neil Hartley. Screenplay: Allan Scott and Chris Bryant. (Woodfall–UA.) Rel: May 14. Colour. 104 Mins. Cert. AA.

Keep It Up Downstairs
Minor British sex comedy. Life at 'Cockshute Towers'! with sexual frolics up and down and around the stairs. Cast: *Diana Dors, Jack Wild, William Rushton, Aimi MacDonald, Françoise Pascal, Neil Hallet, Mark Singleton, Julian Orchard, Simon Brent, Sue Longhurst, John Blythe, Carmen Silvera, Anthony Kenyon, Olivia Munday, Seretta Wilson.* Dir: Robert Young. Pro & Screenplay: Hazel Adair. (EMI.) Rel: Floating. Colour. 94 Mins. Cert. X.

The Killer Inside Me
Tragic-ending story about a small-town deputy sheriff schizophrenic who, normally a nice chap, has his violent other self triggered off by a prostitute who, after starting an affair with him, tries to embroil him in an extortion racket which leads to murder. Cast: *Stacy Keach, Susan Tyrell, Tisha Sterling, Keenan Wynn, Don Stroud, Charles McGraw, John Carradine.* Dir: Burt Kennedy. Pro: Michael W. Leighton. Screenplay: Edward Mann and Robert Chamblee; based on the novel by Jim Thompson. (EMI.) Rel: May 8. Colour. 95 Mins. Cert. X.

King Kong
Re-make of the classic 1933 'monster' thriller, about the discovery and capture of a mountainous ape which, brought back to New York for exhibition, breaks out of his cage and is finally cornered and killed on the roof of the World Trade Centre. Faithfully following the original but making more definite the sexual attraction between the ape and the girl. Technically expert, spectacular and, as with the original, oddly moving in parts. Cast: *Jessica Lange, Jeff Bridges, Charles Grodin, John Randolph, Rene Auberjonois, Ed Lauter, Mario Gallo, Jorge Moreno, Jack O'Halloran, Julius Harris.* Dir: John Guillermin. Pro: Dino De Laurentiis. Screenplay: Lorenzo Semple, Jr. (EMI.) Rel: Dec. 26. Colour. 134 Mins. Cert. A.

The Last Hard Men
Classical confrontation Western with *Charlton Heston* the 'retired' lawman in the Arizona territory in 1909, who with a sigh straps on his guns again when he hears that a killer he sent to jail some while back has broken out and, he knows, will come searching for him to get his revenge. And how eventually the two men face each other in the rugged country of the Indian reservation where the law cannot follow them. Well acted against lovely backgrounds, and beautifully tempoed. Rest of cast: *James Coburn, Barbara Hershey, Christopher Mitchum, Jorge Rivero, Michael Parks, Larry Wilcox, Morgan Paull, Thalmus Rasulala, Bob Donner, John Quade.* Dir: Andrew V. McLaglen. Pro: Russell Thacher and Walter Seltzer. Screenplay: Guerdon Trueblood; based on the novel *Gun Down* by Brian Garfield. (Belasco/Seltzer/Thacher–Fox.) Rel: July 11. Colour. 97 Mins. Cert. X.

The Last Shot
Franco-Italian crime thriller about a highly successful crook who, forced out of Paris by the police, starts up again in Nice but is finally caught and killed after successfully stealing an armoured truck and its two

hundred million franc cargo! Cast: *Robert Hossein, Charles Aznavour, Virna Lisi, Genevieve Thenier, Albert Minski, Marcel Bozzufi, Antonio Passalia, Madeleine Sologne, Fred Ulysse.* Dir & Screenplay: Sergio Gobbi. Pro: Raymond Damon. (Golden Era.) Rel: Floating; first shown London, Dec. 1976. Colour. 105 Mins. Cert. A.

The Last Snows of Spring – Ultima neve di Primavera
Sad little Italian film about the sudden realisation of a busy widower father how much his small son means to him – realised only when he learns that the child has developed leukaemia and will die very soon. Cast: *Bekim Fehmiu, Agostina Belli, Renato Cesti, Nino Segurini, Margherita Horowitz, Margherita Melandri, Carla Mancini, Filippo de Gara, Raika Juri, Giovanni Petrucci.* Dir: Raimondo del Balzo. Pro: Ovidio G. Assonitis and Giorgio C. Rossi. Screenplay: Antonio Troisio and Raimondo del Balzo. (G.T.O. Films.) Rel: Floating. Colour. 90 Mins. Cert. A.

The Last Tycoon
Rather slow, stodgy, technically conventional, solidly entertaining screen adaptation of F. Scott Fitzgerald's last – unfinished – novel about a Hollywood movie mogul of the 1930s, with suggestions of David O. Selznick in the character of the humbly born celluloid dictator with impeccably good taste, which he indulges to the concern of the 'front office' in New York who eventually, when his passion for a girl who reminds him of his wife is thwarted and momentarily interferes with his dedicated concentration, dismiss him as summarily as he has dismissed others. Like nearly all Hollywood films about Hollywood it finally fails to live up to the promise of the material. Cast: *Robert de Niro, Tony Curtis, Robert Mitchum, Jeanne Moreau, Jack Nicholson, Donald Pleasence, Ingrid Boulting, Ray Milland, Dana Andrews, Theresa Russell, Peter Strauss, Tige Andrews, Morgan Farley, John Carradine, Jeff Corey, Diane Shalet, Seymour Cassell, Angelica Huston, Bonnie Bartlett, Sharon Masters, Eric Christmas, Leslie Curtis, Lloyd Kino, Brendan Burns, Carrie Miller, Peggy Feury, Betsey Jones-Moreland, Patricia Singer.* Dir: Elia Kazan. Pro: Sam Spiegel. Screenplay: Harold Pinter; based on the novel by F. Scott Fitzgerald. (Spiegel/Kazan–CIC.) Rel: March 27. Colour. 124 Mins. Cert. AA.

The Last Woman
Extremely explicit Italian sex film which crosses new frontiers in its detailed love play and full frontal nudity but has a valid basis in its theme of male egotism (and the apparent need for the Italian male to constantly prove his virility) which eventually makes a woman, however much she may physically and mentally love a man, turn from him when she feels she has become just an object for him; a variation on the incompatibility of the sexes idea. The story of a young engineer with a small baby – retained when his wife left him – and his torrid affair with a young girl at his office whom he takes from her more mature lover, an affair which leads – not entirely comprehensibly – to the final horrifying scene where he castrates himself with an electric carving-knife. Cast: *Gerard Depardieu, Ornella Muti, David, Michel Piccoli, Renato Salvatori, Zouzou, Giuliana Calandra, Carole Lepers, Nathalie Baye, Daniela*

Silverio. Dir: Marco Ferreri. Pro: Edmondo Amati. Screenplay: Marco Ferreri and Rafel Azcona. (Les Productions Jacques Roitfeld, Paris–Flaminia Produzini Cinematografiche, Rome–Columbia.) Rel: Floating. Colour. 109 Mins. Cert. X.

Le Gang
Alain Delon as the gangster chief whose daring exploits in a series of robberies lead to his becoming a legend. He is finally shot by a woman during a raid on a jewellers after his good luck has deserted him and everything begins to go wrong. Rest of cast: *Nicole Calfan, Roland Bertin, Adalberto Maria Merli, Maurice Barrier, Xavier Depraz, Laura Betti, Giampiero Albertini, Raymond Bussières, Catherine Lachens, François Lalande, Jacques Sereys, Marc Eyraud, Dominique Davray, Lionel Vitrant, Jacques Pisias, Albert Augier, Robert Dalban, Albert Michel, André Falcon.* Dir: Jacques Deray. Pro: Henri Jaquillard. (Screenplay: Alphonse Boudard and Jean-Claude Carrière; based on the novel by Roger Borniche. (Warner.) Rel: Floating. Colour. 103 Mins. Cert. AA.

Len Deighton's Spy Story
Intricate, confusing espionage piece about an unfortunate young man – a nuclear submarine officer apparently – who is involved in a dubious CIA, MI5 and Russian double-crossing and even triple-crossing plot as they try to outsmart each other in their War Games exercises. Cast: *Michael Petrovitch, Philip Latham, Don Fellows, Michael Gwynne, Nicholas Parsons, Tessa Wyatt, Toby Robins, Ciaran Madden, Nigel Plaskitt, Bernard Kay, Derren Nesbitt.* Dir & Pro: Lindsay Shonteff. Screenplay: Len Deighton. (Gala.) Rel: Floating. Colour. 103 Mins. Cert. A.

Les Violins du Bal
Somewhat needlessly intricately contrived and gimmicky telling of a delightful, simple story of a small Jewish boy and his mother's adventures as they move around France trying to escape the Vichy Police and Germans during the last war, and finally, with Grandma, make their exciting escape into Switzerland. And director Michel Drach (who admits the story is autobiographical) gives his drama both humour and charm. Beautifully acted, too. Cast: *Michel Drach, Jean-Louis Trintignant, David Drach, Marie-José Nat, Gabrielle Doulcet, Christian Rist, Nathalie Roussel, Yves Afonso, Guido Alberti, Paul le Person.* Dir & Screenplay: Michel Drach. (Contemporary Films.) Rel: Floating; first shown London, Feb. 1977. Colour and Monochrome. 108 Mins. Cert. A.

Let's Do It Again
A follow-up to *Uptown Saturday Night*, directed by and co-starring *Sidney Poitier*, who is persuaded by pal *Bill Cosby* into hypnotising puny little pugilist *Jimmy Walker* into winning an impossible victory, gaining them a fortune and a battle of wits with the racketeers whose money they've taken. Rest of cast: *Calvin Lockhart, John Amos, Denise Nicholas, Lee Chamberlain, Mel Stewart, Julius Harris, Paul E. Harris, Val Avery, Ossie Davis.* Dir: Sidney Poitier. Pro: Melville Tucker. Screenplay: Richard

Wesley. (Warner.) Rel: Oct. 17. Colour. 113 Mins. Cert. U.

Lies My Father Told Me
About a small boy growing up and discovering the bitter truth about death in Montreal in 1925. Cast: *Yossi Yadin, Len Birman, Marilyn Lightstone, Jeffrey Lynas, Ted Allan, Barbara Chilcott, Magnon Elkins, Henry Gamer, Carole Lazare, Cleo Paskal, Roland Bedard, Judith Gault, Raymond Benoit, Sylvie Heppel, Bertrand Gagnon, Victor Knight, Guy L'Ecuyer, Diana Leblanc, E. M. Margolese, Harry Mayerovitch, Les Nirenberg, Dave Raboy, Howard Ryshpan, Norman Taviss, Jean Dubost, Ruth Thomas.* Dir: Jan Kadar. Pro: Anthony Bedrich and Harry Gulkin. Screenplay: Ted Allan. (Pentimento and Pentacle VIII–Columbia.) Rel: July 4. (Included in 1967–68 *Film Review* as a Floating Release.)

Lifeguard
The problems of thirty-two-year-old Californian beach Lifeguard Rick – whether to stay at his lovely, lazy, girl-filled job or, for the extra money, trek into the hot and dusty town, become a car salesman and move into his ex-girlfriend's lovely house. In fact he opts for the sun and the sand and the easy sex, for a few more years, anyway! A summer film; leisurely, simple and cool! Cast: *Sam Elliott, Anne Archer, Stephen Young, Parker Stevenson, Kathleen Quinlan, Steve Burns, Sharon Weber, Lenka Peterson, George D. Wallace, Paul Kent, Susan Anderson, Beatrice Colen, Linda Gillin, Jody Gilbert, Russ Marin, Allan Gruener, James Beach, James D. Graham, Oaky Miller, Larry Mitchell, David McKnight, Bill Joyce, Erick Hines, Peter Canon, Christian Haren, Mark Hall, Scott Lichtig, Mary Betten, Wallace Earl, Sari Price, Jimmy Van Patten, Scot Wada, Marc Sayer, John Meyers, Marc Winters, Vivian Brown, Sam Kwasman, Louise Golding, Pedro Martinez.* Dir: Daniel Petrie. Pro: Ron Silverman. Screenplay: Ron Koslow. (Paramount–CIC.) Rel: Aug. 8. Colour. 96 Mins. Cert. AA.

Lina Braake
Delightful West German film (with the 1975 'Best of the Year' award there) about a sprightly eighty-two-year-old who, when the bank forces her to leave her house and enter an old people's home, plots a neat revenge on it with the help of one of the home's smarter inmates. A wonderful performance by *Lina Carstens* as the old girl and an almost as good one by *Fritz Rasp* as the wily bankrupt! Rest of cast: *Herbert Botticher, Erica Schramm.* Dir, Pro & Screenplay: Bernhard Sinkel. (Cinegate.) Rel: Floating; first shown Sept. 1976. Colour. 85 Mins. Cert. U.

Linda Lovelace for President
Thoroughly whacky comedy about the re-election of the US President; a sort of pastiche on the whole Presidential election campaign hocus-pocus, with lots of sex and nudity thrown in for full measure. Cast: *Linda Lovelace, Fuddie Bagley, Val Bisoglio, Jack de Leon, Mickey Dolenz, Joey Forman, Danny Goldmann, Garry Goodrow, Roberta Kent, Monte Landis, Morgan Upton, Rod Arrants, Kent Browne, Robert Burton, Jack Collins, Scatman Crothers, Robert Emmett II, Alfredo Fetchuttini, Stanley*

Myron Handleman, Marty Ingels, Richard (Diki) Lerner, Vaughn Meader, Arthur Metrano, Barbara Minkus, John Myhers, Louis Quinn, Joe E. Ross, Patricia Stich, Roy Stuart, Robert Symonds, David Ankrum, Earl Jolly Brown, Edwin Cook, Gene Elman, Hank Grant, Jack Grapes, Diane Lee Hart, Ralph Hoopes, Laura Justin, Bo Kaprall, Richard Kleiner, Georgia Lee, Robbie Lee, Paul Lichtman, Tommy Madden, Oaky Miller, Gus Peters, David Blatt, Christopher Pray, Jamie Reidy, Stafford Repp, Phil Roth, Bob Schott, Michael Schwartz, Marlene Selsman, Philip Simms, Charles Stroud, Lila Teigh, William Tusher. Dir: Claudio Guzman. Pro: David Winters and Charles Stroud. Screenplay: Jack S. Margolis. (New Realm.) Rel: July 4. Colour. 86 Mins. Cert. X.

Lipstick
Story of brutal rape and consequences for the victim. Serious but rather too glossy to be convincing. Fine performances from *Margaux* and *Mariel Hemingway* as the girl and her kid-sister. Rest of cast: *Chris Sarandon, Perry King, Robin Gammell, John Bennett Perry, Francesco, Meg Wyllie, Inga Swenson, Lauren Jones, Bill Burns, Way Bandy, Harry King, Sean Byrnes, Catherine McLeod, Macon McCalman, Mary Margaret Lewis, Nick Masi, Jr., Peggy Rea, Bill Zuckert, Tamara Chaplin, Lisa Walford, Betty Sinow, Ruth Teitel, Mary Ann Kellogg, Sharon Rubin.* Dir: Lamont Johnson. Pro: Freddie Fields. Screenplay: David Rayfiel. (Dino De Laurentiis–Paramount–CIC.) Rel: Aug. 8. Colour. 90 Mins. Cert. X.

The Little Girl Who Lives Down the Lane
Screen version of the Laird Koenig thriller about a thirteen-year-old girl who lives alone in a house by the sea with an imaginary father and copes smartly with a number of curious callers, including the woman from whom the house is leased (she kills her), the kindly cop (she chats up), a young cripple boy (she takes as lover) and a sexually kinky and sadistic young man who has unpleasant designs on her. A remarkably mature performance by *Jodie Foster*. Rest of cast: *Martin Sheen, Alexis Smith, Mort Shuman, Scott Jacoby, Dorothy Davis, Clesson Goodhue, Hubert Noel, Jacques Famery, Mary Morter, Judie Wildman.* Dir: Nicolas Gessner. Pro: Zev Braun. Screenplay: Laird Koenig, based on his own story. (Canadian/Franco Productions–Rank.) Rel: March 13. Colour. 82 Mins. Cert. AA.

Live Like a Cop – Die Like a Man
An all-action cops and robbers thriller; a sort of Italian equivalent to America's 'Starsky and Hutch' with *Marc Porel* and *Ray Lovelock* as two élite incognito Rome detectives determined to bring the powerful local crime boss to book and using some pretty unorthodox ways to do it. Rest of cast: *Adolfo Celi, Franco Citti, Renato Salvatori, Silvia Dionisio, Mavino Masè, Sergio Ammivata, Bruno Covazzavi, Daniele Dublino, Flavia Fabiani, Tom Felleghy, Margarita Horowitz, Zina Mascetti, Marcello Monti, Claudio Nicastro, Gino Pagani, Enzo Pulavano, Aluavo Vitali.* Dir: Ruggero Deodato. Pro: A. Marras and V. Salviani. Screenplay: Fernando Di Leo. (Variety.) Rel: Jan. 30. Colour. 95 Mins. Cert. X.

Logan's Run
Spectacular, gimmicky and pretty gloomy glance into the twenty-third century, when a life of endless pleasure is carried on under a domed, wholly artificial city until the inhabitants' thirtieth birthday – when they are rewarded by being ceremonially exploded into a new life (!) on the giant carousel! Dissident disbelievers who would like extra time are tracked down and exploded by the Sandmen cops, one of whom (*Michael York*) along with a girlfriend (*Jenny Agutter*) ventures into the outside world and discovers Old Man *Peter Ustinov* and the Truth! Rest of cast: *Richard Jordan, Roscoe Lee Browne, Farrah Fawcett-Majors, Michael Anderson, Jr., Randolph Roberts, Lara Lindsay, Gary Morgan, Michelle Stacy, Laura Hippe, David Westberg, Camilla Carr, Gregg Lewis, Ashley Cox, Bill Couch, Glen Wilder.* Dir: Michael Anderson. Pro: Saul David. Screenplay: David Zelag Goodman; from the novel by William F. Nolan and George Clayton Johnson. (MGM/CIC.) Rel: Oct. 31. Colour. 119 Mins. Cert. A.

The Lost Honour of Katharina Blum
Generally gripping and well made West German film about five very important days in the life of Miss Blum, who meets a young man on the run from the cops the first day, takes him home with her then denies on the second day that she knows anything about him (actually she's hidden him in the country house of her boyfriend!) and then becomes the subject, along with her relatives and friends, of the persecution by the yellow press, whose chief persecutor she shoots dead on the fifth day, just as the police find out that the young man is not the anarchist they suspected but just a deserter from the army who has robbed a safe! A generally jaundiced portrait of police and press. Cast: *Angela Winkler, Mario Adorf, Dieter Laser, Heinz Bennent, Hannelore Hoger, Harald Kuhlmann, Karl Heinz Vosgerau, Jürgen Prochnow, Rolf Becker, Regine Lutz, Werner Eichhorn.* Dir: Volker Schlöndorff. Screenplay: Schlöndorff and Margarethe von Trotta; based on the novel by Heinrich Böll. (Contemporary.) Rel: Floating; first shown London, May 1977. Colour. 105 Mins. Cert. AA.

Ludwig: Requiem for a Virgin King
Very odd, fascinating German film which tells the story of Ludwig of Bavaria by means of a series of something like *tableaux-vivant*, seen against painted backcloths and with an integral musical background of Wagner's most impressive melodies. Something for the collector of the cinematic curious. Cast: *Harry Baer, Balthasar Thomas, Peter Kern, Peter Moland, Günter Kaufmann, Waldemar Brem, Gert Haucke, Eynon Hangstaengl, Siggi Graue, Oscar von Schab, Rudi Scheibengrabber, Gerhard März, Annette Tirier, Ingrid Caven, Hanna Kohler, Ursula Strätz.* Dir & Screenplay: Hans Jürgen Syberberg. Pro: not credited. (Contemporary.) Rel: Floating; first shown London, Feb. 1977. Colour. 139 Mins. Cert. AA.

Lust in the Sun – Dans la Poussière du Soleil
1971 Franco-Spanish co-production, a Western which models itself very closely on the story of Shakespeare's *Hamlet*, with nearly all the cast meeting violent death in

the closing scenes! Cast: *Maria Schell, Bob Cunningham, Daniel Beretta, Karin Meier, Pepe Calvo, Colin Drake, Perla Cristal, Manuel Otero, Lorenzo Robledo, Jerome Jeffrys, Jack Anton, André Thevenet, Odile Astie, Pilar Vela, Angel del Pozzo, Santiago Ontanon, Marisa Porcel, Henry Bydon, M. Quesada, Amarilla.* Dir & Screenplay: Richard Balducci. Pro: Jean-Charles Carlus. (Kerfrance, Paris–IMF, Madrid–Golden Era.) Rel: Floating; first shown London, Mar. 1977. Colour. 84 Mins. Cert. X.

Man Friday
A new, 'reversed', and much too socially conscious version of the old Defoe story, with the black servant now becoming the master of the weak white Crusoe, who eventually pleads to join Friday's tribe but is refused because they feel that his influence would corrupt their purity! Cast: *Peter O'Toole, Richard Roundtree, Peter Cellier, Christopher Cabot, Joel Fluellen, Sam Seabrook, Stanley Clay.* Dir: Jack Gold. Pro: David Korda. Screenplay: Adrian Mitchell, based on his own play which was derived from *Robinson Crusoe* by Daniel Defoe. (Keep Films–Avco Embassy–Fox/Rank.) Rel: Floating. Colour. 108 Mins. Cert. A.

The Man on the Roof
Swedish Bo Widerberg's cool and factual, needlessly bloody and at times rather nasty, re-working of the story about a nuthouse case who sets himself up with a gun on a point of vantage and starts to pick off the people below. In this case the sniper is an ex-cop who bears the Force a grudge and confines his ammunition to killing his former comrades. Quite brilliantly done and providing an impressive picture of ordinary cops who, worried by the increasing violence opposing them, do what they have to with little complaint and, sometimes, quiet heroism. Cast: *Carl-Gustav Lindstedt, Gunnel Wadner, Hakan Serner, Sven Wollter, Eva Remaeus, Thomas Hellberg, Carl Axel Heiknert, Torgny Andenberg, Birgitta Valberg, Harald Hamrell, Ingvar Hirdwall, Gus Dahlstrom, Bellan Roos.* Dir & Screenplay: Bo Widerberg; from the novel by Sjowall/Wahloo. Pro: Per Berglund. (Svensk Filmindustri–Connoisseur.) Rel: Floating; first shown London, April 1977. Colour. 115 Mins. Cert. AA.

Marathon Man
Highly complicated and initially horribly confusing but always extremely watchable and latterly very exciting (if incredible and fashionably bloody) convoluted John Schlesinger thriller. A Nazi war criminal comes out of his South American hiding-place in order to collect from the New York bank his considerable deposits of ill-gotten gains, and how this emergence is discovered, leading to the murder of a double-agent and some unpleasant moments for the wholly innocent agent's young brother. And this devotee of the sport of the title finds his prowess useful when friends turn out to be enemies and even the girlfriend is uncovered as one of the gang. Cast: *Dustin Hoffman, Laurence Olivier, Roy Scheider, William Devane, Marthe Keller, Fritz Weaver, Richard Bright, Marc Lawrence, Allen Joseph, Tito Goya, Ben Dova, Lou Gilbert, Jacques Marin, James Wing Woo, Nicole Deslauriers, Lotta Andor-Palfi, Lionel Pina, Church, Tricoche, Jaime Tirelli,*

Wilfredo Hernandez, Tom Ellis, Bryant Fraser, George Dega, Gene Bori, Annette Claudier, Roger Etienne, Ray Serra, John Garson, Charlott Thyssen, Estelle Omens, Madge Kennedy, Jeff Palladini, Scott Price, Harry Goz, Michael Vale, Fred Stuthman, Lee Steele, William Martel, Glenn Robards, Ric Carrott, Alma Beltran, Daniel Nunez, Tony Pena, Chuy Franco, Billy Kearns, Sally Wilson. Dir: John Schlesinger. Pro: Robert Evans and Sidney Beckerman. Screenplay: William Goldman; based on his own novel. (Paramount–CIC.) Rel: Dec. 19. Colour. 126 Mins. Cert. X.

Mayday: 40,000 feet!
A minor air disaster epic (or, perhaps near-disaster would be more realistic) which was, it appears, originally made for TV. About the incident-packed flight of 'Flight 602', with its worried pilot, ailing federal cop and his dangerous prisoner – who finally manages to shoot the pilot and some passengers as well as putting the plane's hydraulics out of action. Cast: *David Janssen, Don Meredith, Christopher George, Ray Milland, Lynda Day George, Marjoe Gortner, Broderick Crawford, Jane Powell, Maggie Blye, William Bryant, John Pickard, Steven Marlo, Jim Chandler, Phillip Mansour, Al Molinaro, Kathleen Bracken, Bill Catching, Norland Benson, Philip Baker Hall, Bert Williams, Buck Young, Bill Harlow, Alan Foster, Garry McLarty, Tom Drake, Christopher Norris, Harry Rhodes, Warren Vanders, Shani Wallis.* Dir: Robert Butler. Pro: Andrew J. Fenady. Screenplay: Austin Ferguson, Dick Nelson and Andrew J. Fenady; based on the novel by the first-named. (A. J. Fenady Associates–Warner.) Rel: June 5. 94 Mins. Colour. Cert. A.

The Message (originally made and announced as Mohammad, Messenger of God)
Long, leisurely and very sincere treatment of the story of Mohammad, who in the seventh century A.D. began the preaching in Mecca which was to triumph over all adversity until today his followers add up to some 700 million souls. Plenty of lavishly staged battles, lovingly photographed backgrounds and impressively spoken extracts from The Koran. Cast: *Anthony Quinn, Irene Papas, Michael Ansara, Johnny Sekka, Michael Forest, Damien Thomas, Garrick Hagon, Ronald Chenery, Michael Godfrey, Peter Madden, Habib Ageli, George Camiller, Neville Jason, Martin Benson, Robert Brown, Wolfe Morris, Bruno Barnabe, John Humphry, John Bennett, Donald Burton, Andre Morell, Rosalie Crutchley, Ewen Solon, Elaine Ives Cameron, Nicholas Amer, Gerard Hely, Hassan Joundi, Earl Cameron, Ronald Leigh-Hunt, Leonard Trolley, Salem Gedara, Mohammad Al Gaddary.* Dir & Pro: Moustapha Akkad. Screenplay: H. A. L. Craig. (Filmco International–EMI.) Rel: Floating. Colour. 182 Mins. Cert. A.

The Middle Man
With ironic detachment, subtle humour and without judgement Satyajit Ray continues his examination of the less pleasant facets of urban Indian commercial life; the wheeling-dealing, bribery and accepted lack of morals seen in a story about a young man who fails to get honours when he passes his University exams – because of a tired and short-sighted examiner – and decides to go into business. The crowning humiliation comes when he has to become pimp for the sake of landing a big order, and the girl he engages to amuse his client turns out to be the sister of his best friend. Delightful performances. Cast: *Pradip Mukherjee, Satya Banerjee, Dipankar Dey, Lily Chacravarty, Aparna Sen, Gautam Chacravarty, Sudeshna Das, Utpal Dutt, Bimal Chatterjee, Soven Laheri, Robi Gosh, Arati Bhattacharya.* Dir & Screenplay (& Music): Satyajit Ray. Pro: Subir Guha. (Indus–Connoisseur.) Rel: Floating; first shown London, Feb. 1977. Black and white. 131 Mins. Cert. AA.

The Missouri Breaks
An authentic collector's Western from Arthur Penn; a beautifully assembled, artistically set, leisurely paced and generally fascinating story about an infuriated horse rancher who when his stock is stolen and his foreman hanged brings in a hired killer, 'The Regulator', who patiently whittles down the rustling gang one by one until only the leader is left . . . and the situation is complicated by a love affair between the rancher's daughter and the rustler leader and the grim undercurrent between the father and daughter. And *Marlon Brando* as the Regulator contributes an extraordinary, eccentric performance right outside the story, the film and everything else; fascinating nonetheless! Rest of cast: *Jack Nicholson, Randy Quaid, Kathleen Lloyd, Frederic Forrest, Harry Dean Stanton, John McLiam, John Ryan, Sam Gilman, Steve Franken, Richard Bradford, James Greene, Luana Anders, Danny Goldman, Hunter Von Leer, Virgil Frye, R. L. Armstrong, Dan Ades, Dorothy Neumann, Charles Wagenheim, Vern Chandler.* Dir: Arthur Penn. Pro: Elliott Kastner and Robert M. Sherman. Screenplay: Thomas McGuane. (UA.) Rel: Sept. 5. Colour. 126 Mins. Cert. AA.

Moon Over the Alley
Brave little British musical, made on 16 mm film in black and white and concerned with showing something of the multi-racial, sad, shocking and sweet life in the Notting Hill area. Some good little tunes by '*Hair*' composer Galt MacDermot, excellent performances; a fairly deft mixture of sentiment and realism. Cast: *Doris Fishwick, Peter Farrell, Erna May, John Gay, Sean Caffrey, Sharon Forester, Patrick Murray, Lesley Roach, Basil Clarke, Bill Williams, Vari Sylvester, Joan Geary, Norman Mitchell, Leroy Hyde, Miguel Sergides, Debbie Evans.* Dir: Joseph Despins. Pro: not credited. Screenplay: William Dumaresq. (BFI–Fair Enterprises.) Rel: Jan. 2. Black and white. 107 Mins. Cert. A.

Moses
Large-scale and lavish (filmed for the main part on the actual locations involved) this story of Moses, from his discovery in the bullrushes to his release from his onerous task by God some century and a quarter later, has only the occasional lapse in the dialogue to dispel the atmosphere of sincerity and care. Powerful performance by *Burt Lancaster* in the title role. Rest of cast: *Anthony Quayle, Ingrid Thulin, Irene Papas, Aharon Ipale, Yousef Shiloah, Marina Berti, Shmuel Rodensky, Mariangela Melato, Laurent Terzieff, William Lancaster, Jacques Herlin, Galia*

Kohn, Jose Quaglio, Umberto Raho, Mario Ferrari, John Francis Lane, Dina Doronne, Melba Englander, Marco Steiner, Michel Placido, Antonio Piovanelli, Yossi Warjansky. Dir: Gianfranco de Bosio. Pro: Vincenzo Labella. Screenplay: Anthony Burgess, Vittorio Bonicelli and Gianfranco de Bosio. (ITC/RAI–Scotia Barber.) Rel: July 18. Colour. 141 Mins. Cert. A.

Mother, Jugs and Speed
Minor American comedy which with its mish-M.A.S.H. of comedy, violent death and agony is often vaguely reminiscent of a similar, better film of a few years back. Cast: *Bill Cosby, Raquel Welch, Harvey Keitel, Allen Garfield, Dick Butkus, Bruce Davison, L. Q. Jones, Larry Hagman, Valerie Curtin, Allan Warnick, Arnold Williams, Ric Carrott, Toni Basil, Robert Lussier, Ross Durfee, Read Morgan, Karole Selmon, Bobbie Mitchell, Brenda Venus.* Dir: Peter Yates. Screenplay: Tom Mankiewicz. Pro: Peter Yates and Tom Mankiewicz. (Fox.) Rel: June 30. Colour. 98 Mins. Cert. AA.

Mr Billion
About the simple garage mechanic who suddenly finds that he has inherited a million dollars – and lots of headaches along with them! Cast: *Terence Hill, Valerie Perrine, Jackie Gleason, Slim Pickens, William Redfield, Chill Wills, Dick Miller, R. G. Armstrong, Dave Cass, Sam Laws, Johnny Ray McGhee, Kate Heflin, Leo Rossi, Bob Minor, Frances Heflin, Ralph Chesse, Bob Herron, Helen Bentley, Martin Kove, Laurence Somma, Robert Statts, Frank Barone, Mary Woronov, Paul Bartel, Eric Barnes, Earl Boen, Julie Hare, Clay Braden, Stan Ritchie, Dan Lee Gant, Neil Summers, Henry Kinji, Denver Mattson, Walt Davis, Gavin James, George W. Cumming, Also Rendine, Gianna Dauro, Maurizio Fiori, Massimiliano Filoni, Marco Tulli, Cesare Nizzica, Vicky George, Polky (the dog).* Dir: Jonathan Kaplan. Pro: Steven Bach and Ken Friedman. Screenplay: Ken Friedman and Jonathan Kaplan. (Pantheon Pictures–Kaplan/Friedman–Fox.) Rel: May 28. Colour. 92 Mins. Cert. A.

Mr Klein
Joseph Losey's first French film, and a remarkably artistic and stylish achievement. A subtle and compelling story of a rich antique dealer in occupied Paris (the time is 1942) who buys cheaply from Jews who need the money to get out of the country. Then suddenly he becomes involved with another Mr Klein, a Jewish Resistance mystery man who uses his namesake as a cover and provokes him into an increasingly obsessive search in order to confront him, a search that leads him finally to become the victim and be deported to the prison camps in Germany. A film full of hints and nuances and haunting images with one of his best performances in the title-role by *Alain Delon*. Rest of cast: *Jeanne Moreau, Suzanne Flon, Michel Lonsdale, Juliet Berto, Francine Berger, Louis Seigner, Michel Aumont, Massimo Girotti.* Dir: Joseph Losey. Pro: Raymond Danon, Ralph Baum and Alain Delon. Screenplay: Franco Solinas. (Gala.) Rel: Floating; first shown London, April 1977. Colour. 122 Mins. Cert. AA.

The Releases of the Year in Detail

Murder By Death

An amusing idea motivates this Neil Simon screenplay: the story of a highly eccentric millionaire who invites five of the world's more famous fictional detectives (a thinly disguised Nick Charles – with Nora and Asta – Hercule Poirot, a Bogartian Sam Spade, Charlie Chan and Miss Marples) to his gloomy and electronically-gimmicked mansion for a week-end, offering as bait a mysterious murder and a million tax-free dollars to the one who can satisfactorily solve the case. Flashes of wit, quite a lot of laughs from a good deal of crazy humour with the tale twisting into more knots than one would think possible. For the most part smoothly and superbly acted – and most ably impersonated! Cast: *Peter Falk, David Niven, Maggie Smith, James Coco, Peter Sellers, Elsa Lanchester, Eileen Brennan, Alec Guinness, Nancy Walker, Estelle Winwood, James Cromwell, Richard Narita, Truman Capote*. Dir: Robert Moore. Pro: Ray Stark. Screenplay: Neil Simon. (Columbia.) Rel: Oct. 3. Colour. 95 Mins. Cert. A.

Mustang Country

Joel McCrea makes a pleasing return to the screen in a minor Western with some fine scenery and the story of a retired rancher who sets out to win the $500 reward (the year is 1925) offered for the capture of a wild and elusive mustang. And it takes place among the scenic grandeurs of the Montana–Canadian border. Rest of cast: *Nika Mina, Robert Fuller, Patrick Wayne*. Dir, Pro. & Screenplay: John Champion. (Universal–CIC.) Rel: Dec. 26. Colour. 79 Mins. Cert. U.

My Name is Nobody

Sergio Leone, originator of the new-type European Western, with its bloody brutality, beautiful photography and distinctive style, here takes the mickey out of himself in a story about a gunfighter on the way out (to Europe and a more peaceful life) who's 'persuaded' by a young gunman (and great fan) to do battle alone with the 150-strong 'Wild Bunch' gang of outlaws and so become a legend of the Old West! Witty touches include a wayside tombstone engraved with the name of Sam Peckinpah and Wagner's 'Ride of the Valkarie' as a theme tune for the 'Bunch'! Cast: *Henry Fonda, Terence Hill, Jean Martin, Piero Lulli, Leo Gordon, R. G. Armstrong, Remos Peets, Mario Brega, Antoine St Jean, Benito Stefanelli, Mark Mazza, Franco Angrosano, Alexander Allerson, Angelo Novi, Tommy Polgar, Carla Mancini, Antonio Luigi Guerra, Emile Feist, Geoffrey Lewis, Antonio Palombi, Neil Summers, Steve Kanaly, Humbert Mittendorf, Ulrich Muller, Klaus Schimdt*. Dir: Tonino Valerii. Pro: Sergio Leone. Screenplay: Ernesto Gastaldi; from a story by Fulvio Morsella, Ernesto Gastalfi and Sergio Leone. (Rafran, Rome–Alcinter, Paris–Leitenne, Paris–Rialto, Berlin–La Soc. Imp. Ex. CI, Nice–Gala.) Rel: Feb. 20. Colour. 115 Mins. Cert. A.

Mysteries of the Gods – Botschaft der Götter

German interest film supporting the theories of Erich von Däniken's proposition that the ancient gods worshipped in mysteriously vanished old civilisations were in fact visitors from another planet whose impact on our own time is still considerable. Dir: Harald Reinl. Pro & Screenplay: Manfred Barthel. Based on von Däniken's several books on the subject; with English commentary. (Hirschberg/Kalowicz–EMI.) Rel: Oct. 10. Colour. 97 Mins. Cert. U.

Network

That unusual cinematic paradox, a remarkably good movie built upon pretty shaky foundations: a highly professional piece of filmcraft made from a script short on logic, low in credibility and theatrically overblown both as to motivation and characterisation. A loosely bound story about a television newscaster (American) who, when he is sacked because his ratings have fallen, announces that in his last telecast he will shoot himself on camera! Persuaded not to and retained because of the upsurge in popularity, he becomes something of an angry TV Messiah, daily biting the hands that feed him until, again changed, he begins to angrily support the Establishment and his ratings once again at a point when something must be done about him, the executives dream up a dotty plan to have him assassinated during his programme and thus end an embarrassment now too much for them to bear! Superb direction, good performances, fine entertainment. Cast: *Faye Dunaway, William Holden, Peter Finch, Robert Duvall, Wesley Addy, Ned Beatty, Arthur Burghardt, Bill Burrows, John Carpenter, Jordan Charney, Kathy Cronkite, Ed Crowley, Jerome Dempsey, Conchata Ferrell, Gene Gross, Stanley Grover, Cindy Grover, Darryl Hickman, Mitchell Jason, Paul Jenkins, Ken Kercheval, Kenneth Kimmins, Lynn Klugman, Carolyn Krigbaum, Zane Lasky, Michael Lipton, Michael Lombard, Pirie MacDonald, Russ Petranto, Bernard Pollock, Roy Poole, William Prince, Sasha von Scherler, Lane Smith, Theodore Sorel, Beatrice Straight, Fred Stuthman, Cameron Tomas, Marlene Warfield, Lydia Wilen, Lee Richardson*. Dir: Sidney Lumet. Pro: Howard Gottfried. Screenplay: Paddy Chayevsky (Howard Gottfried/Paddy Chayevsky–MGM–UA.) Rel: May 1. Colour. 121 Mins. Cert. AA.

Next Stop Greenwich Village

The story of the hard won film success of gentle Jewish lad Larry Lepinsky, who moves away from his cloying family in Brooklyn to a ramshackle room in Greenwich Village and there mixes with a typical group of young people; loses his girlfriend, becomes involved in a suicide, goes to acting classes, survives auditions and wins through to – just possibly – film fame. Cast: *Lenny Baker, Shelley Winters, Ellen Greene, Lois Smith, Christopher Walken, Dori Brenner, Antonio Fargas, Lou Jacobi, Mike Kellin, Michael Egan, Denise Galik, John C. Becher, John Ford Noonan, Helen Hanft, Rashel Novikoff, Joe Madde, Joe Spinnell, Rochelle Oliver, Gui Adrisano, Carole Manferdini, Jeff Goldblum, Rutanya Alda*. Dir & Screenplay: Paul Mazursky. Pro: Paul Mazursky and Tony Ray. (Fox.) Rel: Mar. 27. Colour. 111 Mins. Cert. X.

Nickelodeon

Peter Bogdanovich's warm and endearing if, alas, not entirely successful, tribute to the old silent movies and their makers; paid in a thin and pretty loose story about a young lawyer acting on behalf of one of the first independent movie moguls. Sent to Hollywood to represent the boss, he soon finds himself forced into writing, directing and producing a whole string of silent movies. Within this framework there are a number of more personal stories to provide romantic and humorous content. A lot of – perhaps too much – slapstick and knockabout but a serious ending when at the première of D. W. Griffith's *Birth of a Nation* everyone involved realises that the movies have lost their innocence and in future offer endless opportunities to be respected as an art form. Delightful work from newcomer *Jane Hitchcock*, and very nice ones from *Ryan O'Neal, Brian Keith, Burt Reynolds, Tatum O'Neal* and *Stella Stevens*. Rest of cast: *John Ritter, Brian James, Sidney Armus, Joe Warfield, Jack Perkins, Tamar Cooper*. Dir: Peter Bogdanovich. Pro: Irwin Winkler and Robert Chartoff. Screenplay: W. D. Richter and Peter Bogdanovich. (Columbia–British Lion–EMI.) Rel: April 3. Colour. 122 Mins. Cert. U.

No Deposit, No Return

Disney comedy which rumbles along the line of a good idea but turns aside too often to be fully successful. The story of the comic kidnapping of two youngsters on the way to their grandfather for their Easter holidays; and their adventures before, with a lot of self-help, they eventually reach him. Cast: *David Niven, Darren McGavin, Don Knotts, Herschel Bernardi, Barbara Feldon, Kim Richards, Brad Savage, John Williams, Charlie Martin Smith, Vic Tayback, Bob Hastings, Louis Guss, Richard O'Brien, Barney Phillips, Ruth Manning, Olive Dunbar, James Hong*. Dir: Norman Tokar. Pro: Ron Miller. Screenplay: Arthur Alsberg and Don Nelson, from a story by co-producer Joe McEveety. (Disney.) Rel: Oct. 31. Colour. 112 Mins. Cert. U.

Norman . . . Is That You?

Screen adaptation of a play about the humours of homosexuality which flopped in New York and London but apparently was a hit elsewhere. The film switches to black comedy by giving the three main roles, father, mother and son, to coloured performers: *Redd Foxx, Pearl Bailey* and *Michael Warren*. The motivation is the reaction of the parents to the discovery that their son is living with another man! Best performance in fact comes from *Dennis Dugan* as the gay pal; and it all varies from the mildly amusing to the highly tasteless. Rest of cast: *Tamara Dobson, Vernee Watson, Jayne Meadows, George Furth, Barbara Sharma, Sergio Aragones, Sosimo Hernandez, Wayland Flowers, Allan Drake*. Dir & Pro: George Schlatter. Screenplay: Ron Clark, Sam Bobrick and George Schlatter, based on the play by the first two. (MGM–CIC.) Rel: Mar. 20. Colour. 92 Mins. Cert. X.

A Nous Les Petites Anglaises!

Another French contribution – and one of the best – to the 'growing up' cycle, with a story about two young Parisian boys who fail their English exams and are sent to England – Ramsgate – for their holidays (instead of St Tropez!) with the idea of repairing their failure. After sampling the

English girls they turn to the small French colony in the town for their fun, develop crushes, learn jealousy and swear vows of everlasting love, vows which time will cancel out. Charming, and at the same time ironical and wittily cruel in the way it depicts the English family: tea and brown ale drinking, blancmange eating, Cockney speaking and insufferably vulgar. Superbly atmospheric. Cast: *Remi Laurent, Stéphane Hillel, Veronique Delbourg, Sophie Barjac, Brigitte Bellac, Michel Melki, Julie Neubert, Rynagh O'Grady, Eric Deacon, David Morris, Aina Walle.* Dir & Screenplay: Michel Lang. Pro: Irene Silberman. (Fox.) Rel: Floating; first shown London, Feb. 1977. Colour. 112 Mins. Cert. AA.

Number Two
Jean-Luc Godard lecturing and illustrating his ideas about the place of male/female relationships in industrial society etc. All strictly for Godardians! Cast: *Sandrine Battistella, Pierre Oudry, Alexandre Rignault, Rachel Stefanopoli.* Dir & Screenplay: Jean-Luc Godard. Pro: Anne-Marie Miéville and Jean-Luc Godard. (The Other Cinema.) Rel: Floating; first shown London, Jan. 1977. Colour. 89 Mins. Cert. X.

Obsession
Hitchcock-reminiscent thriller about a man whose wife and daughter have apparently been killed when a ransom plot goes wrong, faced some fifteen or so years later with what appears to be a repeat performance! A mixture of genuine thrills, unabashed contrived situations and overall competent tailoring. Cast: *Cliff Robertson, Genevieve Bujold, John Lithgow, Sylvia 'Kuumba' Williams, Wanda Blockman, Patric McNamara, Stanley J. Reyes, Nick Krieger, Stocker Fontelieu, Don Hood, Andrea Esterhazy, Thomas Carr, Tom Felleghy, Nella Barbieri, John Creamer, Regis Cordic, Loraine Despres, Clyde Ventura, Fain M. Gogrove.* Dir: Brian de Palma. Pro: George Litto and Harry N. Blum. Screenplay: Paul Schrader. (Yellow Bird Films–Columbia.) Rel: Nov. 28. Colour. 98 Mins. Cert. AA.

Ode to Billy Joe
The film based on the popular song about a seventeen-year-old youth in the early 1950s Mississippi who sets his cap at a fifteen-year-old-girl but because of an escapade (added to the film and not in the song) commits suicide. Cast: *Robby Benson, Glynnis O'Connor, Joan Hotchkis, Sandy McPeak, James Best, Terence Goodman, Becky Bowen, Simpson Hemphill, Ed Shelnut, Eddie Taylor, William Hallberg, Frannye Capelle, Rebecca Jernigan, Ann Martin, Will Long, John Roper, Pat Purcell, Jim Westerfield, Jack Capelle, Al Scott.* Dir: Max Baer. Pro: Max Baer and Roger Camras. Screenplay: Herman Raucher; based on the Bobbie Gentry song. (Warner.) Rel: Floating. Colour. 106 Mins. Cert. AA.

The Office Party
Sex film set against the background of a somewhat permissive party held in the office of a sex movie-making firm. Cast: *Alan Lake, Pamela Grafton, Steve Amber, Ellie Reece-Knight, Chris Gannon, Johnny Briggs, Julia Bond, David Rodigan, Caroline Funnell, David Rayner, Jeanne*

Starbuck, Vicky Hamilton-King, Jason White, Teresa Wood. Dir: David Grant. Pro: Michael McKeag. Screenplay: Gordon Exilby and David Grant. (Oppidan Films.) Rel: July 4. Colour. 56 Mins. Cert. X.

The Omen
Somewhat controversial shocker, a cut above the normal run of 'after-Exorcist' movies in that it is put across with precision and conviction by a top-drawer cast that includes *Gregory Peck* as the American Ambassador in London who finds that his small son is a real little Devil! Rest of cast: *Lee Remick, David Warner, Billie Whitelaw, Leo McKern, Harvey Stephens, Patrick Troughton, Anthony Nicholls, Martin Benson, Sheila Raynor, Holly Palance, Robert McLeod, John Stride.* Dir: Richard Donner. Pro: Harvey Bernhard. Screenplay: David Seltzer. (Fox.) Rel: Sept. 26. Colour. 111 Mins. Cert. X.

The Outlaw Josey Wales
Well-directed, technically good, violent and death-filled Western about the cold killer of the title, a farmer who, when at the outset of the American Civil War, he sees his wife and family murdered, joins the Army and subsequently, when the war is over, refuses to surrender (and be traitorously killed, as are his companions) and takes the hard and dangerous road of the outlaw with a big price on his head. Cast: *Clint Eastwood, Chief Dan George, Sandra Locke, Bill McKinney, John Vernon, Paula Trueman, Sam Bottoms, Geraldine Keams, Woodrow Parfrey.* Dir: Clint Eastwood. Pro: Robert Daley. Screenplay: Phil Kaufman and Sonia Chernus; based on the book by Forrest Carter, *Gone to Texas.* (Malpaso–Warner.) Rel: Aug. 29. Colour. 135 Mins. Cert. AA.

Pete, Pearl and The Pole
Good old (minor) gangster melodrama, bringing a whiff of the 1930s in its brutal and lead-punctuated story of the struggle between the first and last-named racketeers to get away with a half-million dollars which in the end their girlfriend Pearl – the survivor – walks off with! Background is Farmington, West Virginia, hit by the Great US Depression and the bootleg liquor racket. Cast: *Tony Anthony, Lucretia Love, Adolfo Celi, Richard Conte, Lionel Stander, Irene Papas.* Dir: Vance Lewis. Pro: Tony Anthony. Screenplay: Norman Thaddeus Vane. (Scotia-Barber.) Rel: Floating. Colour. 93 Mins. Cert. X.

Picnic at Hanging Rock
Another fascinating, densely textured Australian film from the maker of *The Cars That Ate Paris*: Peter Weir. The story of an unsolved mystery about a party of schoolgirls who in Victoria (in 1900), set out for a picnic at the volcanic rocks which are a local attraction and give the film its title. And the strange events that follow, including the unexplained vanishing of a mistress and some of her pupils. Beautifully atmospheric. Cast: *Rachel Roberts, Dominic Guard, Helen Morse, Jacki Weaver, Vivean Gray, Kirsty Child, Anne Lambert, Karen Robson, Jane Vallis, Christine Schuler, Margaret Nelson, John Jarrat, Ingrid Mason, Martin Vaughan, Jack Fegan, Wyn Roberts, Garry McDonald, Frank Gunnell, Peter Collingwood, Olga Dickie, Kay Taylor, Anthony Llewellyn Jones, Faith Kleinig.* Dir:

Peter Weir. Pro: Hal and Jim McElroy. Screenplay: Cliff Green; based on the novel by Joan Lindsay. (Picnic Productions in assoc. with BEF, S. Australian Film Corp. and Australian Film Commission–GTO Films.) Rel: Oct. 31. Colour. 110 Mins. Cert. A.

The Pink Panther Strikes Again
The further comic adventures of the bumbling French detective Inspector Clouseau (now raised to Chief Inspector!) as he tries to catch his now completely crazy ex-Superior, C. I. Dreyfus, before the latter can blackmail the world, with a holocausting new laser-beam weapon, into killing Clouseau and reinstating him in his old job! Another good comedy performance by *Peter Sellers* as the luckiest – and funniest – blunderer alive. Rest of cast: *Herbert Lom, Colin Blakely, Leonard Rossiter, Lesley Ann Down, Burt Kwouk, André Maranne, Marne Maitland, Richard Vernon, Michael Robbins, Briony McRoberts, Dick Crockett, Byron Kane, Paul Maxwell, Jerry Stovin, Phil Brown, Bob Sherman, Robert Beatty, Dudley Sutton, Vanda Godsell, Norman Mitchell, Patsy Smart, Tony Sympson, George Leech, Murray Kash, April Walker, Hal Galili, Dinny Powell, Terry Richards, Bill Cummings, Terry York, Terry Plummer, Peter Brace, John Sullivan, Cyd Child, Eddie Stacey, Rocky Taylor, Fred Haggerty, Joe Powell, Jackie Cooper, Priceless McCarthy, Fran Fullenwider.* And very funny main titles sequence by the Richard Williams Studio. Dir, Pro and Co-Screenplay (with Frank Waldman): Blake Edwards. (UA.) Rel: April 3. Colour. 103 Mins. Cert. U.

The Pink Telephone
Familiar little French film about a middle-aged out-of-town industrialist (from Toulouse) who comes to Paris to complete a takeover deal with some Americans, who dine, wine and whore him into signing. And then he, not knowing the girl's trade, falls in love with her, with some unfortunate results for himself and his wife! Cast: *Mireille Darc, Pierre Mondy, Michel Lonsdale, Daniel Ceccaldi, Gérard Hérold, Françoise Prévost.* Dir: Edouard Molinaro. Pro: Alain Poiré. Screenplay: Francis Veber. (Gaumont–Gala.) Rel: Floating; first shown London, Feb. 1977. Colour. 93 Mins. Cert. X.

Pleasure at Her Majesty's
Straightforward, cinema verité style, recording of a special stage show presented by a number of first-class comics in aid of Amnesty International. With all the high and less high spots inseparable from such a production. Cast: *Alan Bennett, John Bird, Eleanor Bron, Tim Brooke-Taylor, Graham Chapman, John Cleese, Carol Cleveland, Peter Cook, John Fortune, Graeme Garden, Terry Gilliam, Barry Humphries, Neil Innes, Des Jones, Terry Jones, Jonathan Lynn, Jonathan Miller, Bill Oddie, Michael Palin.* Narrated by Dudley Moore. Dir: Robert Graef. Pro: Roger Graef for Amnesty International. (Essential Cinema.) Rel: Floating; first shown London, Mar. 1977. Colour. 105 Mins. Cert. A.

Private Pleasures
Glossy Swedish sex film with plenty of nude couplings and a slim little theme underneath them about what would

happen if we all threw off our inhibitions and gave rein to our secret desires. Extremely well if – in the clinches – artily photographed, lots of production quality and nice performances from a cast including *Elona Glenn* as the comely heroine. Rest of cast: *Per-Axel Arosenius, Ulf Brunnberg*. Dir & Screenplay: Paul Gerber. Pro: Goran Sjostedt. (New Realm.) Rel: Floating; first shown in London, Nov. 1976. Colour. 95 Mins. Cert. X.

Private Vices and Public Virtues
Miklos Jancso departs from his usual style of constant movements and patterns of large numbers of horsemen and herded peasants but retains all his superb artistry and sense of form in this highly personal interpretation of the 'Mayerling' legend; concentrating on sex and nudity but doing it, or so it appears, more for the patterns than the passion of love-making. Overlong, otherwise self-indulgent (especially in its voyeurism) but still magnificently stylish, individualistic and artistic. Cast: *Lajos Balazsovits, Pamela Villoresi, Franco Branciaroli, Therese Ann Savoy, Laura Betti, Ivica Pajer, Umberto Silva, Zvonimir Crnko, Demeter Bitenc, Susanna Javicoli, Anikó Sáfár, Ilona Staller, Gloria Piedmonte, Cesare Barro, Luigi Marturano, Marino Matota, Andrija Tunjic and the Lado Ballet of Zagreb and Vasas Ballet of Budapest*. Dir & Pro: Miklos Jancso. Screenplay: Giovanni Gagliardo. (Filmes S.p.A, Rome–Jadran Film, Sagreb.) Rel: Floating; first shown London, May 1977. Colour. 104 Mins. Cert. X.

Pussy Talk
Pornographic French comedy (!) about a pretty young wife whose sex begins to take on a voluble, foul-mouthed and randy life of its own, and the way that the worried hubbie tries to smother it by violent copulation – with surprising (?) results. English dubbed. Cast: *Penelope Lamour, Beatrice Harnois, Ellen Earl, Nils Hortzs, Vick Messica*. Dir: Frederick Lansas. Pro: Francis Leroi. Screenplay: not credited. (Oppidan Films.) Rel: Floating; first shown London, April 1977. Colour. 86 Mins. Cert. X (London).

Rafferty and the Gold Dust Twins
Something of a collector's piece and a somewhat unusual addition to the American 'on the road' cycle: about three odd loners and their relationship as they motor from Las Vegas to the end of their joint road at Tucson. A comedy that's a little sad around the edges. Cast: *Alan Arkin, Sally Kellerman, Mackenzie Phillips, Alex Rocco, Charlie Martin Smith, Harry Dean Stanton, John McLiam, Richard Hale, Louis Prima, Sam Butera, The Witnesses*. Dir: Dick Richards. Pro: Michael Gruskoff and Art Linson. Screenplay: John Kaye. (Gruskoff/Venture/Linson Production–Warner Bros.) Rel: Mar. 20. Colour. 91 Mins. Cert. X.

Raid on Entebbe
Second of the three major feature films to be made about the famous hostage-releasing, hijacker-defeating raid on Uganda's airport in the summer of 1976, made and shown, like Warner's *Victory at Entebbe* within six months of the

event. In terms of credibility and entertainment, probably the best of the duo. At its exciting best, when detailing the preparation for and actual operation of the raid itself. And, like the Warner film, bearing no obvious evidence of the great speed with which it was made. Cast: *Peter Finch, Charles Bronson, Martin Balsam, Yaphet Kotto, Jack Warden, John Saxon, Robert Loggia, Tige Andrews, Sylvia Sidney, Horst Bucholz, Eddie Constantine, Mariclare Costello, Stephen Macht, Alex Colon, Rene Assa, Harvey Lembeck, Kim Richards, Robin Gammell, Millie Slavin, Allan Arbus, Peter Brocco, Lou Gelbert*. Dir: Irvin Kershner. Pro: Edgar J. Scherick and Daniel H. Blatt. Screenplay: Barry Beckerman. (Hemdale.) Rel: Jan. 2. Colour. 120 Mins. Cert. A.

Rancho DeLuxe
An odd sort of modern Western with an assortment of morally worthless and cynical characters, sexual trimmings, comedy inclination, occasional possible satirical intent and a number of other half-explored, generally abortive points of departure as it follows the story of two layabouts, a rich man's amoral son and an Indian, who get their living by rustling and like lawbreaking and their only pleasures from sex! Cast: *Jeff Bridges, Sam Waterston, Elizabeth Ashley, Charlene Dallas, Clifton James, Slim Pickens, Harry Dean Stanton, Richard Bright, Patti D'Arbanville, Maggie Wellman, Bert Conway, Anthony Palmer, Joseph Sullivan, Helen Craig, Ronda Copland, John Quade, Sandy Kenyon, Joseph Spinell, Wilma Riley, Richard McMurray, Danna Hansen, Doria Cooke, John Rodgers, Paula Jermunson, Patti Jerome, Pat Noteboom, Bob Wetzel, Arnold Huppert, Richard Cavanaugh, Ben Mar, Jr., Angela Cramer, Esther Black, Dwight Riley, Jim Melin, Tim Schaeffer, Oneida Broderick*. Dir: Frank Perry. Pro: Elliott Kastner. Screenplay: Tom McGuane. (Kastner–UA.) Dec. 5 (listed as a Floating Release in the 1976–7 *Film Review*). Colour. 94 Mins. Cert. X.

The Rape
Dutch Fons Rademakers' film about a gang of rich and restless youngsters who get their thrills by breaking into the homes of wealthy people (like those of their own parents) and wantonly destroying them at the behest of an odd character who directs them for the sense of power it gives him. But a gang rape of one of their victims' wife, then the murder of one of their own gang, leads Inspector Van der Valk to uncovering their identities. Made against Amsterdam and environs backgrounds, in English, it is by and large a rather untidy mixture of vague whodunit, psychological mumbo-jumbo and political drama, with some violence and nudity thrown in for good measure. Cast: *Bryan Marshall, Alexandra Stewart, Alex Van Rooyen, Leo Beyers, Martin Van Zundert, George Baker, Liliane Vincent, Sebastian Graham Jones, Sylvia Kristel, Ida Goemans, Guido de Moor, Edward Judd, Anthony Allen, Nicholas Hoye, Delia Lindsay, Roger Hammond, Derek Hart, Christopher Blake, Louis Hensen, Manell Jonas, Louis Borel*. Dir & Pro: Fons Rademakers. Screenplay: Hugo Claus, based on the Nicolas Freeling novel *Because of the Cats*. (Miracle.) Rel: Floating; first shown July 1976. Colour. 98 Mins. Cert. X.

The Red Pony
A truncated re-make of the Steinbeck story. Life at the turn of the century on a lonely horse ranch, where *Henry Fonda* and *Maureen O'Hara*'s young son *Clint Howard* gives them quite a lot of problems before and after the death of his beloved pony 'Gabilan Mountains'. Rest of cast: *Jack Elam, Ben Johnson, Woodrow Chambliss, Link Wyler, Lieux Dressler, Julian Rivero, Rance Howard, Roy Jenson, Warren Douglas, Yvonne Wood, Kurt Sled, Sally Carter-Ihnat, Victor Sen Yung, Jerry Fuentes, David Markham, Clay Radovitch, Clifford Hodge, Heather Totten, Debbie Steele, Verne Ellenwood, Joe Sardello, Bob Roe*. Dir: Robert Totten. Pro: Frederick Brogger. Screenplay: Robert Totten and Ron Bishop. (Omnibus Productions–British Lion.) Rel: Aug. 22. Colour. 68 Mins. Cert. A.

Requiem for a Village
Quite fascinating and imaginative semi-documentary about the way that the bulldozer and the subsequent concrete tide are sweeping over the old English village and its life-style and replacing it with house-boxes and quiet horror. Cast: *Vic Smith and the villagers of Witnesham and Metfield* (Suffolk). Dir & Screenplay: David Gladwell. Pro: Michael Raeburn. (BIF Production Board film.) Rel: Floating. Colour. 68 Mins.

The Return of a Man Called Horse
A follow-up to the 1971 film *A Man Called Horse* in which the English 'milord' who was captured, enslaved and finally accepted as a brave of the Yellow Hands, returns four years later to find the tribe driven off their hunting grounds and decimated by evil white settlers and their Indian allies. So he goes through some horrifying rites to inspire the tribe into throwing off their lethargy and going back to carry on the fight against the enemy in their fort; eventually by guile and good planning, and Horse's leadership, regaining their land and their self-respect. A powerful mixture of blood and thunder and guts (all literally). Cast: *Richard Harris, Gale Sondergaard, Geoffrey Lewis, Bill Lucking, Jorge Luke, Claudio Brook, Enrique Lucero, Jorge Russek, Ana De Sade, Pedro Damien, Humberto Lopez-Pineda, Patricia Reyes, Regino Herrerra, Rigoberto Rico, Alberto Mariscal*. Dir: Irvin Kershner. Pro: Terry Morse, Jr. Screenplay: Jack de Witt. (Sandy Howard/Richard Harris–United Artists.) Rel: Jan. 9. Colour. 125 Mins. Cert. AA.

Ride a Wild Pony
Disney charmer about two children and a pony they both claim to own, set in Australia. Beautifully photographed and winningly acted; a first-class family film package. Cast: *Robert Bettles, Eva Griffith, Michael Craig, John Meillon, Sr., Alfred Bell, Melissa Jaffer, Lorraine Bayly, Wendy Playfair, John Meillon, Jr., Kate Clarkson, Elizabeth Alexander, Peter Gwynne, Graham Rouse, Ron Haddick, Scott Humphries, Jacki Dalton, Dana Moore, Lex Foxcroft, Harry Lawrence, Edward Hepple, Phillip Ross, Jessica Noad, Neva Carr-Glyn, Martin Vaughan, Gerry Duggan*. Dir: Don Chaffey. Pro: Jerome Courtland. Screenplay: Rosemary Anne Sisson; based on the novel *A Sporting Proposition* by James Aldridge. (Disney.) Rel: Dec. 19. Colour. 91 Mins. Cert. U.

The Ritz
Intermittently amusing but often vulgar and tasteless screen adaptation of the New York stage farce about a 'normal' fat man attempting to escape from his brother-in-law – who has sworn to kill him – who takes refuge in a Manhattan hotel which he soon finds is entirely inhabited by queers. But two grand performances by *Jack Weston* (the normal one!) and *Rita Moreno*. Rest of cast: *Jerry Stiller, Kaye Ballard, F. Murray Abraham, Paul B. Price, Treat Williams, John Everson, Christopher J. Brown, Dave King, Bessie Love, Tony de Santis, Ben Aris, Peter Butterworth, Ronnie Brody, John Ratzenberger, Hal Galili, Chris Harris, George Coulouris, Leon Greene, Freddie Earle, Hugh Fraser, Bart Allison, Samantha Weysom, Richard Holmes.* Dir: Richard Lester. Pro: Denis O'Dell. Screenplay: Terence McNally, based on his own play. (Richard Lester–Courtyard Films–Warners.) Rel: Feb. 6. Colour. 91 Mins. Cert. X.

Robin and Marian
Richard Lester's somehow surprisingly serious adaptation of the Robin Hood legend, set at a time that Robin, back in Sherwood, is becoming a little too old for this sort of caper even though he won't admit it, and is poisoned with good intent by Maid Marian after he just about survives a duel with the Sheriff of Nottingham, she taking a dose of the potion herself so that she can die with him! And the performances are for the most part superior to the material: with *Sean Connery* successfully sincere in his Robin portrayal, *Audrey Hepburn* charming as the Maid, *Nicol Williamson* a carefully underplayed Little John and *Robert Shaw* effective as the Sheriff. Rest of cast: *Richard Harris, Denholm Elliott, Kenneth Haigh, Ronnie Barker, Ian Holm, Bill Maynard, Esmond Knight, Veronica Quilligan, Peter Butterworth, John Barrett, Kenneth Cranham, Victoria Merida Roja, Montserrat Julio, Victoria Hernandez Sanguino, Margarita Minguillon.* Dir: Richard Lester. Pro: Denis O'Dell. Screenplay: James Goldman. (Rastar–Columbia.) Rel: Aug. 8. Colour. 107 Mins. Cert. A.

Rooster Cogburn
One-eyed, rumbustious, fearless old US Marshal *John Wayne* carries on bringing swift, lead-filled justice to the wrongdoers (in the manner in which he did it in *True Grit*), assisted by tough missionary's daughter *Katharine Hepburn*, tagging along to see the killers of her dad get their just come-uppance! Superb star teaming and playing lifts this otherwise routine, superbly photographed Western into a class of its own. Rest of cast: *Anthony Zerbe, Richard Jordan, John McIntire, Paul Koslo, Jack Colvin, Jon Lormer, Richard Romancito, Lane Smith, Warren Vanders, Jerry Gatlin, Strother Martin.* Dir: Stuart Millar. Pro: Hal B. Wallis. Screenplay: Martin Julien. (Hal B. Wallis–Universal–CIC.) Rel: July 18. Colour. 108 Mins. Cert. U. (Included in the 1976–77 Film Review as a Floating Release.)

The Sailor Who Fell from Grace With the Sea
A somewhat strange and not altogether happily blended combination of love romance and horror story – based on a Japanese original by Yukio Mishima – about a repressed young widow wooed and won by the sailor who comes from the sea (when a breakdown in his ship's engines force it to put into the port where she lives) and the diabolical plot hatched by the schoolboy gang (of which the woman's small son is a member) which to prove the leader's theories of amorality plan to use the man as the victim in ritual murder! Superbly photographed coast- and sea-scapes. Cast: *Sarah Miles, Kris Kristofferson, Jonathan Kahn, Margo Cunningham, Earl Rhodes, Paul Tropea, Gary Lock, Stephen Black, Peter Clapham, Jenni Tolman.* Dir & Screenplay: Lewis John Carlino. Pro: Martin Poll. (Avco Embassy–Fox.) Rel: Nov. 21. Colour. 105 Mins. Cert. X.

Saturday Night at the Baths
Deceptively titled film which, in fact, against the background of a steamy, gay nightclub tells the permissive-age story of a fine young masculine character from the open spaces who is seduced from his giggly but all-giving girl-friend by the fuzzy-haired half-breed who is MC at the club where our hero has a job playing piano. And the high-spots are the sequences depicting in some close detail the amorous rompings between girl and boy and boy and boy! Cast: *Robert Aberdeen, Ellen Sheppard, Don Scotti, Janie Olivor, Phillip Owens, Steve Ostrow, R. Douglas Brautigham, Paul J. Ott, Paul Vanase, Lawrence Smith, Caleb Ston, J. C. Gaynor, Pedro Valentino, Toyia.* Dir & Co-Pro (with Steve Ostrow) and Co-Written (with Frank Khedouri): David Buckley. (Lagoon Associates.) Rel: Floating. Colour. 90 Mins. Cert. X.

The Scarlet Buccaneer
Roostering pirate melodrama in the good old style; simple, spectacular, broadly acted and directed and just the holiday thing for the kids! Gallant, grinning *Robert Shaw* saving his mates from the hangman's rope, defeating the degenerate acting Governor of Jamaica and winning the lovely, if militant, lady. Rest of cast: *James Earl Jones, Peter Boyle, Genevieve Bujold, Beau Bridges, Geoffrey Holder, Avery Schreiber, Tom Clancy, Anjelica Huston, Bernard Behrens, Dorothy Tristan, Mark Baker, Kip Niven, Tom Fitzsimmons, Louisa Horton, Sid Haig, Robert Ruth, Robert Morgan, Jon Cedar, Diana Chesney, Manuel De Pina, Tom Lacy, Alfie Wise, Harry Basch.* Dir: James Goldstone. Pro: Jennings Lang. Screenplay: Jeffrey Bloom. (Universal–CIC.) Rel: Dec. 26. Colour. 102 Mins. Cert. A.

Schizo
Bloody, conventional thriller which gets wilder as it goes along towards its highly incredible ending: a story about a young wife apparently threatened by the released murderer of her ma – ah, but who killed who? Who is the real schizo in the case? Cast: *Lynne Frederick, Victoria Allum, John Leyton, Stephanie Beacham, John Fraser, Jack Watson, Queenie Watts, Paul Alexander, Trisha Mortimer, John McEnery, Colin Jeavons, Raymond Bowers, Terry Duggan, Robert Mill, Diana King, Lindsay Campbell, Victor Winding, Pearl Hackney, Primi Townsend, Wendy Gilmore, Steve Emerson.* Dir & Pro: Pete Walker. Screenplay: David McGillivray. (Pete Walker–Warner Bros.) Rel: Dec. 5. Colour. 109 Mins. Cert. X.

Sebastiane
Somewhat pretentious historical piece, made in Latin (claimed to be the first movie ever to be so made) concerning the troubles and final martyrdom of the young Roman converted Christian Captain who refuses the homosexual overtures of the Centurion who commands the isolated outpost where he has been sent in disgrace because of his faith. Lots of male nudity and amorous exercises. Cast: *Leonardo Treviglio, Barney James, Neil Kennedy, Richard Warwick, Donald Dunham, Ken Hicks, Janusz Romanov, Steffano Massari, Daevid Finbar, Gerald Incandela.* Dir: Derek Jarman and Paul Humfress. Pro: Howard Malin and James Whaley. Screenplay: James Whaley and Derek Harman. (Cine.) Rel: Floating; first shown London, Oct. 1976. 85 Mins. Cert. X.

The Secret
Tense, finely directed and acted French suspense thriller with *Jean-Louis Trintignant* the escapee from a mysterious political prison where he has been sent prior to being murdered because of a political secret he has accidentally learned. On the run, he becomes the guest of a writer with an apparently fatal disease and his artist mistress, living in a remote old mansion. The tension between the trio, the suspicions and doubts and the final deadly explanation and confirmation makes for a brilliant and memorable movie. Rest of cast: *Marlène Jobert, Philippe Noiret, Jean-François Adam, Solange Pradel, Antoine St. John, Michel Delahaye, Maurice Vallier, Jean-Claude Fel, Patric Melennen, Pierre Danny, Frédéric Santaya.* Dir: Robert Enrico. Pro: Jacques-Eric Strauss. Screenplay: Enrico and Pascal Jardin; based on the Francis Ryck novel, *Le Compagnon Indésirable.* (Contemporary.) Rel: Floating; first shown in August 1976. Colour. 102 Mins. Cert. A.

Section Spéciale
Another Costa-Gavras political 'reconstruction' film, this time based on a particularly shameful event which occurred in France in 1941 when the Pétain judiciary, after the assassination of a German officer by some unknown young communists, made a bargain by which they selected three men in jail, already sentenced and serving their terms, and retrospectively recondemned them to the guillotine in order to stop the execution of a number of seized French hostages. Cast: *Louis Seigner, Michel Lonsdale, Ivo Garrani, François Maistre, Roland Bertin, Henri Serre, Pierre Dux, Jacques François, Claudio Gora, Julien Bertheau, Claude Piéplu, Hubert Gignoux, Jacques Ouvrier, Alain Nobis, Jean Bouise, Jean Champion, Julien Guiomar, Maurice Teynec, Jacques Spiesser, Heinz Bennent, Michel Galabru, Guy Retore, Yves Robert, Jacques Rispal, Eric Rouleau, Guy Mairesse, Bruno Cremer, Jacques Perrin.* Dir: Costa-Gavras. Pro: Jacques Perrin and Giorgio Silvagni. Screenplay: Jorge Semprun. (Reggane Films/ Artistes Associés Productions, Paris–Goriz Films, Rome–Janus Films, Frankfurt–Curzon Films.) Rel: Floating; first shown London (at Curzon Cinema and also on BBC TV), March 1977. Colour. 120 Mins. Cert. A.

The Sentinel
Michael Winner's contribution to the 'Exorcist' cycle; a rip-roaring effort about a mentally strained young lady who finds herself living literally at the gates of hell! They are situated in the old Brooklyn house in which she takes a flat and are guarded by a blind old priest! Cast: *Chris Sarandon, Cristina Raines, Martin Balsam, John Carradine, José Ferrer, Ava Gardner, Arthur Kennedy, Burgess Meredith, Sylvia Miles, Deborah Raffin, Eli Wallach, Christopher Walken, Jerry Orbach, Beverly D'Angelo, Hank Garrett, Robert Gerringer, Nana Tucker, Tom Berenger, William Hickey, Gary Allen, Tresa Hughes, Kate Harrington, Jane Hoffman, Elaine Shore, Sam Gray, Reid Shelton, Fred Stuthman, Lucie Lancaster, Anthony Holland, Jeff Goldblum, Zane Lasky, Mady Heflin, Diane Stilwell, Ron McLarty*. Dir. Michael Winner. Pro & Screenplay: Michael Winner and Jeffrey Konvitz, based on the latter's novel. (Michael Winner–Universal–CIC.) Rel: May 31. Colour. 92 Mins. Cert. X.

Seven Nights in Japan
Highly romantic, 'old-fashioned' story along *Madame Butterfly* lines about a handsome young Naval Prince (George!) and the lovely young Japanese girl he meets, loves and finally leaves (after escaping some assassination attempts) to return to his world (actually his ship) while she goes back to her's (bus conducting!). Cast: *Michael York, Hidemi Aoki, Charles Gray, Ann Lonnberg, Eleonore Hirt, James Villiers, Yolande Donlan, Peter Jones, Lionel Murton*. Dir & Pro: Lewis Gilbert. Screenplay: Christopher Wood. (Gilbert–Anglo–French–EMI.) Rel: Sept. 26. Colour. 104 Mins. Cert. A.

Seven Beauties
Wickedly funny Italian black comedy, English dubbed, about an obstinate survivor who has to pay quite a high price at times for staying alive. From Naples, he (inadvertently) kills his sister's ravisher, escapes death by pleading insanity, escapes from the asylum into the army, escapes the Russian front by feigning wounds, escapes the army – to be thrown into a German Concentration Camp – where his debasing escape is by agreeing to preside over the death of his fellow inmates! And all this directed with great skill and bitter irony by Fellini's ex-assistant Lina Wertmüller, a lady of much talent. Cast: *Giancarlo Giannini, Fernando Rey, Shirley Stoler, Elena Fiore*. Dir, Pro (with Giancarlo Giannini & Arrigo Colombo) & Screenplay: Lina Wertmüller. (Medusa–Warner.) Rel: Floating; first shown London, April 1977. Colour. 115 Mins. Cert. X.

Sex in Sweden
Routine, minor Swedish sex film with plenty of nudity, bed-hopping, reprehensible characters and a sudden, astonishing happy-ever-after ending. Cast: *Chris Chittell, Peter Loury, Maria Lynn, Eva Axen, Darby Lloyd Rains, Kim Pope, Rob Everett, Anita Eriksson*. Dir: Bert Torn. Pro: Inge Ivarson. Screenplay: Edward Mannering. (Fiminvest–Variety.) Rel: Floating; first shown London, May 1977. Colour. 82 Mins. Cert. X.

Shadowman – L'Homme Sans Visage (also known as *The Man Without a Face* and *Nuits Rouges*)
Georges Franju thriller about the criminal Mastermind of the title, who with his real and robot assistants tries to defeat the small band of Knight Templars still guarding their fabulous treasure. Cast: *Jacques Champreux, Gayle Hunnicutt, Gert Froebe, Ugo Pagliai, Josephine Chaplin, Patrick Préjean, Yvon Sarray, Clément Harari, Henry Lincoln*. Dir: Georges Franju. Pro: Raymond Froment. Screenplay: Jacques Champreux. (Terra Films, Paris–SOAT, Milan–Connoisseur.) Rel: Floating; first shown London, Feb. 1977. Colour. 105 Mins. Cert. A.

Shattered
Exciting French/Italian chase thriller about a man who picks up his schoolboy stepson in Rome with the idea of driving him to his mother in Paris, but soon after they set out notices they are being followed by a blue van, which clings to them throughout the latterly eventful drive, culminating in the deadly confrontation at journey's end. Superb building and holding of tense atmosphere, very well acted by *Jean-Louis Trintignant* as the followed, *Bernard Fresson* as follower, *Richard Constantini* the son and *Mireille Darc* the wife. Also *Adolfo Cell*. Dir: Serge LeRoy. Pro: Leo L. Fuchs. Screenplay: Christopher Frank and Serge LeRoy. (Viaduc Productions S.A.–Trianon Productions, Paris–P.I.C., Rome–Warner Bros.) Rel: Floating; first shown London, May 1977. Colour. 103 Mins. Cert. AA.

The Shootist
Quiet, chamber Western and a curiosity of its kind. Following the last few days in the life of ace gunslinger J. B. Books, in Carson City where his old friend the doctor confirms that he has a terminal cancer and only a few weeks to live. With a weary and more craggier than ever *John Wayne* (himself a cancer victim but a winner, at the cost of a lung) giving a magnificent performance in what might almost be a valediction to himself. Rest of cast: *Lauren Bacall, Ron Howard, James Stewart, Richard Boone, Hugh O'Brian, Bill McKinney, Harry Morgan, John Carradine, Sheree North, Richard Lenz, Scatman Crothers, Gregg Palmer, Alfred Dennis, Dick Winslow, Melody Thomas, Kathleen O'Malley*. Dir: Don Siegel. Pro: M. J. Frankovich and William Self. Screenplay: Miles Hood Swarthout and Scott Hale; based on the novel by Glendon Swarthout. (Dino de Laurentiis–Frankovich/Self-Paramount–CIC.) Rel: Nov. 7. Colour. 100 Mins. Cert. A.

Shout at the Devil
Supposedly based on fact, this adaptation of the Wilbur Smith story obviously has plenty of fictional trimmings as it tells the story of the struggle between an Irish adventurer, a true-blue young Britisher and a sadistic German commissioner in Africa prior to and just after the start of the First World War; lots of action and broad comedy, several climaxes and highly spectacular sequences. Cast: *Lee Marvin, Roger Moore, Barbara Parkins, Ian Holm, Rene Kolldehoff, Gernot Endemann, Karl Michael Vogler, Horst Janson, Gerard Paquis, Maurice Denham, Jean Kent, Heather Wright, George Coulouris, Renu Setna, Murray Melvin, Bernard Horsfall, Robert Lang, Peter Copley, Geoff Davidson, Simon Sabela, Shalimar Undi, Joe Mafela, Paul Mafela, Solomon Dungane, Ray Msengana, Nicholas Kourtis*. Dir: Peter Hunt. Pro: Michael Klinger. Screenplay: Wilbur Smith, Stanley Price and Alastair Reid, based on the novel by Wilbur Smith. (Klinger–Hemdale.) Rel: Aug. 29. Colour. 147 Mins. Cert. A.

Silent Movie
Mel Brooks' generally affectionate spoof of the old silent movie slapstick comedies, with only one word ('No') along its entire length, lots of star participation and an uneven level of humour as it tells a tale about a failing movie mogul about to be taken over by a conglomerate who escapes the axe by the success of a silent film. Gags vary from rich to thin, just as the good taste gets a little ragged at times, but for Brooks fans it is obviously satisfyingly funny all along the line. Cast: *Mel Brooks, Marty Feldman, Dom DeLuise, Bernadette Peters, Sid Caesar, Harold Gould, Ron Carey, Carol Arthur, Liam Dunn, Fritz Feld, Chuck McCann, Valerie Curtin, Yvonne Wilder, Arnold Soboloff, Patrick Campbell, Harry Ritz, Charlie Callas, Henny Youngman, Eddie Ryder, Al Hopson, Rudy DeLuca, Barry Levinson, Howard Hesseman, Lee Delano, Jack Riley, Inga Neisen, Sivi Aberg, Erica Hagen, Robert Lussier*. Guest stars: *Burt Reynolds, James Caan, Liza Minnelli, Anne Bancroft, Marcel Marceau and Paul Newman*. Dir: Mel Brooks. Pro: Michael Hertzberg. Screenplay: Mel Brooks, Ron Clark, Rudy DeLuca and Barry Levinson; from a story by Ron Clark. (Mel Brooks–Crossbow Productions–Fox). Rel: Feb. 13. Colour. 87 Mins. Cert. A.

Silver Streak
Extremely well-made and entertaining comedy-thriller set against a background of the Los Angeles to Chicago express train of the title, on which publisher *Gene Wilder* finds romance with the girl in the adjoining compartment, and mystery when he sees her murdered boss hanging outside her window! Winning performances by *Jill Clayburgh* and *Richard Pryor* and a neatly villainous one by *Patrick McGoohan*. The film selected for the 1977 Royal Film Performance. Rest of cast: *Ned Beatty, Clifton James, Ray Walston, Stefan Gierasch, Len Birman, Valerie Curtin, Richard Kiel, Lucille Benson, Scatman Crothers, Fred Willard, Delos V. Smith, Matilda Calnan, Nick Stewart, Margarita Garcia, Jack Mather, Henry Beckman, Steve Weston, Harvey Atkin, Lloyd White, Ed Macnamara, Ray Guth, John Day, Jack O'Leary, Lee McLaughlin, Tom Erhart, Gordon Hurst, Bill Henderson*. Dir: Arthur Hiller. Pro: Thomas L. Miller and Edward K. Milkis. Screenplay: Colin Higgins. (Frank Yablans/Martin Ransohoff–Fox.) Rel: April 24. Colour. 113 Mins. Cert. A.

Some Call it Loving
A weird fantasy which emerges as a rather messy mixture of poetry and pretention: the story of a filthy-rich young man (living in a fabulous rococo mansion with two women and acting out his fantasies with them) who sees a

'Sleeping Beauty' sideshow at the fair, buys it on the spot and takes it home, waking the drugged girl and then, finding no fulfilment, himself readministering the drugs and taking the show back on the road! Cast: *Zalman King, Carol White, Tisa Farrow, Richard Pryor, Veronica Anderson, Logan Ramsey, Brandy Herred, Pat Priest, Ed Rue, J. de Meo*. Dir, Pro & Screenplay: James B. Harris; based on the short story, *Sleeping Beauty* by John Collier. (Pleasant Pastures.) Rel: Floating; first shown London, Oct. 1975. Colour. 103 Mins. Cert. X.

The Spider's Strategem
Brilliant, artistic Bertolucci film actually made before *The Conformist* but only now (Dec. 1976) shown in Britain. Based on an outline sketch by Jorge Luis Borges, it is the story of the son of an anti-fascist martyr who, going back to the town where his father was murdered, discovers a mystery surrounds the killing: was it done by the local fascists? Or an out-of-town assassin? Or could it have been by his friends? Was the man the hero his statue in the town square suggests, or a self-confessed traitor or . . . A wonderful study in ambiguity, lifted by the lovely backgrounds of the sun-drenched town and a constant sense of poetry. Cast: *Giulio Brogi, Alida Valli, Tino Scotti, Pippo Campanini, Franco Giovanelli, Allen Midgett*. Dir: Bernardo Bertolucci. Pro: Giovanni Bertolucci. Screenplay: Bernardo Bertolucci, Eduardo de Gregorio and Marilu Pavolini; based on a story by Jose Luis Borges. (RAI–Artificial Eye Co.). Rel: Floating; first shown Dec. 1976. Colour. 97 Mins. Cert. A.

The Spoilers – Thong (STAB)
Run-of-the-mill Thailand action melodrama set in 1935 and concerning adventurer *Greg Morris's* efforts to carry out his assignment to recover the shipment of gold bullion seized by the Thai police and subsequently hijacked into communist territory. Rest of cast: *Sombat Metanee, Krung Srivilai, Tham Thuy Hang, Anoma Palalak, Krisana Amnueyporn, Darm Daskorn, Dolnapa Sopir*. Dir & Pro: Chalong Pakdivijt. Screenplay: not credited. (Paragon–Golden Harvest–Cathay.) Rel: Floating. Colour. 91 Mins. Cert. X.

The Squeeze
Rough, tough and four-letter word abounding British crime thriller about a drunken ex-cop who becomes involved with crime again when his wife and the daughter of her lover are kidnapped and used as a means to force the man to agree to assist in the theft of a million pounds from his own firm. Unpleasant characters all (with the exception of that played by *Freddie Starr*, who walks away with the acting honours), unpleasant dialogue and action, but all very ably directed. Rest of cast: *Stacy Keach, Edward Fox, Stephen Boyd, David Hemmings, Carol White, Alan Ford, Roy Marsden, Stuart Harwood, Hilary Gasson, Alison Portes, Keith Miles, Lee Strand, Lucinda Duckett, Lucita Lijertwood, Rod Beacham, Leon Greene, Maureen Sweeney, Mordelle Jordine, Pam Brighton, Michael O'Hagan, Ken Sicklen*. Dir: Michael Apted. Pro: Stanley O'Toole. Screenplay: Leon Griffiths. (Warner.) Rel: March 20. Colour. 106 Mins. Cert. X.

Squirm
Nasty, minor thriller about an electric storm along the desolate Georgia coastline which, felling the power lines, electrifies thousands of man-eating worms into horrid activity. Cast: *John Scardino, Patricia Pearcy, R. A. Dow, Jean Sullivan, Peter MacLean, Fran Higgins, William Newman, Barbara Quinn, Carl Dagenhart, Angel Sande, Carol Jean Owens, Kim Iocouvozzi, Walter Dimmick, Julia Klopp*. Dir & Screenplay: Jeff Lieberman. Pro: George Manasse. (American International.) Rel: June 26. Colour. 92 Mins. Cert. X.

St Ives
Charles Bronson and *John Houseman* in pursuit of some stolen ledgers – and nothing will halt them, neither the cops nor the string of corpses which bestrew their path. Rest of cast: *Jacqueline Bisset, Maximilian Schell, Elisha Cook, Burr de Benning, Harry Guardino, Harris Yulin, Joe Roman, Robert Englund, Mark Thomas, Jeff Goldblum, Dick O'Neill, Daniel Travanti, Val Bisoglio, Tom Pedi, Joseph de Nicola, Michael Lerner, Dana Elcar, George Memmoli, Don Hanmer, Bob Terhune, Norman Palmer, Walter Brook, Jerome Thor, George Sawaya, Glen Robards, Jerry Brutsche, Dar Robinson, Lynn Borden, Stanley Brock, Larry Martindale*. Dir: J. Lee Thompson. Pro: Pancho Kohner and Stan Canter. Screenplay: Barry Beckerman. (Kohner/Beckerman–Columbia–Warner.) Rel: Aug. 1. Colour. 94 Mins. Cert. AA.

Stand Up Virgin Soldiers
A follow-up to the first *Virgin Soldiers* film: the story of a group – and two in particular – of National Service soldiers caught by the 1950 extension of the period and forced on the eve of demobilisation to spend a further six months in Singapore, in which time they go a-whoring, take two nurses to their beds, have other fun and then suddenly come up against the shooting war, which sorts out the men from the boys! Broad barrack-room comedy and rough barrack-room dialogue. Cast: *Robin Askwith, Nigel Davenport, George Layton, John Le Mesurier, Warren Mitchell, Robin Nedwell, Edward Woodward, Irene Handl, Fiesta Mei Ling, Pamela Stephenson, Lynda Bellingham, David Auker, Robert Booth, Peter Bourke, Leo Dolan, Brian Godfrey, Paul Rattee, Patrick Newell, Miriam Margolyes, Arnold Diamond, Leonard Woodrow, David Kellar, John Clive, Monica Grey, Rosamund Greenwood, Pearl Hackney, Ken Nazarin, Michael Halsey, Arnold Lee, Denis Chin, John Wu, Dino Shafeek*. Dir: Norman Cohen; Pro: Greg Smith. Screenplay: Leslie Thomas; based on his own novel. (Warner.) Rel: April 24. Colour. 91 Mins. Cert. AA.

Stay Hungry
Bob Rafelson's perceptive expedition into the strange world of body-building; seen through the experience of a rich and idle young man from Alabama who – not without some hesitation – becomes involved in it when he tries to buy a small gymnasium for redevelopment. A film that emerges as being far better than its second feature bracket might lead one to believe. Cast: *Jeff Bridges, Sally Field, Arnold Schwarzenegger, R. G. Armstrong, Robert Englund, Helena Kallianiotes, Roger E. Mosley, Woodrow Parfrey, Scatman Crothers, Kathleen Miller, Fannie Flagg, Joanna Cassidy, Richard Gilliland, May Nutter, Ed Begley, Jr., John David Carson, Joe Spinell, Cliff Pellow, Dennis Fimple, Garry Goodrow, Bart Carpinelli, Bob Westmoreland, Brandy Wilde, Laura Hippe, John Gillgreen, Murray Johnson, Dennis Burkley, Autry Pinson*. Dir: Bob Rafelson. Pro: Harold Schneider and Bob Rafelson. Screenplay: Charles Gaines and Bob Rafelson; based on the former's novel. (Outov–UA.) Rel: Oct. 17. Colour. 102 Mins. Cert. X.

Stoner
Typical Hong Kong action melodrama concerning criminals, drugs and the cops. Cast: *George Lazenby, Angela Mao, Betty Ting Pei, Whonh In-Sik, Joji Takagi, Hung Chin-Pao, Chin Lu, Romanlee Rose, Samuel J. Peake, Yang Wei, Sun Lan, Hung Hsing-Chung, Su Hsiang, Chin Chi-Chu, Szu-Ma Hua-Lung*. Dir: Huang Feng. Pro: Raymond Chow. Screenplay: Ni Kwang. (Golden Harvest–Cathay.) Rel: Floating. Colour. 105 Mins. Cert. X.

The Strongest Man in the World
Back to Medfield College (background for two previous Disney fantasies – *The Computer Wore Tennis Shoes* and *Now You See Him Now You Don't*) where an accident in the lab reveals a vitamin-charged cereal which makes men physical giants. Basis for a typical, formula but laughter-charged comedy. Cast: *Kurt Russell, Joe Flynn, Eve Arden, Cesar Romero, Phil Silvers, Dick Van Patten, Harold Gould, Michael McGreevey, Dick Bakalyan, William Schallert, Benson Fong, James Gregory, Ann Marshall, Don Carter, Christina Anderson, Paul Linke, Jack Derrel Maury, Matthew Conway Dunn, Pat Fitzpatrick, David Richard Ellis, Larry Franco, Roy Roberts, Fritz Feld, Ronnie Schell, Raymond Bailey, John Myhers, James E. Brodhead, Dick Patterson, Irwin Charone, Roger Price, Jack Bailey, Larry Gelman, Eric Brotherson, Jonathan Daly, Kathleen Freeman, Iggie Wolfington, Ned Wertimer, Milton Frome, Laurie Main, Mary Treen, Eddie Quillan, Jeff DeBenning, Henry Slate, Bryon Webster, Burt Mustin, Arthur Space, Bill Zuckert, Larry J. Blake, William Bakewell, Art Metrano, Pete Renoudet, Lennie Weinrib, Danny Wells, James Beach*. Dir: Vincent McEveety. Pro: Bill Anderson. Screenplay: Joseph L. McEveety and Herman Groves. (Disney.) Rel: Aug. 1. Colour. 92 Mins. Cert. U.

Sunday Too Far Away
Quite outstanding Australian film about the hard life of the travelling, expert sheep-shearer in the dry, dusty and isolated interior some twenty years ago; a vivid portrait of a man and a way of life presented without dramatics, without a climax but with complete credibility. Cast: *Jack Thompson, Phyllis Ophel, Reg Lyle, John Charman, Gregory Apps, Max Cullen, Ken Shorter, Robert Bruning, Jerry Thomas, Laurie Rankin, John Ewart, Sean Scully, Peter Cummins, Graeme Smith, Ken Weaver, Lisa Peers, Hedley Cullen, Wayne Anthony*. Dir: Ken Hannam. Pro: Gil Brealey and Matt Carroll. Screenplay: John Dingwall. (Warner.) Rel: Aug. 29. Colour. 95 Mins. Cert. AA.

The Releases of the Year in Detail

Supervixens

Highly coloured mixture of melodrama and comedy satire set in the American rural South-West and concerning a garage mechanic hero, the brutal and ruthless cop who frames him for the murder that he himself has committed, and the big-busted heroine who manages to survive the outrageous end planned for her to enjoy a happy-ever-after ending. Cast: *Shari Eubank, Charles Pitts, Charles Napier, Uschi Digard, Henry Rowland, Christy Hartburg, Sharon Kelly, John La Zar, Stuart Lancaster, Deborah McGuire, Glenn Dixon, Haji, Big Jack Provan, Garth Pillsbury, Ron Sheridan, John Lawrence, F. Rufus Owens, Paul Fox, E. E. Meyer.* Dir, Pro & Screenplay: Russ Meyer. (September 19 Productions–Anthony Balch.) Rel: Floating; first shown April 1977. Colour. 105 Mins. Cert. X.

Survive

Consistently grim, and in the butchery scenes grisly, Mexican (but American adapted) film based on the Clay Blair Jr. book about the air disaster that occurred when a plane chartered by a Uruguayan rugby team to fly them across the Andes to a game in Chile, smashed into one of the peaks and the survivors were eventually reduced to eating their dead companions in order to stay alive. Cast: *Hugo Sitlitz, Norma Lazareno, Luzma Aguilar, Fernando Larranaga, Lorenzo de Rodas.* Dir & Screenplay: Rene Cardona (English adaptation of the Mexican original by Martin Sherman). Pro: Conacine and Rene Cardona. (Robert Stigwood/Robert Carr–EMI.) Rel: Nov. 14. Colour. 86 Mins. Cert. X.

Sweeney

A rough, tough British detection thriller which gives an unflattering (and, one hopes, unrealistic!) picture of police and politicians as it tells a story about a British Minister of Energy blackmailed by his OPIC (Oil Producers International Conference) – employed PRO into reversing our stated dear-oil policy. And when anyone seems likely to object the PRO has them murdered – until hard-drinking, foul-mouthed DI Regan gets suspicious and though framed and suspended from the Force escapes the assassin's bullets (well, most of them!) long enough to be reinstated, smash the plan and see the PRO get his come-uppance at the hands of his own thugs! Cast: *John Thaw, Dennis Waterman, Barry Foster, Ian Bannen, Colin Welland, Diane Keen, Michael Coles, Joe Melia, Brian Glover, Lynda Bellingham, Morris Perry, Paul Angelis, Nick Brimble, John Alkin, Bernard Kay, Antony Scott, Anthony Brown, John Oxley, Peggy Aitchison, Hal Jeayes, Sally Osborne, John Kane, Chris Dillinger, Peter Childs, Alan Mitchell, Leonard Kavanagh, Anthony Woodruff, Michael Latimer, Matthew Long, Joyce Grant, Johnny Shannon, Nadim Sawalha.* Dir: David Wickes. Pro: Ted Childs. Screenplay: Ranald Graham; based on *The Sweeney*, created by Ian Kennedy Martin. (Nat Cohen–Euston Films–EMI.) Rel: Jan. 30. Colour. 98 Mins. Cert. X.

Sweet Kill

The story of the impotent physical education teacher whose violent sexual desires finally tip him off his trolley and convert him into something like a mass murderer, with a score of six! Cast: *Tab Hunter, Cheri Latimer, Nadyne Turney, Roberta Collins.* Dir & Screenplay: Curtis Hanson. Pro: Tamara Asseyev. (Focus Distributors.) Rel: Floating, first shown in August 1976. Colour. 76 Mins. Cert. X.

Taxi Driver

Martin Scorsese's Cannes Festival prize-winner; a technically brilliant story of an alienated young insomniac who takes a job as a night taxi-driver in the seamier parts of New York and develops a psychotic hatred for the sleazier characters, a hatred which eventually bursts into frightful violence as he guns down the pimp of the schoolgirl prostitute he has met, the manager of the hotel where she works and her client of the moment; escaping death himself to survive as something of a hero. A film one can admire but at the same time dislike. Cast: *Robert De Niro, Cybill Shepherd, Peter Boyle, Leonard Harris, Albert Brooks, Diahnne Abbot, Jodie Foster, Frank Adu, Gino Ardito, Garth Avery, Albert Brooks, Harry Cohn, Copper Cunningham, Brenda Dickson, Harry Fischler, Nat Grant, Richard Higgs, Beau Kayser, Harvey Keitel, Vic Magnotta, Robert Maroff, Norman Matlock, Bill Minkin, Murray Moston, Harry Northup, Gene Palma, Carey Poe, Steven Prince, Peter Savage, Martin Scorsese, Robert Shields, Ralph Singleton, Joe Spinell, Maria Turner, Robin Utt.* Dir: Martin Scorsese. Pro: Michael Phillips and Julia Phillips. Screenplay: Paul Schrader. (Columbia.) Rel: Sept. 18. Colour. 113 Mins. Cert. X.

The Telephone Book

A film labelled 'nearer to obscenity than any other film submitted' to the BBFC and refused even a GLC certificate, yet nothing like so disgusting as many of the films seen around with the X blessing. In fact without the needless, scabrous cartoon sequences, rather an amusing and at times even moving pornographic picture about an unfortunate astronaut whose experiences have made any sexual satisfaction, other than what he gains by making obscene telephone calls, quite impossible! And his bizarre romance with the pretty little blonde who falls for his hot line – so to speak! Cast: *Sarah Kennedy, Norman Rose, James Harder, Jill Clayburgh, Ondine, Barry Morse, Ultra Violet, Gerti Miller, Roger C. Carmel, William Hickey, Matthew Tobin, Jan Farrand, David Dozer, Lucy Lee Flippen, Dolph Sweet, Joan Ziehl, Margaret Brewster, Arthur Haggerty.* Dir & Screenplay: Nelson Lyon. Pro: Merwin Bloch. (Bloch–Rosebud–Essential.) Rel: Floating; first shown London, May 1977. Colour. 89 Mins. No cert.

The Tenant

Roman Polanski returns to his obsession with paranoia in a story about a timid young man who rents the flat from the window of which a girl has for no obvious reason lately jumped to her death. Once installed, he begins to get complaints about the noises he has not made, actions which are not his and gradually becomes convinced there is a conspiracy by the landlord and other tenants to drive him to do the same thing as the girl – which, now well off his head, he in fact does: and with an encore! Fascinating if below his *Repulsion* standard. Cast: *Roman Polanski, Isabelle Adjani, Shelley Winters, Melvyn Douglas, Jo Van Fleet, Bernard Fresson, Lila Kedrova, Claude Dauphin, Claude Piéplu, Rufus, Romain Bouteille, Jacques Monod, Patrice Alexsandre, Jean Pierre Bagot, Josiane Balasko, Michel Blanc, Florence Blot, Louba Chazel, Jacques Chevalier, Jacky Cohen, Alain Davis, Bernard Donnadieu, Alain Frérot, Raoul Guylad, Eva Ionesco, Gérard Jugnot, Helena Manson, Maite Nahyr, André Penvern, Gérard Pereira, Dominique Poulange, Arlette Reinerg, Jacques Rosny, Serge Spira, Vanessa Vaylord, François Viaur.* Dir: Roman Polanski. Pro: Andrew Braunsberg. Screenplay: Gerard Brach and Roman Polanski. (Polanski–Paramount–CIC.) Rel: Floating. Colour. 126 Mins. Cert. X.

Tentacles

A very poor Italian relation to *Jaws* with a vast man-eating Octopus after decimating the population around his lair being killed by two well-disposed whales! Cast: *John Huston, Shelley Winters, Bob Hopkins, Henry Fonda, Delia Boccardo, Cesare Danova, Alan Boyd, Claude Akins, Sherry Buchanan, Franco Diogene, Mark Fiorini, Helena Makela, Alessandro Poggi, Roberto Poggi, Giancarlo Nacinelli, Consolata Marcinao, Philip Dallas, Leonard C. Lightfoot, John White, William Van Raaphorst, Patrick Mulvihill, Joanne Van Raaphorst, Janet Myers, Krisha M. Brekke, Janet Raycraft, Kenneth Lundeen, Rita Real, Alan Scharf, Ross Gordon, Ronald Shapiro, Joseph Johnson.* Dir: Oliver Hellman (Sonia Assonitis). Pro: E. F. Doria. Screenplay: Jerome Max, Tito Carpi, Steve Carabatsos and Sonia Molteni. (A-Esse Cinematografica–Fox.) Rel: May 28. Colour. 102 Mins. Cert. A.

The Texas Chainsaw Massacre

Well made but bloodily repelling story of a horrible crime. Cast: *Marilyn Burns, Allen Danziger, Paul A. Partain, William Vail, Teri McMinn, Edwin Neal, Jim Siedow, Gunnar Hansen, John Dugan, Jerry Lorenz.* Dir, Pro & Screenplay (the last with Kim Henkel): Tobe Hooper. (Excalibur Films.) Rel: Floating. Colour. 81 Mins. Cert X (London).

That's Entertainment Part Two

A second package of extracts, sequences, snippets from MGM's very rich celluloid mine of the Golden Age of Hollywood, very high in entertainment and nostalgia value, with plenty of big spectacle, fun and memorable music and performances. Stars included: *Abbott and Costello, Eddie 'Rochester' Anderson, Louis Armstrong, Fred Astaire, John Barrymore, Lionel Barrymore, Robert Benchley, Constance Bennett, Jack Benny, Jack Buchanan, Louis Calhern, Leslie Caron, Marge and Gower Champion, Cyd Charisse, Maurice Chevalier, Joan Crawford, Bing Crosby, Doris Day, Robert Donat, Fifi D'Orsay, Melvyn Douglas, Marie Dressler, Margaret Dumont, Jimmy Durante, Nelson Eddy, Nanette Fabray, W. C. Fields, Bob Fosse, Clark Gable, Greta Garbo, Judy Garland, Greer Garson, Hermione Gingold, Cary Grant, Kathryn Grayson, Georges Guetary, Carol Haney, Jean Harlow, Katharine Hepburn, Judy Holliday, Lena Horne, Betty Hutton, Howard Keel, Gene Kelly, Grace Kelly, June Knight, Laurel and Hardy, Vivien*

Leigh, Oscar Levant, Myrna Loy, Jeanette MacDonald, Marx Bros., Roddy McDowall, Ann Miller, Robert Montgomery, Donald O'Connor, Maureen O'Sullivan, Walter Pidgeon, Eleanor Powell, William Powell, Tommy Rall, Debbie Reynolds, Ginger Rogers, Mickey Rooney, Dinah Shore, Frank Sinatra, Red Skelton, James Stewart, Lewis Stone, Elizabeth Taylor, Robert Taylor, Franchot Tone, Spencer Tracy, Lana Turner, Bobby Van, Gwen Verdon, Ethel Waters, David Wayne, Johnny Weissmuller, Esther Williams, Keenan Wynn, and 'Lassie'. Introduced by Fred Astaire and Gene Kelly. New sequences directed by Gene Kelly. Pro: Saul Chaplin and Daniel Melnick. Narration written by Leonard Gershe. (MGM–CIC.) Rel: Floating. Colour. 126 Mins. Cert. U.

Tibet
Felix Greene's fascinating feature-length look at the country before the Chinese invasion in 1950 and now, when, he suggests, so much has been achieved for this land which until 1946 did not even know about the wheel! Dir, Pro, written and filmed by Felix Greene. (Contemporary.) Rel: Floating; first shown London, May 1977. Colour. 60 Mins. Cert. U.

Trackdown
On the now familiar theme of the citizens taking the law into their own hands when the cops won't or can't help, this is the story of a rancher who comes to town and takes a pretty grim revenge on the racketeers who have raped and lured his kid sister into prostitution and resultant tragic death. And the most fascinating thing about all this is *Jim Mitchum's* extraordinary likeness to dad Robert; in appearance, action and expressions. Rest of cast: *Karen Lamm, Anne Archer, Erik Estrada, Cathy Lee Crosby, Vince Cannon, John Kerry, Roberto Rodriguez, Ernie Wheelwright, Zitto Kazann, Elisabeth Chauvet, Rafael Lopez, Gilbert De La Pena, Joe La Due, Ray Sharkey, James R. Parkes, Frederick Rule, Don Reed, Tony Burton, Lanny Gustavson, Leslie Simms, Jim Stathis, Larry Gabriel, Robert Forward, Simmy Bow, Gus Peters, John Rayner, Junero Jennings, Dick De Cott, Russell Shannon, Joe Tornatore, Evelyn Guerrero, Rebecca Winters.* Dir: Richard T. Heffron. Pro: Bernard Schwartz. Screenplay: Paul Edwards, from a story by Ivan Nagy. (Essaness–UA.) Rel: Dec. 5. Colour. 97 Mins. Cert. X.

The Travelling Players – O Thiassos
Assured, winning and in its way highly remarkable Greek film, with honestly left-wing political leanings, which relates the travels and travails of a group of strolling players in Greece between those years of turmoil, 1939 and 1952. It is for once a film which can be seen to have enough quality to deserve the 1976 Cannes Film Festival Critics' Prize. And worthy of somebody's Oscar is *Eva Kotamanidou* in the central role. Rest of cast: *Aliki Georgoulis, Statos Pachis, Maria Vassiliou, Petros Zarkadis, Kiriakos Katrivanos, Yannis Firlos, Nina Papazaphiropoulou, Alekos Boubis, Kosta Stiliaris, Greg Evaghelathos, Vanghelis Kazan.* Dir & Screenplay: Theodor Angelopoulos. Pro: Georges Papalios. (Academy.) Rel: Floating; first shown London, Sept. 1976. Colour. 130 Mins. Cert. X.

The Treasure of Matecumbe
Disney 'family trade' film about treasure-hunting among the Florida Keys a century ago; the 'team' consisting of two lads and four adults, opposed by a very persistent villain who's after the gold for himself. Cast: *Robert Foxworth, Joan Hackett, Peter Ustinov, Vic Morrow, Johnny Doran, Billy Attmore, Jane Wyatt, Robert DoQui, Mills Watson, Val de Vargas, Virginia Vincent, Don Knight, Dub Taylor, Dick Van Patten.* Dir: Vincent McEveety. Pro: Bill Anderson. Screenplay: Don Tait; based on the novel *A Journey to Matecumbe* by Robert Lewis Taylor. (Disney.) Rel: April 17. Colour. 117 Mins. Cert. U.

25 Years
The Silver Jubilee film which in various ways, newsreel shots, etc., covers the Queen's first twenty-five years on the throne. Dir & Pro: Peter Morley. (London Celebrations Committee for the Queen's Silver Jubilee–EMI.) Rel: Floating. Colour. 77 Mins. Cert. U.

21 Hours At Munich
Careful and reasonably convincing reconstruction of the Black September attack on the Israeli athletics team at the 1972 Munich Olympics. Cast: *William Holden, Shirley Knight, Franco Nero, Anthony Quayle, Richard Basehart, Gunther Halmer, Paul Smith, Maryin Gilat, Noel Willman, Georg Marishka, James Hurley, Michael Degen.* Dir: William A. Graham. Pro: Robert Greenwald and Frank Von Zerneck. (Filmways–Moonlight–Alpha Films.) Rel: Floating; first shown London, April 1977. Colour. 101 Mins. Cert. AA.

Two-Minute Warning
Slow-starting but progressively bloody and exciting story about a sniper who takes up his position in an almost impregnable tower commanding a Los Angeles sports stadium in which a big football match is taking place, presumably with the idea of killing the US President guest of honour. When this plan is thwarted, he starts to shoot at will into the crowds, causing a horrifying panic before being killed by Captain Cop *Charlton Heston* assisted by Sergeant *John Cassavetes* and his tough SWAT team. Rest of Cast: *Martin Balsam, Beau Bridges, Marilyn Hasset, David Janssen, Jack Klugman, Gena Rowlands, Walter Pidgeon, Brock Peters, David Groh, Mitchell Ryan, Joe Kapp, Pamela Bellwood, Jon Korkes, William Bryant, Allan Miller.* Dir: Larry Peerce. Pro: Edward S. Feldman. Screenplay: Edward Hume; based on the novel by George La Fountaine. (Universal–CIC.) Rel: Feb. 6. Colour. 116 Mins. Cert. AA.

Vampyres
Shot dead in a lonely house in the woods, lesbians Fran and Miriam return to the scene of the crime as a couple of ghostly blood-suckers, getting their revenge on the male of the specie by luring them to their lair by their charms and then sucking them dry . . . but there's a little ambiguity in the tail! Cast: *Marianne Morris, Anulka, Murray Brown, Brian Deacon, Sally Faulkner, Michael Byrne, Karl Lanchbury.* Dir: Joseph Larraz. Pro: Brian Smedley-Aston. Screenplay: D. Daubeny. (Fox–Rank.) Rel: Sept. 18. Colour. 84 Mins. Cert. X.

Vanessa
German film about a young girl's adventures – sexual and otherwise but considerably the former! – in Indonesia, where she goes to take over her large inheritance. Cast: *Olivia Pascal, Anton Diffring, Uschi Zech, Günter Clemens, Eva Eden, Eva Leuze, Tom Garven.* Dir: Hubert Frank. Pro: Erich Tomek. Screenplay: Joos de Ridder. (Lisa–Film-SF.) Rel: Floating. Colour. 91 Mins. Cert. X.

Victory at Entebbe
The first of at least three films to be made on this thrilling Israeli exploit to reach the (British) screen, having been planned, made and shown all within six months! And the result? Variable; very exciting when concerned with the details of the raid, more routine when concerned with the hostages and their stories, and embroidered with some needless sequences, such as the one shared by *Kirk Douglas* and *Elizabeth Taylor*. Rest of cast: *Helmut Berger, Theodore Bikel, Linda Blair, Richard Dreyfuss, Stefan Gierasch, David Groh, Julius Harris, Helen Hayes, Anthony Hopkins, Burt Lancaster, Jessica Walters, Harris Yulin.* Dir: Marvin Chomsky. Pro: Robert Guenette. Screenplay: Ernest Kinoy. (David L. Wolper–Warner.) Rel: Jan. 2. Colour. 119 Mins. Cert. A.

Vigilante Force
Another of these American films which beneath the polished and superficial surface of excitement and violence imply that with the forces of law and order losing control, it is up to the citizen to take up his gun and go out and clean the place up by force. Seen in the story of a Korean war veteran called in by the worried citizens of a racketeer-controlled, small oil-boom town, who double-crosses his employers and takes the place over himself with his small private army and squeezes the place as it has never been squeezed before. And it is his clean-living young brother who eventually has to cry halt, with the aid of his gun and his friends. Cast: *Kris Kristofferson, Jan-Michael Vincent, Victoria Principal, Bernadette Peters, Brad Dexter, Judson Pratt, David Doyle, Antony Carbone, Andrew Stevens, Shelly Novack, Paul X. Gleason, John Steadman, Lilyan McBride, James Lydon, Peter Coe, Charles Cyphers, Debbie Lytton, Carmen Argenziano, Don Pulford, Suzanne Horton.* Dir & Screenplay: George Armitage. Pro: Gene Corman. (Corman–UA.) Rel: Floating. Colour. 89 Mins. Cert. X.

The Violation of Justine
French adaptation of the Marquis de Sade story *Justine*; about the sad adventures of two sisters, one who builds success and happiness on ruthlessness and the other who achieves nothing but misery and a violent end by her goodness! Cast: *Alice Arno, France Verdier, Yves Arcanel, Georges Beauvillier, Dominique Santarelli, Diane Lepvrier, Christian Chevreuse, Mauro Parenti, André Rouyer, Marco Perrin.* Dir & Pro: Claude Pierson. Screenplay: Huguette Boisvert. (Garpalm–Tigon.) Rel: Floating; first shown London, May 1977. Colour. 85 Mins. Cert. X.

The Releases of the Year in Detail

W. C. Fields and Me
Failing finally to capture the whole man, the film most admirably presents quite a balanced and certainly entertaining portrait of the famous bibulous comic, whose hatred of dogs, family, children and – rather more understandably – tax-gatherers provided so much of the material for his inimitable humour. Fields was said to be the most irascible, anti-social character ever to become a universally loved star and some of that comes across, with *Rod Steiger* wisely settling for an interpretive rather than imitative portrait and making a fine job of it. In the support there's a notable, and surprisingly raw and honest portrait of John Barrymore by *Jack Cassidy*. *Valerie Perrine* as the woman who shared Fields' last sad days. Rest of cast: *John Marley, Bernadette Peters, Dana Elcar, Paul Stewart, Billy Barty, Alan Arbus, Milt Kamen, Louis Zorich, Andrew Parks, Hank Rolike, Kenneth Tobey, Paul Mantee, Elizabeth Thompson, Eddie Firestone, Linda Purl, Clay Tanner, George Loros*. Dir: Arthur Hiller. Pro: Jay Weston. Screenplay: Bob Merrill; based on the book by Carlotta Monti with Cy Rice. (Universal–CIC.) Rel: Floating. Colour. 112 Mins. Cert. AA.

War
Impressive twenty-eight-minute film about an incident in the American Civil War made by two young students of the British National Film School. Obviously made with great economy it lacks nothing in conviction as it portrays the misery and alert terror of the deserter from the Confederate Army as he is tracked down and finally killed by Unionist soldiers who ambushed and massacred his company. Cast: *Brian Shorthouse, Anna Bentinck, Ken Shorthouse, Lionel Digby, Vic Farrer, Peter Straight, and other members of the Southern Skirmishers Association and Société au Cavalier*. Dir & Screenplay: John Sharrad and David Griffith. Pro: David Wollcombe. (National Film School.) Rel: Floating; first shown London, Dec. 1976. Colour. 28 Mins. Cert. A.

What's Up Tiger Lily? – Kizino Kizi
1966 Woody Allen film which took ten years to reach us. A quite amusing dubbing of American voices and American idioms on to a typical Japanese all-action spy thriller. Cast: *Tatsuta Mihashi, Miyi Hana, Eiko Wakabayashi, Tadao Nakamaru, Susumu Kurobe, Woody Allen, The Loving Spoonful, China Lee*. Dir: Senkichi Taniguchi. Pro: Reuben Bercovitch – Woody Allen. (Benedict, Los Angeles–Toho, Tokyo–Focus.) Rel: Floating. Colour. 79 Mins. Cert. A.

When Joseph Returns – Megjon Jozsef
Hungarian film about a young wife who, left alone by her sailor husband, drifts into affairs, has an abortion and only after that develops a slowly increasing intimate relationship with her mother who lives with her and previously could never break through their mutual reserve. Cast: *Lili Monori, Eva Ruttkai, Gyorgy Pogany, Gabor Konez, Maria Ronyeez*. Dir & Screenplay: Zsolt Kezdi Kovacs. Pro: not named. (Budapest Studio–Hungarofilm–Essential.) Rel: Floating; first shown London, April 1977. Colour. 92 Mins. Cert. AA.

146

When the North Wind Blows
Superbly photographed, unusual film about a trapper and wilderness lover who through accidentally killing a man (trying to save him from a tiger) is forced into the winter snows in Alaska and, surviving, decides he cannot return to civilisation, preferring the company of two orphaned tiger cubs who become his 'family'. Some remarkable photography and quite astonishing scenes between the man and the big cats. Cast: *Henry Brandon, Herbert Nelson, Dan Haggerty, Henry Olek, Sander Johnson, Jan Smithers, Dale Ishimoto, Rex Holman, Jack Ong, Fernando Schwartz, Betty Raffill, Jack Rabey, Hal Boxar, Henry Del Giudice, Ernie Misko, Tony Miretti, Gerard Alcan*. Dir & Screenplay: Stewart Raffill. Pro: Joseph and Stewart Raffill. (Sun Classic Productions–Brent Walker.) Rel: Feb. 13. Colour. 113 Mins. Cert. U.

White Rock
Out-of-the-rut film about the 12th Winter Games (held at Innsbruck early in 1976). Star *James Coburn* narrates and the background music is by Rick Wakeman. Dir & Written: Tony Maylam. Pro: Michael Samuelson. (Shueisha Publishing Co., Japan–Worldmark Productions/Samuelson International–EMI.) Rel: Feb. 27. Colour. 76 Mins. Cert. U.

Who's That Knocking at my Door
Earlier (1969) Martin Scorsese film which is something of a sketch for some of his later works: a story about a young man from New York's Little Italy and the girl he worships so much and so spiritually that he loses her; a vivid evocation of New York back-street life. Cast: *Harvey Keitel, Zina Bethune, Anne Collette, Lennard Kuras, Michael Scala, Harry Northrup, Phil Carlson, Wendy Russell, Catherine Scorsese, Martin Scorsese*. Dir & Screenplay: Martin Scorsese. Pro: Joseph Weill, Haig and Betsi Manoogian. (Gate.) Rel: Floating; first shown Aug. 1976. Black and white. 90 Mins. Cert. X.

The Wild Game
1973 West German Fassbinder film about a fourteen-year-old daughter of a middle-class family who once seduced, by a boy five years her senior, becomes obsessed with physical pleasure, cheerfully seeing the boy-friend going to prison because of his intimacy with her and then insisting on renewal of the relationship (though still forbidden) when he is parolled, a situation that leads to her persuading her lover to kill her rigid-moralled, incestuously inclined father when he appears likely to stop her fun! Cast: *Jorg von Liebenfels, Ruth Drexel, Eva Mattes, Kurt Raab, Harry Baer, Rudolf Waldemar, Bren Hedi, Ben Salem, Karl Scheydt, Klaus Lowitsch, Irm Hermann, Marguand Bohm*. Dir & Screenplay: Rainer Werner Fassbinder; based on the stage play *Wildwechsel* by Franz Xaver Kroetz. (Contemporary.) Rel: Floating; first shown Nov. 1976. Colour. 99 Mins. Cert. X.

Winstanley
Semi-documentary, shoestring-budget reconstruction of a lesser-known chapter of British history (*circa* 1649) when

the sober and religious Mr Winstanley tried by action and pamphlet to stir the poor into taking over the common grazing lands, ploughing and sowing them and raising the food they needed to keep alive, a course which took him into conflict not only with the local farmers (whose cattle used the land) but with the law. Made with a passion for authenticity which gives an oddly memorable, muddily convincing realism to the rather gloomy proceedings. With an especially good performance by *Miles Halliwell* in the title-role. Rest of cast: mainly non-actors. Dir: Kevin Brownlow and Andrew Mollo. Pro: The British Film Institute Production Board. Screenplay: not credited. (BFI.) Rel: Floating; first shown at The Other Cinema, Oct. 1976. Black and white. 95 Mins. Cert. A.

Wives
Amusing Norwegian film about a girls' class school reunion and the decision of three of the now young wives – one heavily pregnant – to opt out of all domestic responsibilities, renew their old friendship and do the town together, which they in fact do. Loosely knit, often witty, meandering but finally in-depth portraits of three rather sluttonly young women dissatisfied with the restrictions of their lives but unable to do anything really constructive about it. Beautifully acted by *Anne Marie Ottersen, Froydis Armand* and *Katja Medbe*, whose performances gives the film a quality it otherwise might not have had. Rest of cast: *Noste Schwab, Helge Jordal, Stein Collett Thue, Alv Nordvang, Sverre Anker Ousdal, Veslemoy Haslund, Grethe Nordra, Julian Strom, Gunnar Alme*. Dir: Anja Breien. Pro: not named. Screenplay: Anja Breien 'and the actors'. (Contemporary.) Rel: Floating; first shown in June 1976. Colour. 84 Mins. Cert. X.

Won Ton Ton, The Dog Who Saved Hollywood
Michael Winner's intermittently amusing and occasionally very funny comedy about Hollywood in the twenties and the canny canine who saved not only the studio from bankruptcy but also brought fame and fortune to some rather undeserving characters; with lots of amusing references and a whole host of glimpsed old-timer stars. Cast: *Dennis Morgan, Shecky Greene, Phil Leeds, Cliff Norton, Madeline Kahn, Teri Garr, Romo Vincent, Bruce Dern, Sterling Holloway, William Benedict, Dorothy Gulliver, William Demarest, Art Carney, Virginia Mayo, Henny Youngman, Rory Calhoun, Billy Barty, Henry Wilcoxon, Ricardo Montalban, Jackie Coogan, Aldo Ray, Ethel Merman, Yvonne de Carlo, Joan Blondell, Andy Devine, Broderick Crawford, Richard Arlen, Jack La Rue, Dorothy Lamour, Phil Silvers, Nancy Walker, Gloria de Haven, Luis Nye, Johnny Weismuller, Stepin Fetchit, Ken Murray, Rudy Vallee, George Jessel, Rhonda Fleming, Ann Miller, Dean Stockwell, Dick Haymes, Tab Hunter, Robert Alda, Eli Mintz, Ron Leibman, Fritz Feld, Edward Ashley, Kres Mersky, Jane Connell, Janet Blair, Dennis Day, Mike Mazurki, The Ritz Brothers, Jesse White, Carmel Myers, Jack Carter, Jack Bernardi, Victor Mature, Barbara Nichols, Army Archerd, Fernando Lamas, Zsa Zsa Gabor, Cyd Charisse, Huntz Hall, Doodles Weaver, Pedro Gonzales-Gonzales, Eddie Le Veque, Edgar Bergen, Ronny Graham, Morey Amsterdam, Regis Toomey, Alice Faye,*

Ann Rutherford, Milton Berle, James E. Brodhead, John Carradine, Keye Luke, Walter Pidgeon and *Won Ton Ton* played by *Augustus Von Schumacher*. Dir: Michael Winner. Pro: David V. Picker, Arnold Schulman and Michael Winner. Screenplay: Arnold Schulman and Cy Howard. (Paramount–CIC.) Rel: July 18. Colour. 92 Mins. Cert. A.

Zoltan – Hound of Dracula
This variation on the old theme has a vampire dog as its mainspring, the canine blood-sucker released from its Transylvanian tomb by a young soldier who after taking the stake from its heart is killed by the beast, who then goes on the rampage. Cast: *Jose Ferrer, Michael Pataki, Reggie Nalder*. Dir: Albert Band. Pro: Albert Band and Frank Ray Perilli, who is also responsible for the Screenplay. (EMI.) Rel: May 8. Colour. 88 Mins. Cert. X.

The Children's Film Foundation

Last year, the twenty-fifth anniversary year of the CFF, this feature was introduced into the annual. This year (or the period covered, 1 July to 30 June) there were more new features premièred than last, including two – *The Glitterball* and *Fern, The Red Deer* – which were presented in a special Royal Première on 22 April. Notes and details about these and all the other new films shown will be found below.

Blind Man's Bluff
Junior detection story with the youngsters tracking the kidnappers of a big pools prizewinner through London's East End and Docks to a successful confrontation. A disused newsagents shop was converted into a set and the upstairs became the production offices! Cable St, Limehouse, the Woolwich Boat Marina and the Guildhall tunnels were all used for location work. Cast: *Patricia Fletcher, Terry Sue Pratt, Steve Fletcher, Chris Ellison, Debbie Ash, David Lincoln, Reg Lye, Ken Watson, Mela White, Richard Parmentier*. Dir: Gerry O'Hara. Pro: Cyril Randell. Screenplay: Patricia Latham; based on a story by her and Benjamin Lee. (Willis Wide World Productions for CFF.) Colour. 58 Mins. Cert. U.

Patricia Fletcher, Chris Ellison and Terry Sue Pratt set off to search for their small kidnapped friend in *Blind Man's Bluff* (Willis Wide World Productions).

The Chiffy Kids

Six-part serial about the adventures in various circumstances of the youngsters. Cast: *Luke Batchelor, Lesley Saunders, Philip Sadler, Wayne Kebell, Tracey Strand.* Dir: David Bracknell. Pro: Hugh Stewart. Screenplay: Mike Gorell Barnes. (Anvil Film and Recording Group Ltd. for CFF.) Colour. Cert. U. Part 1: *Pot Luck.* Additional cast: *Harry H. Corbett, Norman Bird, Judy Cornwall.* 20 Mins. Part 2: *Room To Let.* Additional cast: *Alfie Bass, Irene Handl.* 19 Mins. Part 3: *Decorators Limited.* Additional cast: *Peggy Mount, Ronnie Brody, George A. Cooper, Barbara Cochran, Susan Richards, Peggy Ann Clifford, Roy Barraclough, Roy Seely, William Rushton.* 17 Mins. Part 4: *Shrove Tuesday.* Additional cast: *Suzan Farmer, Patsy Smart, Colin Jeavons, Johnny Vivian.* 18 Mins. Part 5: *The Great Snail Race.* Additional cast: *Marianne Stone, Norman Chappell, Sylvaine Charles, Allan Cuthbertson, Sam Kydd, Kenny Lynch, Valerie Singleton.* 18 Mins. Part 6: *Magpie Lays an Egg.* Additional cast: *George Claydon, Eva Ruber-Staier, Dennis Ramsden, George Hilsden, Harold Goodwin.* 17 Mins.

Chimpmates – Series 2

Seven-part film about the varied escapades by Alice, the Chimp (from Southam Zoo). Cast: *Lynne Morgan, Marcus Evans, Philip da Costa.* Dir & Pro: Harold Orton. Screenplay: Frank Godwin (1), Harold Orton (2, 5 & 6) and Patricia Latham (3 & 4). Colour. (Eyeline Films for CFF.) Cert. U. Part 1: *Alice Goes South.* Additional cast: *Veronica Lang, Godfrey James, Roy Kinnear, Toke Townley, Geoffrey Larder, Candida Dunn.* 17 Mins. Part 2: *Treasure Hunt.* Additional cast: *Ian Allis, Reggie Winch, Ralph Griffin, Neil McDermott, Roger Brierley, Claire Davenport.* 19 Mins. Part 3: *Holiday Spirit.* Additional cast: *Veronica Lang, Godfrey James, Sylvia Coleridge, John Bramwell, Dennis Lawson.* 16 Mins. Part 4: *Waxworks.* Additional cast: *Lucy Griffiths, Leslie Dwyer, Ian Cullen, Chris Hallam.* 14 Mins. Part 5: *Airborne.* Additional cast: *Peter Denis, Steven Lamplugh, Frank Miles, Derek Piggott.* 14 Mins. Part 6: *The Go-Karters.* Additional cast: *Godfrey James, Robert Keegan, Anthony Sympson, Gary Rich, Andrew Pinous, Austin King, John Tucker, Jim Pitt, Larry Pitt.* 18 Mins. Part 7: *Zoo Time.* Additional cast: *Veronica Lang, Godfrey James, Graham Stark, Joe Wadham.* 17 Mins.

Echo of the Badlands

The adventures of two small white children and the black boy they befriend, and help to recover the stolen calf which he has been assigned to guard. And the background is Lesotho (formerly Basutoland) where the film was made entirely on location. Cast: *David Nkena, Clive Sanders, Fiona Sanders, Rosemary Jolly, David Sixishe, Richard D'Aeth, Evelyn D'Aeth, King George, Chief Macheku, Emmanuel Nkena, Stanley Moloi, Paul Mosala, Rose Moshoshoe, 'Gold-Dust'.* Dir: David Eady and Tim King. Pro: Peter Manley and Richard Meyrick. Screenplay: Patricia Latham. (Little, King & Partners–Eady–Barnes Productions Ltd. for CFF.) Colour. 56 Mins. Cert. U.

Tracey Strand, Philip Sadler, Lesley Saunders, Luke Batchelor and Wayne Kebell as the companions in the 'Shrove Tuesday' episode of Anvil Films six-part movie for CFF, *The Chiffy Kids*.

Alice, the Chimp star of the first Chimpmates series, returns to the screen in the new Eyeline Films series *Chimpmates – Series Two*, a seven-part film in which Alice plays the leading role. Here she has a go at Go-Karting!

A general scene from the Little, King & Partners–Eady–Barnes production *Echo of the Badlands*, which was made entirely on location in Lesotho.

Fern, The Red Deer

Two cousins, one from Exmoor and the other from London, are brought together and to mutual understanding by the advent on the remote Exmoor farm of a four-hour-old orphaned deer fawn. And the film was made entirely on Exmoor in two periods: May to June and September to October. Cast: *Candida Prior, Craig McFarlane, Mark Eden, Diana Eden, John Leyton, Madeline Smith, Neil McCarthy*. Dir & Screenplay: Jan Darnley-Smith. Pro: Adrian Worker. (De Lane Lea for CFF.) Colour. 58 Mins. Cert. U.

Craig McFarlane and Candida Prior with the real star of the film, 'Fern' the fawn, in *Fern, The Red Deer*, a De Lane Lea production. Royal premièred in April.

The Glitterball

SF comedy-thriller about the arrival from outer space of a miniature spaceship piloted by a small silver ball with highly advanced powers! Luckily the small son of a RAF sergeant and his pal manage to find the secret of communication and defeat the machinations of villain Filthy Potter whose intentions towards the visitor are highly dubious. And lots of invention and imagination had to be used in the production to get the special effects needed. Made largely on location in Herts. and Suffolk with completion in EMI studios. Cast: *Ben Buckton, Keith Jayne, Ron Pember, Marjorie Yates, Barry Jackson, Andrew Jackson*. Dir: Harley Cocklis. Pro: Mark Forstater. Screenplay: Howard Thompson. (Mark Forstater Productions for CFF.) Colour. 56 Mins. Cert. U.

Ben Buckton and Keith Jayne look on with astonishment as the miniature spacecraft which arrives from outer space in the Mark Forstater production *The Glitterball*, another CFF film Royal premièred in April last.

Jayne Tottman, Graham Fletcher and Bernard Cribbins in the Eady–Barnes Production *Night Ferry*.

Night Ferry
Crime melodrama about three youngsters' efforts to thwart a plot to smuggle out of the country, via the Night Ferry to France, a valuable 'Mummy' and its jewel-studded case. Made entirely on location at Dover. Cast: *Graham Fletcher, Engin Ashref, Jayne Tottman, Bernard Cribbins, Aubrey Morris, Carole Rousseau, Lloyd Anderson, Jeremy Bulloch, Michael Halsey, Colin Jeavons, Richard Montez, Ronald O'Neill.* Dir: David Eady. Pro: Greg Younger. Screenplay: Mike Gorell Barnes. (Eady Barnes Productions Ltd. for CFF.) Colour. 60 Mins. Cert. U.

Nosey Dobson

About a persistent young amateur detective who, in spite of police opposition, finally solves the case of the stolen silver and becomes the hero of the hour. Made by a Scottish director new to children's films (most of his previous work has been for the BBC) on location on the Isle of Arran. Cast: *Joseph McKenna, James Morrison, Gary Rankin, Iain Andrew, Charles Kearney, Mary Ann Reid, Benny Young, James Grant, William Marlowe, Phil McCall, Isobel Gardner, Jean Faulds, Tom Watson.* Dir & Screenplay: Michael Alexander. Pro: Cyril Randell. (Pelicula Films for CFF.) Colour. 59 Mins. Cert. U.

Heavily disguised Nosey (Joseph McKenna) with his Sherlock Holmes magnifying-glass leads his school friends on the search for the stolen silver in *Nosey Dobson*, a Pelicula Films Production.

One Hour to Zero

In fact one hour to the expected explosion of a deserted nuclear research station, and the three small friends know nothing about the threat! Made on location in North Wales. Cast: *Jayne Collins, Toby Bridge, Andrew Ashby, Dudley Sutton, John Forgeham, John Barcroft, Ann Windsor, Mike Lewin, Morris Perry, Frederick Treves, Hazel McBride, Roger Llewellyn.* Dir: Jeremy Summers. Pro: Jean Wadlow. Screenplay: John Tully. (Charles Barker Films for CFF.) Colour. 55 Mins. Cert. U.

John Barcroft, Toby Bridge and Andrew Ashby know that an atomic plant explosion is likely to hit them at any moment in *One Hour to Zero*, made by Charles Barker Films.

Seal Island

The struggle against time by three children to save the seals on an island which though to be designated as a nature reserve is still open for cullers until the Conservation Group and its wardens actually take over. Made in Wales. Cast: *Andrew Dove, Lisa Norris, Joey Clarke, Donald Douglas, John Savident, Wolfe Morris, Janet Davies, Gillian Barge, Cyril Luckham*. Dir & Pro: Ronald Spencer. Screenplay: Patricia Latham. (Pacesetter Productions for CFF.) Colour. 55 Mins. Cert. U.

Nursing one of the stars of *Seal Island*, a Pacesetter film for the CFF.

Sky Pirates

Thriller about a crooks' plot to smuggle a stolen Paris museum diamond across the Channel by means of a radio-controlled model airplane. And how an ex-pilot and three children thwart them. Cast: *Adam Richens, Michael McVey, Sylvia Donnell, Bill Maynard, Reginald Marsh, Jamie Foreman, Kenneth Watson, John Lee*. Dir & Screenplay: Pennington Richards. Pro: Frank Godwin. (Ansus, for CFF.) Colour. 60 Mins. Cert. U.

Michael McVey and Bill Maynard with one of the highly advanced model airplanes (it's a Spitfire) which give the background and excitement to *Sky Pirates* (Ansus Films).

The Film Books of the Year Reviewed by Ivan Butler

The same classification procedure has been followed as in previous years – the three divisions being somewhat arbitrary and apt to overlap.

The compilation of titles is not complete, but is as full as I have been able to make it. Once again, my thanks to all those publishers who have kept me informed about their books.

Prices, as always, are subject to change – and, equally as always, alas – upwards. A point worth noting is that paperback editions nowadays often follow very quickly on hardbacks; so any prospective purchaser should check on this before deciding that a quoted price is way out of reach. It may have come down from hard to soft after these words have gone to press.

BIOGRAPHY, MEMOIRS

Fred Astaire: Michael Freedland; W. H. Allen, £4.95.
Fred Astaire is among the more fully covered stars, but Mr Freedland's warm and enthusiastic biography is a welcome addition to the shelf. Personal and professional lives are given equal weight in his book. The story of Astaire's happy marriage and its tragic termination after over twenty years when his wife Phyllis died of a brain tumour is movingly told; and the myths and rumours surrounding his relationship with his famous partner, Ginger Rogers, are recounted and supplanted by the reality. The films themselves are dealt with briefly – there is surely not much that is new to be said about them now, nor about Astaire's reputation as a perfectionist. But Mr Freedland sets it all out pleasantly and discerningly. Lightweight popular biography, perhaps, and written in a style to match ('Miss Caulfield, who could be a dab dancer in her own way . . .'), but an enjoyable 'read'. An index is included, and two sections of illustrations – some of them very familiar, but also one or two interesting early photographs of the young Fred and Adele.

Jack Benny: Irving A. Fein; W. H. Allen, £4.50.
Mr Fein's 'intimate biography' is lightweight, chatty and full of adulation. The author was Benny's personal manager, producer and close friend for many years, and his warm tribute makes for pleasant reading – even if one is inclined to question statements such as that which closes the book: 'When he died . . . millions cared – and cried'. *Millions?* Never mind – the sentiment is impeccable. The films are mentioned only briefly (though as fully, perhaps, as some of them merit), as this is mainly a personal memoir. Mr Fein is at pains to point out that Jack Benny's comedy reputation as a 'tightwad' meant that he had to distribute much more than anyone else in largesse, to counteract the impression that it extended to his personal life. The author might, however, have been wiser not to include reputedly 'funny' snatches of dialogue – even though one must make allowances for the cold scrutiny of the printed page without the accompanying comic gestures and intonations.
Note: 'War is hell' – 'as *someone* once said' . . . see p. 89. Surely Mr Fein is here feigning ignorance?

Bogart and Bacall: Joe Hyams; Michael Joseph, £4.25.
The appetite for knowledge of the private life of Humphrey Bogart seems insatiable, and this nicely written and produced off-shoot from the same author's biography makes enjoyable – if fairly lightweight – reading for the fans. As regards the films and working lives of both subjects, the ground has already been, of course, well trodden; but as a 'Love Story' (the book's subtitle) this fills the bill as a pleasant addition to the Private-Lives-of-the-Stars shelf. It is indexed, and contains a good selection of rare family photographs, in addition to publicity and film stills.

The Bogart File: Terence Pettigrew; Golden Eagle Press, £4.50.
The Bogart legend is so alive that it is hard to believe he has been dead for twenty years. Mr Pettigrew marks the occasion with a study that ranks high among the proliferating Bogart literature. Very commendably, he confines himself almost entirely to the films themselves, discussing them in detail with authority and discernment, giving praise where he feels it justified, but never hesitating to criticise, and criticise sharply, where this is called for. He makes copious use of a wide variety of

contemporary reviews, American and British, and this adds greatly to the value of his book particularly when regarded as a work of reference. This aspect is enhanced further by the inclusion not only of a very full filmography but also by similar details of Bogart's stage career.

Several sections of illustrations and a good index complete a highly recommendable book.

The Day the Laughter Stopped – The Arbuckle Scandal: David A. Yallop; Hodder & Stoughton, £5.95.
In this horrifyingly engrossing and deeply moving book Mr Yallop tells the full story of the tragedy of Roscoe 'Fatty' Arbuckle – his rapid rise to fame as one of the most brilliant and beloved of silent film comedians, his downfall and trials for manslaughter following the death of Virginia Rappe during a hectic party in a San Francisco hotel, his long struggle for rehabilitation and recognition of the injustice he had undergone. Tragedy is, indeed, scarcely too elevated a word for this victim of the envy, cowardice and spite of those who hounded him. If Mr Yallop's arguments and conclusions are sound (and he puts up a strong case), his story is a searing indictment both of the American legal process and of the pusillanimity, the money-grubbing hypocrisy of Hollywood. But it is also a story of the courage and loyalty of Hollywood: Arbuckle had staunch friends who stood by him throughout – above all fellow-comedian Buster Keaton. Mr Yallop has had access to much hitherto unavailable material and has interviewed many people closely connected with Arbuckle, in particular his first wife, Minta Durfee, who, though already separated from him at the time of the scandal, courageously returned to his side during his ordeal. He explodes many a myth and legend, and induces reliance on his accuracy.

The injustice done to Fatty Arbuckle has never before been really cleared up. As a schoolboy at the time of the scandal I remember (without being allowed fully to understand) the atmosphere of shocked horror which for years surrounded his name. Yet I have no memory of hearing then of his innocence and acquittal. One feels, on finishing this book: 'If only Fatty Arbuckle could have read this complete and warm-hearted vindication . . .' I can think of no higher tribute to Mr Yallop's achievement. On the practical side, the book is very fully illustrated and has a magnificent filmography, together with a full index and bibliography.

Cukor: Carlos Clarens; Secker & Warburg, £4.90 hardback, £2.90 paperback.
This is number 28 in this excellent series of monographs – which have not, regrettably, been appearing recently with their earlier regularity. It is well up to standard. Following concise but very adequate essays on the long and honourable Cukor career (paying particular attention to two points – the effect of his experience as a theatrical director, and his reputation as primarily a director of women), about one-third of the book's 190 pages is taken up with a first-class filmography, including a personal note by Cukor on each production, and commendably full cast lists. One reservation: the absence of an index may be due to the necessity, these austere days, to keep down

costs; but, with no individual films listed on the Contents page, such an aid to discovery would have been helpful. Could not a page reference have been placed next to each title in the Filmography? There are numerous good illustrations, and the paperback edition is stoutly bound.

Doris Day – Her Own Story: A. E. Hotchner; W. H. Allen, £4.95.
For a large part of her professional life Doris Day has suffered (and, it must not be forgotten, flourished) under the label of the healthy, hearty, clean and sporty neighbourhood American girl, and she must often have longed to break out of this restricting if profitable circumscription – and indeed has often said so. This pleasant, generally readable book may do something to redress the balance, for it shows clearly that Miss Day's life has had the ups and downs, the lights and shadows, that may be found in any less publicised existence. Indeed, she points this out forcibly enough in the very first page: one paragraph listing the less 'sweet and virginal' roles she

has played; and the next describing how at ten she discovered a family scandal, at thirteen was deprived by a leg injury in a car accident of her hopes of becoming a dancer, at seventeen was married to a psychopathic sadist – and so on. How many next-door-girls can claim as much? Mr Hotchner states that 80 per cent of the book is in Miss Day's words – enough, perhaps, to justify the use of the description 'autobiography'. Family, friends and colleagues contribute brief memoirs, and the result is an entertaining and warm study of a star and the personality behind the stardom. An index would have been most welcome – particularly as several pages are left irritatingly blank at the end of the book. There are lots of good photographs.

Eisenstein – A Documentary Portrait: Norman Swallow; George Allen & Unwin, £2.95.
A brief but illuminating portrait of the famous director, based on a television film made in collaboration with G. V. Alexandrov, and derived to a large extent from

recollections of those who knew him – in Russia, England and America. The major films, *Potemkin, Nevsky, Ivan, Que Viva Mexico!*, etc. are covered in some detail, but the main interest of the book lies in the comments, personal and professional, from colleagues and critics. It is these that justify another book on this much-written about pioneer. There is a useful bibliographical note, and also a good index. Of particular interest are the many illustrations (stills, sketches and personal photographs) which embellish this useful handbook's 140 pages.

The Fairbanks Album: Douglas Fairbanks Jr. and Richard Schickel; Secker & Warburg, £7.50.
There have been several large-format family album film books recently (notably the Gish sisters), and this must rank among the best. Apart from its fascinating pictorial record of the two Douglases, it presents a splendidly revealing and nostalgic picture of the great Hollywood period of the silent and early sound days. Though the vast number of superb illustrations may be the attraction that first catches the eye of the prospective purchaser (or borrower), the volume has much more to offer than a collection of pictures. It has the great advantage of a text and captions by Richard Schickel – one of the most enjoyable and perceptive of film writers, with an easy style (though he is a bit rough on his infinitives) and a warm appreciation of his two subjects. The tragic decline and fall of the elder Fairbanks in his later years is frankly and movingly told, with the rise of Junior and his reconciliation with his father as a happy contrast. Altogether a most welcome collection of memories of the already almost legendary days of Hollywood.

The Great Garbo: Robert Payne; W. H. Allen, £4.95.
At last, a book on Garbo which takes account of the fact that about half of her films were made during the silent era, and gives them due prominence. Mr Payne is a true worshipper, and in this lively and extremely readable book he is lavish (but by no means totally uncritical) in his praise. Praise of the star, that is. For her 'vehicles' he has hardly a good word to say, with the possible qualified exceptions of *Camille, Queen Christina* and *Ninotchka*. Mr Payne's favourite word for the great majority of Garbo's scripts, directors and fellow players is 'disaster'. Indeed, in his insistence that Garbo alone saved film after film from utter condemnation he seems sometimes to lean a little too far towards total destruction. Allowing for the conventions of the period, Antonio Moreno, for instance, was not *too* dire a performer (*The Temptress*, indeed, for all its absurdities, had some quite effective moments), and as for poor old Ricardo Cortez (Jacob Krantz), to dismiss him out of hand as merely 'potato-headed' is crudely cruel. However, it is always fun to watch a well-informed writer lashing about him – or her – and Mr Payne certainly knows his subject. Almost all the films are dealt with in full detail, and there are some very good illustrations, together with an adequate index and a chronology. There are also some fascinating revelations. For instance, 'GARBO' did *not* 'LAUGH' (as per the publicity) in *Ninotchka*: the sound had to be dubbed in afterwards as she was incapable of

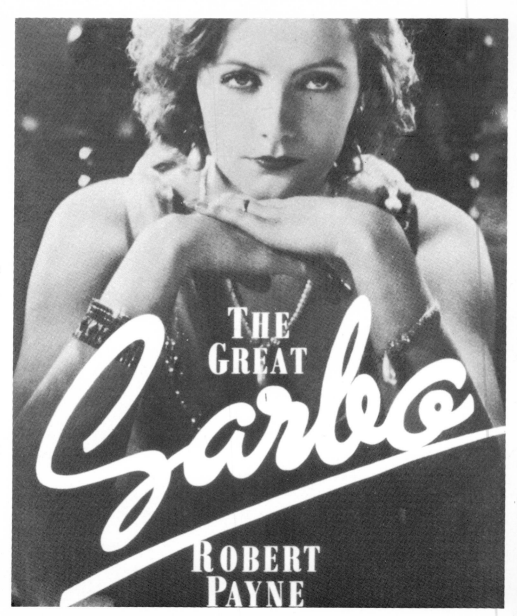

providing it – a case, perhaps, for the Trade Descriptions Act. Oddly, Mr Payne omits all mention of the alternative, 'happy', ending to *The Temptress* which was shown over here.

The book has one or two carelessnesses – 'Monty' Blue and 'Cedrick' Hardwicke, for instance, both names spelt correctly in the index.

Goldwyn: Arthur Marx; The Bodley Head, £4.95.
Sam Goldwyn was one of the most colourful figures of a colourful company, and it is surprising that he has had to wait so long for a really full biography. Now that it has appeared, it is doubtful whether he could have been better served than by Mr Marx in this thoroughly entertaining and engrossing book. The famous 'Goldwynisms' (true or apocryphal) are discussed in a Prologue, and of course appear frequently (together with some magnificently unorthodox name juggling) throughout the book – often capping a story so funny as to cause the unwary reader the happy embarrassment of a sudden guffaw in a public place. Malapropism is, however, reduced to its proper proportion in the make-up of a remarkably contradictory and complex personality. Happy and fortunate as he was during most of his private life, after the dire poverty and notable courage of the early years, it is with his working career that the biographer is mainly concerned: relations with William Wyler, Mabel Normand, Lillian Hellman, Mamoulian, Zukor, Lasky, Harpo Marx, and dozens of others over the long years; the Anna Sten débâcle; the great films, led by *The Best Years of Our Lives*, and those that were something less than great – all these, and a hundred triumphs, disasters, battles and friendships come under Mr Marx's frank but affectionate scrutiny. From *The Squaw Man*, through the Banky/Colman silents of fond memory, *The Children's Hour* (or *These Three*], *Wuthering Heights*, *Porgy and Bess*, the films and their making are brought to life in the recreation of an age – and a world – that will never recur. Only in the illustrations is the book let down. These, meagre and not very well reproduced, seem to me quite unworthy of the text. To compensate, there is an excellent index.

Growing Up in Hollywood: Robert Parrish; The Bodley Head, £4.95.
Extra, apprentice editor, cutter (editor), director, and now lively and witty autobiographer, Mr Parrish has produced a book well in the vanguard of the most entertaining of the vast army of Hollywood memoirs. He started as a child actor in the 1920s (parts including a newsboy in *City Lights*, a chorus boy in *Harold Teen*, a schoolboy in *All Quiet on the Western Front*); turned quite early to editing (including apprentice work on *King Kong*, and winning an Oscar nomination for *All the King's Men* and an Oscar itself for *Body and Soul*) and finished up as director (*Cry Danger*, *The Bobo*, *Duffy*, etc.). From these varied vantage-points he casts an amusing and often astringent eye on such venerated figures as Chaplin, De Mille, Fairbanks Senior, Walsh, and in particular John Ford – not to mention many others less fully considered. A gift of vivid recreation makes the part of the book dealing with the earlier years particularly fascinating. In a tribute quoted

on the jacket Kevin Brownlow describes how he laughed aloud reading Mr Parrish's chronicle: I am happy to have shared the same reaction.

The book is very nicely produced, with a good index. The illustrations are excellent – even overcoming being reproduced in dark blue (perhaps as a reminder of the 'art pages' in old film magazines?)

Fritz Lang: Lotte H. Eisner; Secker & Warburg, £9.75.
In her Preface Miss Eisner remarks that Fritz Lang considered all the monographs published on him previously to be inadequate. It is difficult to imagine that he would have felt the same about the present book. The sorely overworked word 'definitive' must surely be applied here. It is a magnificent 400-page study in detail of all Lang's films, German and American, with two brief but engrossingly illuminating sections on his working methods in each country, a final chapter on *Le Mépris*, and a splendidly detailed filmography. Lang himself is frequently quoted, and there are apt quotations also from other writers. Miss Eisner analyses and comments with the utmost perceptiveness, clarity, and an engaging affection which in no way clouds her critical faculties. Many of the films will be seen (if not in the cinema, then, with luck, on television) with renewed and sharpened appreciation after reading her essays. It was delightful, for instance, to read at last the truth about the marvellously subtle 'dream' ending to *The Woman in the Window* – stupidly dismissed by many unperceptive critics as a let-down. Less pleasant, but equally important reading, is that concerning the horrifying mutilation of film after film at the hands of various cinematic vandals – particularly the disgraceful lopping of the entire last section of *Cloak and Dagger*, which resulted in a complete distortion of the film's true significance. An attractively produced and excellently illustrated book.

Charles Laughton: Charles Higham; W. H. Allen, £4.95.
Mr Higham's warm, appreciative and penetrating study must rank very high among the best biographies of the year. Within a comparatively brief space (230 pages), most generously and unreservedly assisted by Laughton's wife, Elsa Lanchester, he presents an astonishingly full and vivid picture of a complex, often difficult – but as often kindly and generous – man. Something in Laughton's genius (not too strong a word) in his chosen profession is captured in these pages, and it is difficult to imagine them being supplanted. One might, perhaps, have wished for a slightly more detailed account of his early theatrical life, to include even the 'less outstanding' plays. The films, however, are excellently dealt with, particularly Laughton's one magnificent achievement as a director, *The Night of the Hunter*. Mr Higham's account brings it vividly back to the memory; though one is left wondering why he links the murder with Sibelius' *Valse Triste* – certainly the music accompanying the deed has nothing to do with that famous piece.

The author's subtitle, 'An Intimate Biography', is for once justified, and little is withheld concerning Laughton's sexual deviation. He comes across, too, as a man who must at times have been very difficult (to put it mildly) to work

with. Mr Higham is rightly scathing about the quality of such scripts as those of *The Mutiny on the Bounty* and *The Hunchback of Notre Dame*. Here and there an error creeps in – it was J. B. Fagan (not Pagan) who produced *The Greater Love*, which was not about the French Revolution. There are also slips of style – our old enemy the misused 'disinterest' turns up, and also 'aggravate' for 'annoy' or 'anger' (twice in as many pages). 'Due' is used for 'Owing': and were the worldlings of Louis XI's court really 'diffident', i.e. bashful?

Lemmon: Don Widener; W. H. Allen, £4.95.
Chatty but (in the main) pleasantly readable story of the popular and likeable Jack Lemmon. An often subtle actor who has too seldom had the opportunity of demonstrating that he is not *only* a comedian (*Days of Wine and Roses*), Lemmon deserves a full-length study, and though this is admittedly lightweight it will serve as an interim account of his life and fortunes – including an unexpectedly tough

struggle for recognition. Before his career comes to a close he may well be recognised as a performer of greater depth and significance – and of wider range – than has at present been permitted to him. Nicely illustrated and very adequately indexed. Mr Widener indulges in the occasional ugliness ('. . . my wife . . . who *critiqued* every line . . .'): and his final story surely concerned the much earlier clown Grimaldi, and not 'Grok' – thus misspelled.

Living It Up: George Burns; W. H. Allen, £4.95.
Though most of their work was in other media, the Burns and Allen team enlivened a number of film comedies during the early days of sound. Mr Burns has written a most engaging, warm-hearted autobiography, including in it lengthy extracts from some of his scripts with his wife and with Carol Channing. The tragically sudden death of the former is movingly told. Even though the author may not be as well known in Britain as in the United States, this likeable, disarmingly modest story cannot fail to be read with sympathy and enjoyment.
There are plenty of good illustrations: but also some ugly, easily avoidable, end-of-line hyphenations ('ti- tle'; 'wa-ter') – and, sad to say, several blank, index-less pages.

Memoirs of the Devil: Roger Vadim; Hutchinson, £3.95.
It looks as if this delightful brief autobiography may well turn out to be the literary surprise packet of the year. Fed on the lurid publicity put out by the press and other media for a long time past (and, it must be admitted, seemingly not altogether discouraged by its subject) the reader might have expected a sensational account of orgiastic goings-on and colourful sexual encounters. Instead Mr Vadim emerges as a serious, modest, sympathetic and thoughtful man of his era. After a brief account of a highly unconventional, often exciting and at times grim childhood, the main body of the book is concerned with his relationship with the four women who have figured most prominently in his life: Brigitte Bardot, Annette Stroyberg, Catherine Deneuve and Jane Fonda. Pride of place, understandably, goes to B.B. Dispelling many a myth as he goes, he is generous in the extreme to Annette and understanding towards Jane. The section on the fascinating Miss Deneuve is tantalisingly short – he states that a detailed story would fill another book, and perhaps one day he will present it to us.
Well illustrated and indexed, smoothly and readably translated (except for the occasional grammatical slip) by Peter Beglan, this is a charming, amusing, touching – and sometimes even wise – chronicle.

My Heart Belongs: Mary Martin; W. H. Allen, £5.00.
Mary Martin's sojourn in Hollywood was brief (*The Great Victor Herbert, Rhythm on the River,* etc.) and not particularly illustrious, but as star of some famous stage musicals which later became cinema blockbusters, her career will doubtless be of interest to devotees of that *genre*. This is a chatty, rather fulsome, book, full of theatrical anecdotes – of which it seems impossible to tire – and with plenty of names dropped around. Good full index and numerous illustrations.

Musical Stages: Richard Rodgers; W. H. Allen, £5.95.
For any lover of the musical film this is an obviously indispensable addition to the film bookshelf. Most attractively produced (note, for instance, the reproductions of programmes, posters and music covers on the pre-chapter pages), written with wit and generosity and containing a mine of good stories – it is a valuable record of the American world of light music over some fifty years. The birth and growth of such famous productions as *Oklahoma!, South Pacific* and *On Your Toes* are fully described, together with British stage shows such as *Ever Green* and *One Dam Thing After Another.*

On The Way I Lost It: Frankie Howerd; W. H. Allen, £4.50.
An amusing and engaging autobiography, with plenty of good stories of stage and screen for which the demand seems insatiable. Mr Howerd writes of his ups and downs

(from Pompeii to Shakespeare) with equal emphasis and a disarming modesty, and the result should entertain even those filmgoers who would not claim that his pictures have a high place in their Ten Best lists.

The Real F. Scott Fitzgerald: Sheilah Graham; W. H. Allen, £4.95.
One of the less understandable cults is that which has arisen around this small-scale writer and his tiresome Zelda. However, it undoubtedly flourishes, and his devotees will need no recommendation to procure this important addition to its prolific literature: an intimate memoir by someone whose name was closely linked with his and who was present when he died (as the blurb accurately states) literally at her feet. As might be expected, Miss Graham is frank to a degree. In a chapter on his miserable drunkenness she remarks on his 'rage of a spoiled child. Life frustrated him, and when the sweets were taken away, he kicked and screamed and tried to hurt

everyone.' An admirable character indeed around whom to form a cult! Several pages are devoted to his period as a Hollywood scriptwriter, but perhaps the most valuable parts of the book – at least to the researcher – are lengthy sections from an unfinished play the author and Fitzgerald wrote together (not, alas, apparently a very good play), and the photographed typescript of a short story by her, with corrections by him. There are some interesting (though rather smudgy) illustrations, and a good, full index.

Ken Russell: Joseph Gomez; Muller, £5.95.
Mr Gomez's book is not a biography (though there is a brief account of Russell's life) but a study of 'The Adaptor as Creator'. It deals, intelligently and interestingly, and in considerable detail, with both the early television films (in particular *The Debussy Film, Isadora Duncan, Dante's Inferno, Song of Summer* and *Dance of the Seven Veils*), and the full-length feature films, *Women in Love, The Music Lovers, Savage Messiah* and *Mahler*, with two chapters on

The Devils as centrepiece and briefer accounts of the remaining titles. The author makes a spirited defence of Russell's deliberate inaccuracies, self-indulgent sensationalism and determination to shock at all costs, though it is doubtful whether he will convert many to whom the results are anathema. The opening paragraph of his Conclusions (that the 'usual naïve pronouncements of film critics can no longer be considered justified', etc.) remains a personal statement rather than an incontrovertible fact: he does not really reassure those who may wonder whether, when the present murky climate of the cinema changes, these films will appear more than immature japes. There is a brief, somewhat pointless, Foreword in which Mr Russell – famous for his sensitivity to criticism – quotes unfavourable reviews by now forgotten critics on those composers around whom he has himself made films: causing the reader to speculate whether the criticisms or the films would have enraged these victims the more!
The book is very well illustrated, but unfortunately one's pleasure in reading it is somewhat marred by careless proof checking which has resulted in numerous pages spotted with ugly wrong-fount letters.
Note: The Brontës, of course, lived at Haworth, not Howarth. And where did Mr Gomez get hold of the appalling word 'diagonalisation' (p. 40) – from Raymond Durgnat, presumably, as he is referring to that writer – but he might have avoided it himself!

Frank Sinatra: Tony Scaduto; Michael Joseph, £4.25.
Held, almost against one's will, by Mr Scaduto's plain and penetrating biography, one is left exhausted and, perhaps, slightly appalled. The overall impression of an emotional immaturity is astonishing – and unsettling – in so famous and fortune-favoured a figure. On page 81 Bogart is quoted as saying, 'I don't think Frank's an adult emotionally. He can't settle down.' No overstatement, certainly. Yet beneath the childish tantrums, the silly squabbles, the infantile outbursts of violence, there is obviously – as Mr Scaduto strongly brings out – the ability to win the most extraordinary loyalty from many people. Sinatra is quoted as saying – with undoubted truth, 'My personal life is my own business: all I owe you is my performance, my voice.' Well, the personal life is here – alleged Mafia connections, wives, buddies and all. Even those to whom the famous 'voice' is something less than magical will find themselves compelled to stay the course.

Sinatra: Earl Wilson; W. H. Allen, £5.
Written in a somewhat flamboyant style well suited to its subject, this 'unauthorised' biography by a leading American columnist is the best book on Sinatra to have come my way, winning by a short head over Mr Scaduto's which is also reviewed in these columns. In a preface the author explains how, after being closely associated with Sinatra for many years, he was suddenly 'cast aside' on account, apparently, of having been found guilty of 'inaccurate reporting' – a charge he never understood. When asked five years later to write a Sinatra biography he hesitated, but eventually agreed after being told he must 'know his subject from both sides'. The result, he hoped, would be a story that contained no character assassination

while still retaining all the warts. The dichotomy in Sinatra's personality (spoilt immature bully/generous courageous fighter, to simplify outrageously) make him one of the more interesting film people to read about, even for those who do not worship wholeheartedly at his shrine. Mr Wilson presents his public, private and professional life (or lives) in a vivid and sometimes exciting, frank but never malicious, lengthy but always interesting tale. We are given reasonable, not over-generous illustrations, but no index.

Jacques Tati: Penelope Gilliatt; Woburn Press, £2.95.
Surprisingly little material in book form has been available on this inimitable man of the cinema – among the greatest (indeed, some may argue the very greatest) and most subtle comedians of the screen. Here, within the brief space of just under one hundred pages, are packed a wealth of excellent photographs and stills, a splendidly full filmography, and an informative text derived largely from interviews with the great man himself. It has, regretfully, to be admitted that Miss Gilliatt's style is often clumsy and tortuous (and on occasion careless – even the ingenious M. Tati would find it difficult, as described by her, to 'write down the number of a wilful car', while whistling, with his hands on his hips), but otherwise this is a most welcome introductory study, attractively produced.

Rudolph Valentino: Alexander Walker; Elm Tree Books, £2.75.
Mr Walker wrote most interestingly and perceptively on Valentino in his earlier book, *Stardom*. This enlargement and embellishment is a brief but admirably comprehensive biography of the man and study of the legend – frank but fair, appreciative but critical. He painstakingly sifts fantasy from fact (as far as anyone can, now), and leaves us with a portrait in depth drawn with sympathy and understanding – all in 120 pages, many of which are filled with illustrations. Even to those of us old enough to remember at any rate the later films as they first appeared, he has something fresh to reveal. The splendid illustrations – many of them rare and never seen before – deserve a special mention.

The Westmores of Hollywood: Frank Westmore and Muriel Davidson; W. H. Allen, £5.
Directors, stars, composers, writers, stuntmen, producers, all these have been covered – at times over-covered – in film literature. Now comes the turn of the make-up artist, and a worthy tribute it is. Frank Westmore is the son of George Westmore and the last survivor of a great family of Hollywood creators. His father founded the first movie make-up department in 1917, and from the earliest days to *The Towering Inferno* he and his family were responsible for some of the most famous feats of beautification – transformation – and uglification, in the cinema. Among hundreds of fascinating stories, some of the most interesting deal with the polishing of Valentino, the marvellous Hyde-transformation of Fredric March, the making of Harold Lloyd's artificial hand after he lost the thumb and a finger (*before* doing most of his great acrobatic stunts), and the Japanning – if I may be

pardoned – of Shirley MacLaine in *My Geisha*. The Westmores know most of the stars – often literally – in 'undress', and their story abounds in illuminating incidents, such as the devastating paragraph on the often unpleasant Spencer Tracy.

The book is engagingly written and beautifully produced, with an illustrated family tree, informative photographs, and a first-rate full index. It is fervently to be hoped that the unfamiliarity of the name on the jacket will not deter anyone from opening the pages: the merest glance inside should ensure an immediate decision to acquire this captivating memoir.

HISTORY, CRITICISM, ANALYSIS

The Best of Buster: Edited by Richard J. Anobile; Elm Tree Books, £5.95 hardback, £3.50 paperback.
Another of Mr Anobile's painstaking and patience-demanding forays into the world of the frame blow-ups, containing lengthy extracts from *The Goat, Sherlock Junior, The Navigator, Go West, Seven Chances* and *The General*. Riches indeed! Keaton devotees may lament that only portions of their favourites are present instead of the whole lot (for my part, I would plump for *Sherlock Junior* and *Seven Chances*) but this would be to cry for the moon, and one can only be thankful that Mr Anobile's skill and sensitivity manages to convey so much of the spirit of these scenes, and – most importantly – something of the very essence of this great and enduring comedian. *The General* is, of course, available in full in another Anobile volume, and might perhaps have been replaced here by the great and lesser-known *Steamboat Bill, Jr*. However, let us not niggle: here are hundreds of pictures, every one of them able to conjure up treasured memories. Mr Anobile includes a brief, splendidly laudatory preface, in which he rightly advises the reader (or scanner) not to hurry through the pages, but to turn them leisurely enough to capture at least something of Keaton's superb sense of timing.

The Best of Laurel and Hardy: Ed. Richard J. Anobile; Michael Joseph, £3.50.
On the whole, the Anobile 'blow-up' books which are devoted to a single film may perhaps be the most satisfying, but of those restricted to highlights from a number of pictures this marvellous collection of Laurel and Hardy treasures is undoubtedly the best. In his preface Mr Anobile says that he has broken his usual rule of economy in his frames selection, and included enough in a single sequence to show every nuance of expression and gesture. His decision is amply justified. The result, in some thousand blow-ups covering about half a dozen sequences, enables something of the exquisite comedy timing of the illustrious pair to be preserved even on the immobile page. The wonderful scene from *Swiss Miss* involving the St Bernard dog and its brandy barrel is alone worth the price of the book – even if in this instance Mr Hardy is replaced by the brilliantly expressive and superbly unflappable dog.

The Blue Dahlia: Raymond Chandler; Elm Tree Books, £3.95.
This is the complete film-script, all that remains from an unfinished novel, and obviously of the greatest interest to anyone anxious to learn more of Raymond Chandler, the Los Angeles of the forties, film history or the tough American novel of the period. The book is very well produced and readably set out. Included are several integrated illustrations and a set of the dreadful display stills of the time. It also contains an interesting memoir by John Houseman, and an even more interesting critical analysis by Matthew J. Bruccoli, who edited the script. Very wisely, he has made a minimum of alterations – e.g. typing errors and some repetitions have been corrected. He has left in the inconsistencies and two major (and ludicrous) plot failures, which go to make the finished film such a confused jumble. The circumstances of its making were appalling: no ending decided on even when the script was half shot, Chandler writing in a deliberately induced state of drunkenness. His original murderer was – incredible to say – disallowed by the US Navy because it might reflect on the integrity of a Service man – all American sailors, presumably, wearing haloes! Chandler disliked the film, partly because of the poor performance by the actress he kindly described as Miss Moronica Lake. Unbelievably, the screenplay was nominated for an Academy award. The whole thing is a sobering reminder of the sort of stuff we were prepared to spend good money on in the so-called Golden Years. An even more sobering thought perhaps is that we are frequently no more discriminating in our expenditure today!

The Cinema of Federico Fellini: Stuart Rosenthal; Barnes/Tantivy, £5.50.
A scholarly and perceptive study, this could be described as essential reading for anyone anxious to enlarge his understanding of this sometimes difficult director's work. All the films are fully analysed, dealt with under such headings as 'The Personal Vision', 'A World of Symbols' and 'Characters and Identity'. Of particular interest are the pages on Fellini's first all-colour film – often underrated and awarded an unduly low place in his work – the subtle, haunting, and visually ravishing *Juliet of the Spirits*. Mr Rosenthal makes the valid and interesting point that, in contrast to the other films, 'in $8\frac{1}{2}$ and *Juliet of the Spirits* we assume that the principal characters will keep growing and maturing after the film has ended'. Plenty of fine stills and commendably full cast and credit lists combine with penetrating but lucid discussion to make this the most valuable study of Fellini's work that has come my way.

Cinema of Mystery: Rose London
Freaks, Cinema of the Bizarre: Werner Adrian
Swastika, Cinema of Oppression: Baxter Phillips
All published by Lorrimer at £1.95.
Three further volumes in the odd, but often original and stimulating, Lorrimer series of 'aspect studies'. All follow the general pattern of including much material about the derivations and sidelines of the respective *genres* – both in the comparatively brief texts and in the lavish illustrations.

Mr Phillips' *Swastika* is perhaps the most important of the present trio, concerning itself not only with Nazi films, but with those of Stalin's Russia, Mussolini's Italy and Franco's Spain – and even starting off with *The Birth of a Nation*. A useful, if necessarily fairly superficial, survey. (Brando's film was *The Wild One*, not *The Wild Ones*.) Werner Adrian's *Freaks* is really one more horror/science-fiction notebook, but including quite a lot of information on circus and fairground curiosities – particularly in the illustrations. (*Underworld* was certainly not von Sternberg's first film, nor even his first American film.) *Cinema of Mystery* is almost wholly concerned with Edgar Allan Poe – possibly the most complete study of his films inside one cover. A large proportion of the illustrations are not film stills but excellent reproductions of those drawn for Poe's books by Arthur Rackham (to whom she rightly accords high praise), Beardsley and – very interestingly – Heath Robinson before his 'comic inventions' days. It seems, however, totally unnecessary to drag in a still from *The Clockwork Orange* – minimally connected with the text, and apparently inserted merely for its presumed sensational value. Miss London proves her point that Poe – in the main shockingly mangled in the cinema – has been best served 'in spirit' by those films that strayed furthest from his text.

Costume Design: David Chierichetti; Studio Vista, £7.95.
For many years, throughout its heyday, Hollywood was proclaimed as the great arbiter and trendsetter of fashion. To some extent the claim may have been exaggerated, but there is no doubt it had substance: witness only the furore over the vestlessness of Clark Gable in *It Happened One Night*. It is fully time, therefore, that a survey of the world of fashion should join those of practically every other film activity and this splendidly researched book does this *par excellence*. Divided into sections on each studio, it covers the Hollywood scene from the 1920s to date, with an informed and informative text and a magnificently detailed Designers' Filmography, dominated by the gargantuan output of Edith Head. The all-important illustrations are lavish and well reproduced, consisting of stills, posed portraits, and line drawings, with a section in colour. By making the necessary, if often difficult, effort to overcome the inevitable instinct to regard a recently *passé* fashion as the last word in ugliness, one can fully admit the skill and artistry that has gone into the costuming of each passing year during the half-century or so of epic Hollywood glamour.

Deeper into Movies: Pauline Kael; Calder & Boyars, £3.95.
I welcomed the appearance of this latest collection of reviews in its hardback edition (£6.95, same publishers) in last year's *Film Review*, in the following words: 'With the possible exception of John Simon, Miss Kael is arguably the most lively and vital of contemporary film critics – at any rate of those whose work crosses the Atlantic . . . Though she seems to be almost wilfully perverse in her judgements at times, it is as stimulating to disagree as it is satisfying to agree with so witty and pointed a critic.' This nicely produced paperback edition is an essential addition to the shelves of all those who have not availed themselves

of the considerably more costly hardback. It covers a large number of films from 1969 to 1972, together with an occasional brief essay, and is excellently indexed. The reviews originally appeared in *The New Yorker*.

Documentary: A History of the Non-Fiction Film: Erik Barnouw; Oxford University Press, £2.50.
Perhaps the most interesting aspect of Mr Barnouw's wholly excellent study is the way in which he sets the 'history' of his subject into the 'history' of the events surrounding it. It could, indeed, be read with almost equal profit as general history as documentary film history. It is also a model of conciseness; in under 300 pages of text he covers the whole field – from Lumière to Vietnam – and sets his sights wide enough to include such fictional documentaries (or documentary fictions) as *The Search*. A glance at the Index may be enough to give some idea of the width of the book – but it should be read with care (and it is a joy to read) in order to appreciate the depth. In earlier volumes of *Film Review* I have extolled the virtues of two earlier paperbacks on Documentary – R. M. Barsam's *Nonfiction Film* and the more restricted *Studies in Documentary* by Alan Lovell and Jim Hillier. Together with these, Mr Barnouw's book form an indispensable trio of first-class handbooks on the subject. The illustrations, incidentally, are many, fresh and well produced. Highly recommended.

Double Takes: Alexander Walker; Elm Tree Books, £5.95.
Subtitled 'Notes and Afterthoughts on the Movies 1956–76', this is a selection of contemporary film reviews with comments added from hindsight. Mr Walker has always been one of the liveliest, on occasion one of the most provocative, of critics, and his book – dealing mainly with American and British productions – is a welcome complementary volume to his excellent *Hollywood, England*. One may differ from some of his opinions and verdicts while at the same time appreciating his essential fairness, and the refreshing absence – in his often severe condemnations – of spleen.
It is particularly pleasant to read his defence of a number of underrated films such as *The Sergeant, Three into Two Won't Go*, and, especially, Lindsay Anderson's *O, Lucky Man!* He expresses the hope that he will be there when the latter film 'makes its comeback and finds its audience': I hope I may be there with him, and that we are shown the full version instead of the shamefully mutilated copy sent around the country. As a lightweight bonus there is an entertaining account of his famous rolled-newspaper encounter with Ken Russell on television, when he suffered an assault similar to that inflicted on theatre critic Hannen Swaffer (and joyously capitalised by him) many years ago.

Ealing Studios: Charles Barr; Cameron & Tayleur/David & Charles; £6.95.
Of all past British films, the Ealing series were probably most closely a reflection of their period (as Sir Michael Balcon's plaque inscription indicates) and Mr Barr rightly places them against their historical and sociological background in his first-rate, scholarly yet always

entertaining study. He concentrates mainly on the films themselves rather than the business side of the studios, though obviously the two threads of his story are often interlinked. Most of the films are referred to (he places in their proper perspective the Ealing comedies which are often unduly emphasised in accounts of the total output), and the most significant productions are discussed in detail. It is here that Mr Barr's book is so valuable. His analyses of such films as *Passport to Pimlico, Kind Hearts and Coronets* and particularly the superb *Man In The White Suit* are perceptive, persuasive, and stimulatingly fresh. He is also excellent on the often underrated *Went the Day Well?*
On two points only I would take issue. His attitude towards the British *theatre* of the thirties is unfairly (though perhaps trendily) patronising. One day perhaps a book will be written on the memorable productions of these years – they will compare favourably with much of the more recent permissiveness-burdened era! Then there

is his apparent admiration for Raymond Durgnat's *A Mirror for England* – one of the most turgid, carelessly written, tediously splenetic and inaccurate film books it has ever been my misfortune to come across: at least Mr Barr admits the inaccuracies!
Ealing Studios is indexed for film titles, and has a first-rate filmography.

Elvis – The Films and Career of Elvis Presley: Steven and Boris Zmijewsky; Citadel, dist. LSP Books, £8.50.
Blurb-described as 'definitive', this contains 100 pages of biographical details and analyses, followed by just over 100 pages of film credits, synopses and song titles – this latter section being (perhaps wisely) almost innocent of criticisms. It is well-made, quite readable, and lavishly illustrated.

Face to Face: Ingmar Bergman; Marion Boyars Publishers, £4.95 (hardcover), £1.95 (paperback)
With *Face to Face* Bergman is back to his most spell-binding form – as subtle and tantalising as ever, yet more immediately approachable and lucid than in some of his recent films. His account of a woman psychiatrist's sudden breakdown and attempted suicide, her nightmares and hallucinations, are gripping and at times terrifying; while his portrayal of her ageing grandparents is among the most moving of all studies of approaching loneliness and dissolution seen on the screen. Bergman's published film-scripts have always obviously been prepared with great care – clearly set out and eminently readable – and this example (very smoothly translated by Alan Blair) is among the very best. Indeed, it could well prove no mean substitute for those unable to see the film itself, and in its own right provides a moving and memorable experience.

Fifty Major Film-makers: Ed. Peter Cowie; Barnes/Tantivy, £8.25.
Last year I welcomed the announcement that the 'Directors of the Year' sections from Peter Cowie's *International Film Guide* were to be published in an embellished and permanent form. This has now been achieved, and the result amply fulfils all expectations. Of coffee-table size, well-illustrated (film stills, production photographs and portraits), it is an excellent introduction (all that is modestly claimed for it) to the work of the film-makers it includes. Directors from sixteen countries are covered. They range from Kubrick to Haanstra, Polanski to Rohmer, Bergman to Kazan, Welles to Němec, Tati to Hitchcock. The illustrations are notably well reproduced, and there is an index of film titles. The price is, perhaps, in the higher range for books of this size – but what is offered is well worth the extra.

The Films of Jeanette MacDonald and Nelson Eddy: Eleanor Knowles; Barnes/Tantivy, £10.
The professional reputation of the Eddy/MacDonald team has had its vicissitudes, and many a critical nose turns up sharply at the mention of their romantical–musical–fantastical epics: but there is no denying that their popularity over some twenty years was unprecedented, unswerving and universal. This enormous book, a work of

sheer devotion on the part of its author and her generously acknowledged helpers, is a tribute that must surely satisfy even the most ardent of devotees. It has over 450 large pages, filled with lavish illustrations, a huge and detailed index, *really* complete filmographies and statistical data (compiled by John Cocchi), some sixty double columns of discographical details (J. Peter Bergman), reviews, synopses and full biographies. The mind boggles at the amount of research that must have gone into the putting together of so gargantuan a tome.

The Films of Norma Shearer: Jack Jacobs and Myron Braum: Barnes/Tantivy, £8.
A 'Films of . . .' book on this important star of the Hollywood twenties and thirties (as actress, and as wife of the powerful Irving Thalberg) has long been overdue. Messrs Jacobs and Braum provide a large number of exciting rare stills (especially of the silent days) and full cast, credit, synopsis and review details which are particularly valuable for a period in which research is often difficult.
The opening biographical section is, unfortunately, marred by an irritatingly facetious and fulsome approach, and also by some inexcusably slipshod writing: 'Two other performances that stood out besides Chaney's was Tully Marshall . . .' etc.; 'Shearer soon curbed her dogmatism and prima-donnaish ways . . .'; 'Although she was never a tomboy in the sense of the word . . .' (how else can one be a tomboy?); 'Sidney Franklin rang all the pathos at his command . . .', etc. Another black mark must be given for the absence of both an index and a list of film titles on the Contents page.
Recommended, therefore, for the reference matter (if it can be found) and the stills. These, as stated, are splendid, and very generous – in some cases half a dozen or more to a single film.

The Films of Lana Turner: Lou Valentino; Citadel, dist. LSP Books, £8.50.
This is a manifest labour of love, very beautifully designed (by the author) and radiating adulation. Opinions as to Miss Turner's skill as an actress may vary, but it is indisputable that, in Mr Valentino's words, she was 'a contemporary legend who, both on screen and off, epitomized ideals of glamour and sophistication in a Hollywood that we will never see again'. After a fairly brief biographical prelude, he covers all her films (the number of which may surprise some cinemagoers) in detail, with commendably full cast lists. Throughout, while never masking the fact that an appreciable number of her pictures were something less than memorable, Mr Valentino's affection for his subject is disarmingly apparent. In his biography he dismisses the tragic scandal over her daughter and the killing of Johnny Stompanato in a brief, discreet paragraph – and rightly: the sorry episode has been written about luridly and fully enough already. It has small place in a study such as this.
The illustrations have always been a notable part of the Citadel/LSP series – but here they are outstanding, whether film stills, publicity glamour portraits, or production and personal shots. Director Mervyn LeRoy

contributes a brief foreword, and there are sections on television appearances and stage shows. A nostalgically engaging book.

Finnish Cinema: Peter Cowie; Barnes/Tantivy, £3.25.
This is a very attractively produced introductory handbook to a district of world cinema too little known (as Mr Cowie forcefully persuades us) outside its own country. It is fairly certain to come as a considerable surprise to most filmgoers just how flourishing a concern the Finnish cinema is – yet almost the only director whose name is likely to be at all familiar (and then only in the unfortunately named 'art' theatres) is Jörn Donner (*Black on White*), a proportion of whose work was done in the wider-known Swedish cinema. Although the book inevitably – and tantalisingly – deals with a great many films we are never likely to see, there is always a chance that, with the BBC's generally enlightened attitude towards 'foreign' films, one or more may be shown on the television screen. The owner of this very attractive (and well illustrated) little volume may well find that he or she is the owner of a reference book of practical as well as theoretical use – and at any rate can spend the intervening period practising the pronunciation of the Finnish names!

From Hollywood: DeWitt Bodeen; Barnes/Tantivy, £6.50.
Mr Bodeen is one of the most informative of all writers on the stars of the silent and early talkie eras, and it was an excellent idea to collect these brief but fact-packed career articles (updated and revised) from 'Films in Review' and other magazines and issue them in one handsomely made volume. Seventeen stars are covered – from Theda Bara, through Wallace Reid, Betty Compson and Richard Dix, to Douglas Fairbanks, Sr. Filmographies are included in every case – and these are of special value on account of the difficulty often encountered in tracing details of early movies. For older filmgoers these pages will revive fond memories: for younger ones they should stimulate interest in the germinal years of the cinema's growth, particularly as there is always a chance (though not nearly so often as there should be) of meeting these great mythical figures on television. A companion volume is promised.

The Great Adventure Films: Tony Thomas; Citadel, dist. LSP Books, £8.50.
Mr Thomas selects fifty films – from *The Mark of Zorro* (1920) to *The Man Who Would be King* (1975) in this handsome volume. It is, of course, a personal choice, but he justifies it with style and wit, ranging from *The Crusades*, through *Tarzan and His Mate*, *Robin Hood* (Flynn, not Fairbanks), *Tom Sawyer*, *Henry V*, *Scott of the Antarctic*, *War and Peace*, to *The Naked Prey*. Four silents are included – *The Mark of Zorro*, *Don Juan*, Keaton's *The General* and *Wings*. The many stills are up to the usual high standard, and Mr Thomas's fairly full reviews are discerning and informative. This is a most welcome addition to the second string of the Citadel/LSP series (companions to 'The Films of . . .') and the wide coverage and lively presentation should assure it a place in most collections.

Heroes of the Horrors: Calvin Thomas Beck; Collier Macmillan, £3.80.
Without doubt it is the illustrations that are the chief attraction of this handsomely produced paperback – the best collection on the subject that I have yet come across in a single volume, lavish, stunningly reproduced, and in many cases very rare. Such discoveries, for instance, as that of Bela Lugosi as Christ in a 1915 stage production are real treasures – and this is only one among many.
The text is, at times, less satisfactory. It starts off with a useful summary of horror divided into decades, and continues with lengthy biographies of six stars – the two Chaneys, Lorre, Lugosi, Karloff and Price. Unfortunately Mr Beck's style (sometimes pedestrian, sometimes facetious, sometimes careless) is not always up to his eye for a good photograph. There are errors of fact, illiteracies, and sometimes questionable judgments. No index is provided, nor is there any documentation, except in a few instances. He does not credit his sources

– and a closer study of some of those sources might have helped to avoid, for instance, the misstatements concerning the early stage productions of *Dracula*. However, such strictures made, there is much of interest to be found: and, to repeat, the illustrations are superb, by themselves worth the price of the book.

Hollywood and the Great Stars: Editor – Jeremy Pascall; Phoebus Publishing Company, £4.95.
It would be a pity if the emphasis on the jacket on the 'Great Stars' part of the title led any prospective reader to think this collection of articles was one more account of over-written Hollywood personalities; because in fact the second (and most interesting) half is concerned with a variety of aspects of the Film Capital – censorship, early days, scandals, camera trickeries, the great silents, location work, stunts, etc. The twenty-odd stars include regulars such as Bogart, Dietrich, Gable and Davis – but also Valentino, McQueen, Bronson and Connery. For the rest, there is much to interest and inform, including a multitude of excellent illustrations. Some of these, inevitably, are old friends, but there are many less frequently reproduced. Here, again, the early days come off best, with covers of old fan magazines, posters, newspaper headlines, and production stills – all well printed, whether colour, tinted or black and white.
At the end of each star section is a list of his or her 'Best Films' – any such preferential choosing is, of course, open to attack from dissenters – but how good to see at last Garbo's early *The Temptress* given such recognition.
A very handsomely put together 'coffee-tabler', and reasonably priced for today.

Hollywood Directors 1914–1940: Richard Koszarski; Oxford University Press, £9.50 hardback, £2.50 paperback.
It was an excellent idea of Mr Koszarski's to collect together contemporary articles written by fifty Hollywood directors from the earliest days, and the arduous research he must have put into this project is amply justified by the result. For this is a fascinating digest of what film-makers thought, experienced, attempted and expected – stated *without* benefit of hindsight. If at times the ghost-writer's presence haunts the page and a 'written-to-order' piece has slipped by, it was, as the editor says, undoubtedly issued with authority.
The directors included range from Edwin S. Porter and Sidney Olcott to George Cukor and Frank Tuttle; and the articles are by no means culled from fan or trade magazines only. *The Ladies' Home Journal, Travel* and the *New York Times*, for instance, are among those represented. All the Big Four comedians are here – Keaton, Chaplin, Lloyd and Langdon, and most of the other directors are well known. There are, however, a number of less familiar names, such as Alice Guy-Blaché, who in 1914 wrote a spirited attack on sex-discrimination in the cinema. One of the most enjoyable sections is not, as it happens, a written article, but an excerpt from a lecture given in 1929 by the British pioneer (and director of *The Glorious Adventure*) J. Stuart Blackton. What is apparent throughout is the inspiring belief in the potentialities and power of the new

medium. It would be interesting, if sobering, to hear the comments of these trail-blazers on some of the films taking up screen time in the cinemas today.
The author provides a brief note on each contributor; François Truffaut adds a pleasant Foreword; and the book (a most pleasant volume to handle, incidentally) contains a number of excellent production photographs. Highly recommended to all film historians, and to anyone interested in the formative years of Hollywood.

The Hollywood Exiles: John Baxter; MacDonald & Jane's; £5.95.
It would seem that every angle of Hollywood must have been covered by now – but this is a most interesting and entertaining account of yet another special corner: the many foreigners who chose – or were driven – to work in the great film city from earliest days to its declining years, and the very great influence they had in different ways on the making of movies in its heyday. Not only actors and directors are included, but also others such as musicians and writers – in this last category it is pleasant to note one more particular kindness from that kindest and most generous of authors, Hugh Walpole.
As the blurb on the jacket remarks, pride of place goes to the Germans. Of particular interest are the sections on Emil Jannings, Lubitsch and Paul Leni – but indeed throughout the book the reader is regaled with items of interest and information, and probably surprised at the extent of the list of those who brought from different countries their skills, attitudes, experience and personalities to make Hollywood the great amalgam that it was. Special mention must be made of the illustrations – many of them of rare historical interest.

The Hollywood Professionals, Vol. 4: Stuart Rosenthal and Judith M. Kass; Tantivy/Barnes; £1.25.
The fourth volume in this useful little series consists of studies of two directors, Tod Browning (Mr Rosenthal) and Don Siegel (Miss Kass). The procedure is as before – lengthy critical essay followed by a filmography which includes a one-sentence synopsis. Mr Rosenthal takes his horror seriously, and Miss Kass justifies the recent Siegel cult. Reproduction of the stills is not always up to the usual high standard (which is a pity, as some of the Browning ones in particular are rare and interesting), but they are at least adequate for this reasonably priced and intelligent addition to a valuable series.

Holmes of the Movies: David Stuart Davies; New English Library, £6.96.
A useful, well-researched and excellent study of all the Sherlock Holmes films – from the early silent days, through the great Eille Norwood series, the Clive Brook and Basil Rathbone productions, to the 1976 impertinence *The Seven Per Cent Solution*, on which he most tartly comments. It is good to see the silent movies given prominence, and also to find the often neglected Arthur Wontner receiving due regard. On stage and screen, he was undoubtedly the truest and closest impersonator of the great detective, whatever the quality of the films in other respects. One need only glance at the excellent photographs here reproduced to appreciate this.

Though far from uncritical, Mr Davies is still too indulgent towards the shameful Rathbone–Universal updated travesties – perhaps the most disgraceful, though by no means the only, liberties taken with a classic creation in the foul name of box-office greed. It is sad to learn that the excellent Clive Brook was the first to perpetrate these abominations.
Mr Davies includes a good filmography but, alas, no index.

The Idols of Silence: Anthony Slide; Barnes/Tantivy, £7.50.
Mr Slide's devotion to the Silent Cinema, even before he left England and joined the staff of the American Film Institute, was well-known to be single-minded, all-embracing, and perhaps surprising in someone born one year before the end of the Second World War. The author of several books on the subject, and editor and co-founder of *The Silent Picture* magazine, his knowledge is as deep as his affection, and anything new from his (doubtless silent) typewriter is to be welcomed. This new volume is divided quite sharply into two parts. The first is a series of essays on a dozen stars of the twenties (an interestingly off-the-beaten-track selection) and three chapters on fan magazines and their writers. The second part is an extremely extensive bibliography (perhaps 'magazineo-graphy' would be more accurate, though it is to be hoped no one ever uses such a word again) of over one hundred players. They are arranged in alphabetical order, and each list of entries is accompanied by a still or studio portrait. Obviously this second half of the book is aimed very much at the serious researcher, as it is unlikely that many people would have the means of access to the vast number of publications quoted. As an aid to fact-finding for those within reach of the BFI or the AFI, of course, these lists are a marvellous time-saver. For anyone, though, the pictures are a treasure to be relished – many of them rare, and some decidedly uncharacteristic. How many people, for instance, would recognise Clara Bow from a quick glance at page 125? Oddly, most of the stills of Bebe Daniels and Ben Lyon are from the sound period.
Of course, complaints will inevitably reach Mr Slide about favourites having been omitted. I'll send him one myself for a start: why is so little notice taken of the delightful Miss Vera Reynolds?
An excellent book, then, but I am surprised at Mr Slide passing a misspelling of Alma Rubens' name *twice* in picture captions!

King Lear – The Space of Tragedy: Grigori Kozintsev; Heinemann Educational Books, £8.50.
King Lear (1972) was Kozintsev's last film before his death in 1973. Reviewing it on its first showing in Britain I wrote that 'sight and sound combine to make this a film to remember'. The final words could equally well be applied to the present book. Its subtitle – 'The Diary of a Film Director' is over-modest. Linked by a factual account of the practical problems encountered in the making of the film – the defeats suffered and the triumphs achieved during four hard years work – the major part of the book consists of comments and thoughts on this greatest and most complex of tragedies. In addition there are personal

memories, and sections on film history; in particular the work and influence of such figures as Eisenstein, Stanislavsky, Gordon Craig, Peter Brook and others. As a bonus, there is a full account of the composing of Shostakovich's marvellous score.

Lest all of this might seem likely to result in a work of formidable density, let it be said at once that the whole book (lovingly and lucidly translated by Mary Mackintosh) is easy to read, refreshingly unpretentious, and absorbing from the first page to the last. The jacket blurb claims that it 'will be of great interest to all concerned with Shakespeare criticism and also to cinema enthusiasts and to the theatre world'. On this occasion, at any rate, advertisement does not exaggerate. To readers of these columns it can be wholeheartedly recommended, for educational and recreational reading alike.

A good index and several pages of stills are included.

The Major Film Theories: J. Dudley Andrew; Oxford University Press, £2.50.

Mr Andrew's book is 'designed for anyone with a serious interest in the art of the film', and his extremely skilful condensation of the outpourings of the major theorists is very welcome, and of great value, either as a straight 'read-through' or as a work of reference. Even more useful is it, however, as a revelation of the preposterous pretentiousness and deadening solemnity of much lunatic-fringe film writing. One's strongest reaction is astonishment that so much turgid incomprehensibility is indulged in to arrive at conclusions which, to lesser (but more lucid) mortals appear so obvious. To take at random one quotation – from arch-priest André Bazin: 'If slapstick comedy succeeded before the days of Griffith and montage, it is because most of its gags derived from a comedy of space, from the relation of man to things and the surrounding world. In *The Circus* Chaplin is truly in the lion's cage, and both are enclosed within the framework of the screen.' How much deep, midnight-oil thought – how many hours of brooding were necessary to hatch so minuscule (and obvious) an egg? Or is it that we (or at least those among us with a 'serious interest in the art of the film') have been gently conned? On the next page, a still of Laurel and Hardy hanging for dear life on a high girder, is captioned: 'Laurel and Hardy suspended in a space at once deep and comic.' One's immediate reaction is Splendid – so what? In his introduction the author states, with commendable honesty, 'Certainly there is no guarantee that film theory deepens the appreciation of film . . .' True – true. On the last page of the text we are told: 'Seen in this way, the separation between the semiotician and the phenomenologist is narrowed.' Granted – and doubtless a relief to the filmgoer as he forks out his (or her) next 120 pence to see the latest offering at the nearest triple-cubicle picture palace.

There follows what may well be the most formidable-looking bibliography in any book on the cinema. One title, however, offers a gleam of hope: Pauline Kael's 'Is there a Cure for Film Theory?' Maybe, maybe.

The Men who made the Movies: Richard Schickel; Elm Tree Books, £5.95.

Richard Schickel is one of the liveliest writers on the cinema (witness his articles in *The Platinum Years*, published by Studio Vista and reviewed in the *1975–76 Film Review*), and judging by the results gathered here he is also one of the most persuasive interviewers. His book is a collection of talks by eight leading Hollywood directors – Capra, Cukor, Hawks, Hitchcock, Minnelli, Vidor, Walsh, Wellman – put together from his own television series of the same title. Question and answer have been amalgamated into a continuous narrative, broken up into well-spaced sections which are commendably easy to find separately. Each chapter is introduced by Mr Schickel, and the director is then allowed to speak for himself. The skill of the questioner's approach is demonstrated by the way in which the individual personality comes through in each case.

Every reader will of course select his own most interesting contribution. I would personally award Hitchcock first place – always a spellbinding (if at times tantalisingly ambiguous) talker about his work, and in fine form here. Among other points, at last we have his own interpretation of the meaning of *The Birds*! (Incidentally, I am proud to be a member of Our Society – referred to by Mr Hitchcock on p. 281.)

Well illustrated, well indexed, well produced, well recommended.

Monsters and Vampires: Alan G. Frank; Octopus, £2.50.

In appearance this is the most attractive of the Movie Treasury Series to date, which is saying a good deal. Over 190 stills – many rare and all superbly reproduced – are beautifully set out on colourfully variegated pages; and the colour plates, so often a let-down, are of equal standard with the black and white. Mr Frank's text may not delve very deep, but he writes in a lively, readable style (except for a plethora of exclamation marks) well suited to the unadventurous, plain straightforward chronological recording he has chosen to adopt. He does attempt, towards the end in particular, to cram too many titles into a limited space, so that the final pages are a jumble of oddly concatenated movies – *2,001, A Space Odyssey*, for instance, which he stoutly denigrates, being squeezed between *The Gods Hate Kansas* and *The Body Stealers*. He is surprisingly insensitive to the delicious subtleties of Polanski's *Dance of the Vampires* – which, incidentally, he wrongly states was so titled in America: in fact, this is the *British* title, *The Fearless Vampire Killers* being the American. He is guilty of some carelessnesses. The world of Metaluna is brought into the *Quatermass* films; Ronald Colman is spelt Coleman, which would have angered that charming and elegant star.

A final point: to the best of my knowledge I was the first writer to 'reveal' (in my early book *The Horror Film*) the secret of the famous 'change' in the 1932 *Dr Jekyll and Mr Hyde*, having originally read it in a 1930s film magazine. Since Mr Frank does not acknowledge any of his sources, he may have come by his own account from a different one. When I challenged the director, Mr Rouben Mamoulian, personally a few years ago *his* comment was *'No* comment'!

Movies from the Mansion: George Perry; Elm Tree Books (Hamish Hamilton), £6.95.

This large format, splendidly illustrated book is primarily what its subtitle indicates, a history of Pinewood Studios, but inevitably it wanders far afield, and in fact finishes up as a remarkably clear and concise chronicle of the British film scene as a whole, mainly from the business angle, from the thirties to date. The permutations and combinations, partnerships and dissolutions, amalgamations and separations between studios (Pinewood, Elstree, Denham, Ealing and the rest), and their chiefs (Rank, Korda, Woolf, Deutsch) are an impenetrable jungle to the layman, but Mr Perry threads his way staunchly through and leads the reader with at any rate reasonable ease along the maze.

The path of Pinewood has been anything but smooth, and the glorious euphoria of its beginnings soon gave way to the grim reality of shrinking markets and failing finance: but at least, after forty years, it still exists – though, as the author questions with only too obvious cause, 'for how long?'

A sad footnote: 'Kip' Herren, quoted as Managing Director of Pinewood in the last paragraph of the text, died before the book was published.

The Novel and the Cinema: Geoffrey Wagner; Fairleigh Dickinson University Press/Tantivy, £6.25.

For many years Mr Wagner's excellent and entertaining book *Parade of Pleasure* has had an honoured place on my bookshelves, and it was with pleasurable expectations that I looked forward to reading his new work on the cinema. I was not disappointed. *The Novel and the Cinema* is a most scholarly and readable examination – not only of the transference from one medium to another, but of the whole nature of film in its aspect of a narrative form. This is done by means of a number of essays (on, for example, the Trials of Technique; the Norms of Narration, the Psychology of Cinema), interspersed with considerations of particular films, including *Citizen Kane*, *The Blue Angel* (an excellent chapter), *Hunger, Wuthering Heights* (witheringly exposed!), *Last Year at Marienbad*, and a dozen others. This is not a book for quick reading through – it demands, and amply repays, concentrated study. It is, however, by no means another of the dull, portentous and inflated tomes which all too often drop with a heavy thud from the higher reaches of film criticism. Film criticism in some of its aspects, indeed, comes in for some stimulating castigation from the author. He writes wittily and well – except for a (fortunately isolated) use of the nasty vogue-illiteracy 'hopefully'.

Personal Views: Robin Wood; Gordon Fraser, £5.90.

Mr Wood has always had an honourable place among the comparatively few writers on film culture who are able to mount into the rarified atmosphere of the higher criticism without at the same time managing to sink into a bog of pretentious obscurantism – and on occasion, to put it frankly, into circumlocutory nonsense. His early study of Hitchcock still remains the best on this director (with the possible exception of the mammoth Truffaut interview), and there is more on the Master of Suspense in this new modestly titled book. This is however a much wider-flung collection of essays – with chapters ranging from 'In Defence of Art' to 'The Shadow Worlds of Jacques Tourneur', whose notable *The Cat People* is fully discussed. Other directors considered at some length include Orson Welles', Ophüls, Hawks and Sternberg (*The Scarlet Empress*). The once fashionable – now somewhat tarnished – 'auteur' theory is 'reflected on', as is the present favourite term among the theorists, 'semiology': a word, it is wryly interesting to note, which originally referred to the branch of pathology concerned with symptoms. Mr Wood disarmingly combines his scholarship with modesty, wit and – when required – a sharp tongue. His book, though not inexpensive at its price for 250 pages, is obviously required reading (and possessing) for the serious student.

A Pictorial History of Sex in Films: Parker Tyler
Science Fiction Films: Jeff Rovin
The Films of Gene Kelly: Tony Thomas
The Great Romantic Films: Lawrence J. Quirk;
All from Citadel, dist. LSP Books, £3.95.
The first three of these sturdily-built soft-backs were covered in earlier issues of *Film Review* in their hardback form. *Gene Kelly* and *Sex* could be unreservedly recommended (though the unlucky caption misprint on p. 141 of Mr Tyler's book is still uncorrected): *Science Fiction* was considered as a less satisfactory work – but even the best of series may be forgiven an occasional lapse. The *Great Romantic Films* (dealing with sound only – 1932–73) have been chosen and written up by an expert hand – which has also chosen some splendid stills – the only surprises being one or two odd (almost perversely odd) inclusions, e.g. Pasolini's pointless and pretentious *Teorema*, Reisz's turgid and dull *Isadora* (*The Loves of Isadora*), and even Ken Russell's immature and snook-cocking travesty *The Music Lovers. Great Romantic* films? Nonsense! However, among the rest are many to justify the title, from *Smilin' Thru* to *Camille* and *King's Row*. The collection concludes with another surprising but reasonable choice – Pakula's *Love and Pain and the Whole Damn Thing.*

Scarlett, Rhett, and a Cast of Thousands: Roland Flamini; André Deutsch, £4.95.
Whatever its position in the more weighty Ten Best Lists, there is no doubt that *Gone With The Wind* is one of the most famous films ever made, and as such it warrants special attention in the cinematic literature. Mr Flamini's book does it proud: 350 pages, beautifully produced, and packed with superb stills. He follows his subject from the earliest moments of inception of the book itself, provides rare and fascinating snippets of information about its elusive author Margaret Mitchell (Peggy Marsh), and goes far afield in endless stories about people even remotely connected with the production, the frenetic pre-production activities (including of course the famous Hunt for Scarlett), and the post-production junketings. A minor grumble: if only for completeness, we should surely have been given a full list of cast and credits – instead of none at all.
For devotees of the epic movie, of course, this book needs no recommendation, but it should have plenty to interest even those for whom *G.W.T.W.* is something less than the world-shaking masterpiece of all time.

Science Fiction Movies: Philip Strick; Octopus, £2.50.
With production and photographic qualities well up to standard, and so authoritative a writer as Mr Strick at the textual helm, this is a highly recommendable addition to the Movie Treasury Series. Mr Strick frankly confesses the difficulty of defining a sci-fi film, and has inevitably included titles which in other books might appear as horror, thriller, problem, or even social commentary. He does, indeed, cast his net very wide (*Last Year in Marienbad, Belle de Jour, Rashomon*) – indeed, it is perhaps stretching things a bit much to bring in the 1920s farcical thriller *The Gorilla*, though admittedly it enables him to include a rather gorgeous still in full page.
As in all Octopus books on the cinema, these stills are superbly presented, whether in sepia or colour, and here they are accompanied by a worthy commentary. Strongly recommended – not least on account of the price.

The Selznick Players: Ronald Bowers; Barnes/Yoseloff, £6.25.
After a brief biographical chapter, Mr Bowers starts his survey with the best *short* account of *Gone With The Wind* that I have come across. This is followed by sections on eight leading Selznick stars – Ingrid Bergman, Vivien Leigh, Joseph Cotten and Shirley Temple among them – and by brief paragraphs on some lesser lights, and finally by details of awards and rewards. There are filmographies, a reasonable number of good stills, an index and a bibliography. Mr Bowers writes easily and entertainingly. He is guilty, however, of repeating a mistake which has persisted much too long (p. 182): Patrick Hamilton's play, filmed later as *Gaslight* was not (repeat, not) entitled *Angel Street* – it was entitled, simply enough, *Gaslight*. It is time the perpetuation of this error was brought to a halt.

Sleuths: Janet Pate; New English Library, £4.95.
Though it is not solely a 'cinema book', nearly all the portraits in Miss Pate's gallery of detectives have had full screen representation, and the majority of her illustrations are film stills. In brief, business-like style she devotes three or four large pages to each character, including a short descriptive paragraph in the original author's words, a commentary, and a commendably full list of publications and performances. The latter makes her book a very useful work of reference: any filmgoer interested in crime (and what filmgoer is not?) will find it an essential addition to the relevant bookshelf. There are some fascinating reproductions of book illustrations and the film stills are well selected. One interesting point is brought out: a photograph of Will Fyffe adjacent to Edgar Wallace's description of Mr Reeder aptly demonstrates how flagrantly the film-makers disregard the physical appearance of the characters they claim to present. Another example (though to some extent redeemed by Alec Guinness's performance) is the Columbia *FatherBrown*. Miss Pate will inevitably face some criticism from indignant readers whose favourites have been omitted – but obviously not every crime-solver could be included in a book of some 120 pages. Even so, it seems a strange quirk to find room for Rin-Tin-Tin and Rip Kirby, while leaving out those classic creations of John Dickson Carr

and his pseudonym Carter Dickson: 'Dr Fell' and 'Henry Merivale'.

Some Time in the Sun: Tom Dardis; André Deutsch, £5.50.
Of all aspects of Hollywood, one of the least covered is the work of the screenwriter. The author discusses five major writers, famous in other fields, who spent part of their careers in the film factory: long essays on F. Scott Fitzgerald and William Faulkner, shorter ones on Aldous Huxley, Nathanael West and James Agee. His book is wholly compulsive reading – authoritative, scholarly without being dull, perceptive and informative. He pays a lot of attention to the financial details involved (always fascinating), quotes from film-scripts, and presents in each case a penetrating and sympathetic account both of the personal relationships between the authors and the studios, and of the artistic relationships between the writer and the film-maker. Mr Dardis writes lucidly and well (though causing a shudder on p. 65 with the horrible word 'deemphasise'); and the only point where one may differ from him is his apparent opinion that 'datedness' in a film may *of itself* be counted against it. A film is made for its period and in the total circumstances and conventions of its period, and can no more be fairly criticised on that account than for (say) being in black and white before colour came into use, or silent before sound.
Highly recommended – in fact essential reading for all seriously concerned with the American cinema.

Stop the Presses!: Alex Barris; Barnes/Tantivy, £7.50.
There have been plenty of books on film detectives, but this is, to my knowledge, the first to appear on the newspaperman – which is surprising, because the latter has featured in a far greater range of movie stories than the former. As Mr Barris points out, with few exceptions the reporter had to await the advent of sound before coming into his own, but since then almost every well-known player has at some time or other represented the press, and thus finds an honoured place in the author's lively, authoritative and excellently illustrated pages. Apart from the stars (from Adolphe Menjou to Robert Redford and Dustin Hoffman) there are the stalwart, unforgettable regulars: Pat O'Brien, Lee Tracy, Regis Toomey, Roscoe Karns, Stuart Erwin, Wallace Ford and many others who enlivened film after film – not forgetting the ladies, led by the unforgettable Glenda Farrell, crisp wisecracker *par excellence*, who also had her own series, *Torchy Blane*. Some of the earlier newspaper films – the 1931 version of *The Front Page* and *Five Star Final*, for instance – can still hold their own for pace and attack. I can well remember the impact of the climax of *Five Star Final* on its first showing, even while accepting Mr Barris's claim that it is now 'dated'.
And as a crowning glory, of course, one of the greatest films of all time has *the* newspaper setting and *the* newspaperman: *Citizen Kane* and Orson Welles.

Surrealism and the Cinema: Michael Gould; Barnes/Tantivy, £4.
A prospective reader faced with a preliminary quotation in

a study of film theory: 'This is not a book', and an opening to the first chapter: 'Before you lies an open book' may be pardoned a qualm of anxiety as to what sort of facetious pseudo-profundities await him in the text to follow. Such qualms are needless. Mr Gould's survey is one of the best to come my way for a long time – lucid, concise, persuasive, unpretentious and – rarely and mercifully – not without humour. His opening exploratory chapter contains the most comprehensible and convincing description ('definition' is probably impossible) of surrealism I have read. It might by itself win converts to so entertaining and stimulating an art form. Chapters follow on Buñuel, Sternberg, Hitchcock and Samuel Fuller (whose work is interestingly compared with the 'comics', every one of them likely to increase appreciation of the director's films. A chapter on animation follows – excellent on both Betty Boop and Bambi – and then a final, very short one on 'minimal cinema'. Here Mr Gould enters a glum world of tedium, and perhaps does not altogether convince the humbly enquiring reader that three hours of a camera swirling and whirling around a single landscape will be as richly rewarding an experience for him as it is for the writer. Nevertheless even here Mr Gould has a gently persuading hand with which to push the hesitant novice along.

The book is well and aptly illustrated.

They Went Thataway: James Horwitz;
   W. H. Allen, £5.95.
An unashamed trip into nostalgia – the world of the old cowboys – from W. S. Hart and Tom Mix, via the singers (Roger and Autry) to Joel McCrea and Duncan Renaldo, with a final chapter on Tim McCoy at eighty-five years of age. The author, having been brought up on such delights, determined to find out what had become of his boyhood heroes, and set out on a journey of discovery. Racily (at times facetiously) written, this chatty but informative book should conjure up many pleasant memories of juvenile thrills. The illustrations are from posters of the day – a welcome and interesting change from over-familiar stills.

John Wayne and the Movies: Allen Eyles;
   Barnes/Tantivy, £6.00.
Mr Eyles has always been particularly strong on thorough and accurate documentation, and his sixty-page filmography at the end of this large-format book is a model of what such a reference section should be – *really* full cast-lists, and all the essential technical credits: an absolutely essential companion to a study of its subject. The main body of the book consists of brief biographical and general critical chapters, leading to essays of varying lengths on all the films. These latter are succinct and perceptive, of equal interest as evaluation and as history. The prickly matter of *The Green Berets*, for instance, is approached in an admirably level-headed and refreshingly unemotional manner. Bonuses include a wealth of illustrations and a brief Introduction by – of all people – Louise Brooks. One might well say – a 'definitive' study.

Who was that Masked Man? – The Story of the
   Lone Ranger: David Rothel; Barnes/Tantivy, £8.

I must confess that I had no idea of the extent of Lone Ranger interest, and certainly never regarded him as the 'ultimate' hero character. Mr Rothel, however, has no doubts on this point, and also provides ample proof of the extent of the Masked Man's public. For all of them this enormous, fully illustrated book is the 'ultimate' gift. In 256 large pages he covers every aspect of the phenomenon – on radio, or television, or film, or in comics. Interviews with leading people concerned are included in the general narrative, together with an index, a bibliography and – a prize bonus indeed – a transcript of the very first radio episode. Fascinating details emerge on the side – such as the fact that George Seaton (later screenwriter of *The Song of Bernadette*, etc., and director of, among many other films, the first *Airport*) was the original radio Lone Ranger. The many illustrations are splendidly varied – portraits, film stills, publicity photographs, frame blow-ups, pages from comics, posters, newspaper cuttings, etc. It can truly be said that Mr Rothel has done the Masked Man proud.

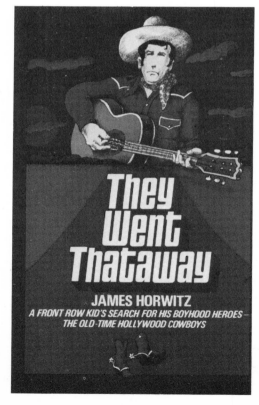

They Went Thataway

JAMES HORWITZ
A FRONT ROW KID'S SEARCH FOR HIS BOYHOOD HEROES – THE OLD-TIME HOLLYWOOD COWBOYS

REFERENCE

Character People – The Stalwarts of the Cinema:
   Ken D. Jones, Arthur F. McClure and Alfred
   E. Twomey; Barnes/Yoseloff, £7.50.
It is always welcome to find attention being paid to the lesser covered film players (often so much more satisfying to watch than the over-publicised 'stars'), and the three authors of this follow-up to their earlier book, *The Versatiles*, have most rewardingly continued their useful work. Nearly 200 actors and actresses of character roles are to be found in these pages – ranging from Adolphe Menjou and Hobart Bosworth to Mala and Dick Purcell. How pleasant to read even a few details (and see a photograph) of such old and tried friends as Claude Gillingwater, Otis Harlan, Louise Fazenda, Tully Marshall, and the magnificently named Gustav von Seyffertitz – though his most memorable performance in the too-little-remembered *The Red Mark* (directed by James Cruze) is not mentioned. How pleasant, too, to find a reasonable proportion of space given to the earlier days. Of course, everyone will regret his or her own particular – but inevitable – omission. Where are Lucien Littlefield, Emily Fitzroy, Craufurd Kent, Martha Mattox? But this is to take a churlish view: and perhaps, who knows, a third volume is in the offing, to include *all* such omissions!

The Film Buff's Bible: Ed. by D. Richard Baer;
   Hollywood Film Archive (8344 Melrose Avenue,
   Hollywood, California 90069), $12.95 paperback
   $12.95 cloth.
13,000 titles (taking the editor at his word) are listed in this large format volume, giving in each case release date, length (very useful for checking TV vandalism), three critical gradings, distributor and, in a few cases, a very brief comment. Understandably, the emphasis is largely on American films, but quite a number of British and foreign productions are included. Silent pictures also are present to some extent. There is also a useful list of alternative titles. Even with so large a spread omissions are bound to be numerous – and are freely admitted: the first two silent films I looked up as a test were absent. One might perhaps have wished that more space had been given to lesser-known films, as against those famous ones which are easy to trace elsewhere – but as its declared aim is to help the television viewer (rather than the historian) this was probably too much to expect. The rating guide provided by the editor and staff is full of surprises. Only 10 out of 13,000 films gain top marks (ten out of ten) – *My Fair Lady*, *The Pawnbroker*, *Tom Jones* and *Z*; strange bedfellows indeed! *Citizen Kane* receives only 6–7, *Les Enfants du Paradis* 5 ('Passable'), Clair's classic *Le Million* 3 ('Not worth watching'). Many of the judgements, indeed, are likely to meet violent disagreement from both lovers and haters – which is, of course, all to the good. Informative (within its limitations of space), and stimulating as well.

Film Directors Guide: Western Europe: James
   Robert Parish; Scarecrow Press, dist. Bailey
   Bros. & Swinfen, £8.80.
From being one of the worst documented 'lively arts', the

cinema is rapidly becoming one of the best, and there will always be room for convenient handbooks such as this, which covers the work (full-length features) of directors based in western Europe. A list of the countries *not* covered includes Denmark, Sweden, Poland, Czechoslovakia, etc., i.e. the 'borderliners'. The compilation is especially commendable on two points: (*a*) it aims for complete listings within its declared limits, and (*b*) in the case of directors whose 'major reputation was first obtained in Europe', American credits are included – e.g. for Lang, Hitchcock, Robert Siodmak. This inclusion is a very welcome addition to the general convenience. Film documentation is a notoriously tricky and nerve-racking activity, and any book is apt to contain its quota of errors and omissions – several titles are missing, for instance, from J. Lee Thompson. On the whole, however, the labour that went to ensure accuracy must have been prodigious – and for fullness one need only suggest a glance at the entry for Michael Curtiz. Even if much of the information *could* be traced elsewhere, the compactness of this sturdy little volume will save any researcher hours of perspiring and dusty delving. There are a number of pleasant illustrations. One looks forward to the future promised volumes.

Hollywood Glamor Portraits: Edited by John Kobal; Constable/Dover, £4.
There are 145 of them, from 1926 to 1949, full page, superbly reproduced (except for, in my copy, a nasty smudge all down Norma Shearer's cheek), taken by the leading still photographers of the Golden Period. About ninety stars are represented – in rough chronology from Lillian Gish, Clara Bow and Louise Brooks to Marlon Brando and Lizabeth Scott. In numbers, Dietrich, Garbo, Crawford and Lombard rate highest – but each reader (or viewer) will rate his or her own choice in aesthetics. The price is fairly high for a slim, soft-back volume; but the quality, range and nostalgic value of these exquisite, admittedly artificial creations justify it.

International Film Guide 1977: Ed. Peter Cowie; Tantivy/Barnes, £2.50.
This 'perennial buff and trade must' (to quote *Variety*) appears this year in a somewhat larger format – all 504 pages of it. After a momentary regret for the friendly squatness of the series to date the reader, or user, can only admit that the increased page size greatly benefits ease of handling, attractiveness of lay-out, and reproduction of stills. The I.F.G. is now a most handsome volume, incredibly modest in price at today's levels. The system is much as before: World Survey taking pride of place, with numerous side issues such as Festivals, Schools, Awards, Book reviews and shops, etc., etc. The Directors of the Year are Woody Allen, Cukor, Kobayashi, Claude Sautet and Lina Wertmüller – a wide range if ever there was one. There is also a TV section – marred for one reader at any rate only by David Wilson's disparaging reference to the fine and thought-provoking BBC series *Survivors* (not, as he has it, *The Survivors* – and not a repeat during the past year, but a second series).
A trenchant Introduction by the editor, Peter Cowie,

castigates the flood of overlong and over-inflated films which have recently dragged their weary length across the screen. 'Elephantiasis' is the word he uses, and it is not only the weary, eye-strained reviewer who will agree with his condemnation of unnecessary, padding-stuffed hours of cinema.

Motion Picture Performers, A Bibliography of Magazine and Periodical Articles, Supplement No. 1: Mel Schuster; Scarecrow Press, dist. Bailey Bros. & Swinfen, £22.
Until fairly recently the film was considered one of the worst documented of the arts – now it looks like becoming one of the best. This welcome progress should certainly get a strong boost from the appearance of this new reference book. To quote the Introduction: 'The basic volume, published in 1971, examined material on 2,900 performers appearing in selected periodicals from 1900 through 1969.' Here, 2,600 additional names are represented, making a total of 5,500, and the whole field of entries vastly widened. In some 800 clearly printed pages literally thousands of entries are included. Volume, issue, page and date of each article in each publication are lucidly set out, making the hunt for references a simple matter. A random example or two will give some small indication of the scope and range: on Spencer Tracy there are some 500 references from 1932 to 1972; on Jean-Louis Trintignant nine from 1960 to 1973; on Alice White twelve from 1927 to 1934; on Pearl White about twenty from 1914 to 1970. If you want to know the story of Susan Larson, this book will tell you exactly where to find it. If you want Barbara Everest's obituary, or to increase your knowledge of Mick Jagger or Rod La Rocque – the way to finding out is put before you.
At its price this is, perhaps, a book for the reference or public library rather than the general private collection; but for the cinema historian, the serious student in depth, the film-star biographer, or even the razor-keen buff, it is an invaluable boon.

The Oxford Companion to Film: Ed. Liz-Anne Bawden; Oxford University Press, £10.
I had been thinking for some time that the Film deserved the ultimate accolade of inclusion among the Oxford Companions – and now I am doubly delighted: first that this has been done, and secondly that it has been done so excellently. Obviously a labour of both love and scholarship, its 750 closely (but always clearly) printed pages covers every aspect of cinema – biographical, historical, national, technical, commercial. The great majority of entries are, of necessity, brief, but skilfully filled with the necessary detail and the essential point. Particularly welcome is the large number of entries on important *films* – from *A Bout de Souffle* to *Zvenigora*. This is, of course, a standard work of reference, and deals mainly, as is to be expected, with the most famous and important subjects in each category. It is best used in conjunction with – rather than as a substitution for – other volumes such as Halliwell's *Filmgoer's Companion*, Truitt's splendid *Who Was Who on the Screen* and the Michael Joseph and Studio Vista encyclopaedias. Illustrations take second place here, but those included (frame enlargements

retaining the correct screen proportions) are at least adequate, and carefully chosen in their context. It is hardly necessary to add that this is an essential addition to the film reference library – it is also a very attractive one.

Screen World 1976: John Willis; Muller, £6.50.
Mr Willis's indispensable annual record continues on its way with undeviating excellence, leaving the admiring reviewer with little to say except that this latest volume is fully up to standard: lavish stills (superbly reproduced), full – really full – cast and credit lists, gargantuan index, obituary (sadly lengthy!) and other features as usual. Back volumes soon become collectors' pieces, and the intelligent enthusiast loses no time in securing each new issue to add to his reference shelf: it should, indeed, be there long before this paragraph can meet his eye!

The Westerns: John Cocchi, Constable/Dover, £2.25.
A welcome addition to the Picture Quiz Book series (Silents, Musicals), consisting of well over 200 stills and questions about them guaranteed to tax the memory of the most self-confident buff. As with the earlier books, the stills alone are worth the price, particularly those (in quite a generous proportion) from the old days, which are valuable for their rarity. All are well produced, and altogether the book offers an enjoyable way of combining the acquisition of knowledge, the stimulation of memory, the tantalising of fellow cinemaniacs, and the passing of a wintry evening by the central-heated radiator.

Soundtrack! –
The Year's Releases on Record

by Derek Elley

A good year in spite of itself – in the sense that, although the overall quality of contemporary film music did not show any appreciable rise, enthusiasts were still supplied with a reasonable flow of old classics to assuage parched ears. Yet the signs of change dimly discernible in 1975–76 began to take visible form during 1976–77. RCA, one of the pioneers in the revival of classic scores, did not issue in Britain any more of their Gerhardt/National Philharmonic series after the Errol Flynn album, despite the fact that two more (Dmitri Tiomkin and David Raksin) have been available in the US for some time; at the time of writing, only an album of leftovers from various sessions is due for release. Polydor, too, came to the end of their remarkable Miklós Rózsa series, with no plans for extending it further despite very successful sales.

There are equally signs, however, that the market is not so much playing itself out as merely changing its appearance. Rózsa recorded a new *Ben-Hur* for Decca Phase 4 last September for release in the summer of 1977, and will tackle *Quo Vadis* this autumn for the same company. In addition, Elmer Bernstein's Film Music Collection (PO Box 261, Calabasas, California 91302), so far restricted to a membership/mail order listenership, has recently been making strenuous efforts to interest a major international company in handling and furthering its series (up to now financially underwritten by Bernstein himself) without compromising any of its hallowed objectives – one of which is the thoroughly laudable idea of presenting original cues as heard in the film, rather than (as with RCA and Polydor) fabricated orchestral suites.

The past year saw the sixth, seventh and eighth releases in Bernstein's series, each of major importance. The first recording of Alfred Newman's enchanting score to William Wyler's *Wuthering Heights* (FMC–6) made it possible to savour at leisure the wealth of material beyond the deservedly famous (and much recorded, e.g. RCA) Cathy's Theme; it is one of Newman's most romantic scores – rather like Steiner with bitters – and shows his gift for continuous development of already highly melodic material. For his own *To Kill a Mockingbird* (FMC–7) Bernstein used the RPO for the first time in his series, restoring this ingenuous and utterly charming score to the catalogues in a version more faithful to the film than the original 'soundtrack release'. The only major flaw in Bernstein's series has been thin string tone (for obvious financial reasons), which no amount of forward recording can hide: in *Mockingbird*, with its delicate, colouristic scoring, this was not serious, but in *The Thief of Bagdad* (FMC–8), coupled with a more concert-hall acoustic, it saps much of the drama from Rózsa's energetic string writing. That apart, however, this is a wonderful release to have on the shelves and reveals the score as one of Rózsa's most inspired, shot through with a relative youthfulness and *esprit* which the later large-scale scores compensate for by greater portentousness. Bernstein gives us only a portion of the very long original, but throws in chorus and baritone and mezzo soli as in the film, the brass and woodwind of the RPO fully attuned to the composer's style.

And well they might be, as Polydor's magnificent series has born witness. Whatever one may think of the concept of presenting arranged suites of old music, it undeniably makes for superb entertainment, especially when conductor (Rózsa himself) and orchestra (RPO) work together with such empathy. The second album (Polydor 2383384), featuring scores like *Lust for Life, Tribute to a Badman, Knight without Armour, The Asphalt Jungle, Double Indemnity* and *Moonfleet*, stressed Rózsa the colourist, adapting his style to a variety of *genres* with equal panache and sensibility, whether Western, Slavic, urban American, French Expressionist, or the war film. The third album, 'Rózsa Conducts Rózsa' (Polydor 2383440), marginally the best recorded of the series, collected together a fascinating collection of *arcana*: the Overture to *Julius Caesar* (unheard for fifteen years, since MGM replaced it with Tchaikovsky's *Capriccio italien*!, a suite from Wyler's *The Private Life of Sherlock Holmes* (with Erich Gruenberg playing excerpts from Rózsa's Violin Concerto, originally written for Jascha Heifetz in 1953), and undiscovered beauties like *Five Graves to Cairo*. Let us hope that Rózsa's collaboration with Decca will be as fruitful and well respected by the company as it has been with Polydor over the past two years. The other major focus of 1976–77, despite his death, was again Bernard Herrmann. Decca continued to honour him with a string of issues, some, like PFS 4363, revealing Herrmann's love for British music as he conducted film scores

by such concert composers as Constant Lambert (*Anna Karenina*), Arnold Bax (*Oliver Twist*), William Walton (*Escape Me Never*), Arthur Bliss (*Things to Come*) and Ralph Vaughan Williams (*The Invaders/49th Parallel*), others, like PFS 4365 and PFS 4337, largely composed of re-issues of him conducting his own music to fantasy spectaculars like *Mysterious Island, Jason and the Argonauts*, and *The Three Worlds of Gulliver*. All were sharply recorded. Of his more recent music, too, the gaps continued to be filled in: least satisfactorily with *Taxi Driver* (Arista ARTY 32), a weak score which no amount of juggling by the record company could disguise, and best of all by *Obsession* (Decca Phase 4 PFS 4381), Herrmann's penultimate assignment and his finest accomplishment of the past decade. Of the late works, this is the score by which I wish to remember him: as an adjunct to De Palma's picture it sums up over thirty years' experience, and as an extended musical essay it bears repeated listenings, by dint of its unclouded, flowing style, in a way that even *Sisters* and *Battle of Neretva* never quite achieve.

The latter two were made available on an enterprising new American label, Entr'acte Recording Society (PO Box 2319, Chicago, Illinois 60690, but available from Henry Stave, 9 Dean Street, London W1), the brainchild of TWA executive John Steven Lasher. Lasher started by making available already recorded material – *Sisters* (ERQ 7001–ST) and *Battle of Neretva* (ERS 6501–ST) – cautiously entered into original recordings with 'Korngold Songs and Arias' (ERS 6502), retreated

into re-mastering in stereo John Green's classic *Raintree County* (ERS 6503–ST, 2 discs), and then, helped by a grant from Max Steiner's widow, burst forth into the field with a new, first recording of Steiner's *King Kong* (ERS 6504), reconstructed from the original sketches with admirable fidelity and played with gusto by the National Philharmonic in St. Giles, Cripplegate. Lasher already has an album of Americana from Herrmann, Newman, Waxman and Friedhofer in the can, and his high standards and professionalism are worthy of support.

Re-issues from other companies have varied from the helpful to serviceable. In the former category are André Previn's *Four Horsemen of the Apocalypse* (Polydor 2353125), one of his more memorable creations, EMI's 'Bands on Film' (World Records SH 197) with Harry Roy on the soundtrack of the 1936 British musical *Everything Is Rhythm*, and United Artists' restoration to the catalogues on the budget Sunset label of reference material like *Thunderball* (SLS 50396) and *Un homme et une femme* (SLS 50409). In the latter came *Dr No* (SLS 50395), 90% composed of calypso music by Monty Berman, and *The Eddy Duchin Story* (MCA Coral CDL 8040), featuring the flying fingers of Carmen Cavallaro on the piano.

There has, too, been the usual musical wallpaper over the year (and I omit so-called 'soundtrack releases' which are entirely reliant on songs – a depressing feature of the market): Michel Legrand's *Ode to Billy Joe* (Warner K 56258) and *Gable and Lombard* (MCA MCF 2754), both showing the musical intelligence of a high-school student; Henry Mancini's *The Pink Panther Strikes Again* (UAS 30012), which re-trod familiar ground with no new initiative – unlike his *W. C. Fields and Me* (MCA MCF 2759), which showed to dazzling effect what Mancini can do when he bothers; Rick Wakeman's *White Rock* (A&M AMLH 64614), an interminable *mélange* of Steinway, mellotron, moog and pipe and Hammond organs; and even John Williams' *The Missouri Breaks* (UAS 29971), with equally interminable harmonicas and various fretted instruments. Inspiration of a kind came from Alex North with an album collecting some of the best music from *Rich Man, Poor Man* (MCA MCF 2767); David Shire with *Farewell, My Lovely* (UAS 29915) despite reliance on Legrand (!) and Herrmann; Pino Donnaggio with *Carrie* (UAS 30033), a thoroughly efficient job done within the awesome shade of the prior De Palma/Herrmann collaboration; and Jerry Fielding with *The Outlaw Josey Wales* (Warner BS 2956), though one expects more than the often vacuous padding from this talented composer. The number of really satisfying scores which reached record were alarmingly few. Laurence Rosenthal's *The Return of a Man Called Horse* (UAS 30007) avoided almost all the Indian music *clichés* in favour of good, workable themes, little more than a conventional symphony orchestra, and musical imagination. John Morris's *Silent Movie* (UAS 30009) further extended his discography of pastiche with a score which amused, entertained and surprised with its endlessly inventive use of two major themes (for the two film com-

panies). John Addison's *The Scarlet Buccaneer* (MCA MCF 2779), like the hugely enjoyable film, did the same, with razzle-dazzle orchestration pointing up an already literate score; one of the year's major triumphs. Equally successful, if with more limited opportunities, was Ernest Gold with *Cross of Iron* (EMA 782), the heartbreaking main Steiner's Theme put to powerful use in the film's final few reels. Jerry Goldsmith, too, regained the momentum of *The Wind and the Lion* with a pair of works which showed a breadth of imagination equal to the films, and a desire to (intelligently and creatively, rather than trendily) explore new resources: *Logan's Run* (MGM 2315376), the more complex of the two, derived tension from the clash of electronic and majestic symphonic orchestrations, representing the worlds of the City and Freedom; *The Omen* (RCA Tattoo BJL1 1888), recalling Ennio Morricone's fake *Sanctus* in the Italian film *Allonsanfàn*, featured a splendidly barbaric *Ave satani* for mixed choir hammering out its message in Orffian vein and a relaxed, sunny melody for the contrasting scenes of family happiness. And the year's most unexpected triumph came from a composer who has jolted us before – Ennio Morricone himself. *Moses* (Pye NSPH 28503) rejected the expected epic orchestral devices in favour of accompanied wordless vocals stressing the vision and longings of the central character. The modalisms which permeate the score give it a folk character which tallies well with Gianfranco De Bosio's overall conception, and Moses' Theme, whether soulfully crooned by Gianna Spagnolo or

played on a solo viola by Dino Asciolla, has the emotive power of anything Newman, Rózsa or Waxman wrote in this vein. Who said Morricone was played out?

Elmer Bernstein conducting the RPO in Rózsa's *The Thief of Bagdad* for his own label, at Olympic Studios, London, last January.

The In-Betweens

It has never been easy to go to press with this annual with the comfortable knowledge that *every* generally released film of the year has been tidily included, more especially towards the end of the 'year' when I have to work something like two months in advance and discover, as this year, the circuits are only working three or four weeks ahead! Another point concerns those films which though premièred have not as yet been given any release date, even an acknowledged Floating Release, even though they have had various showings and, indeed, in some cases will have very little more! The problem always has been where to list such films? There is no completely satisfactory way of doing this but I am hoping that this feature is the next best thing: in it you will find mentioned these (to me) problem films. Those that will earn a general or even restricted release next year will be mentioned in next year's annual in the usual way, so in this manner I hope to cover the whole scene and close all the possible gaps.

Part-time pugilist Rocky (Sylvester Stallone) gets last-minute instructions from his old trainer/manager (Burgess Meredith) before he goes into the ring against the world heavyweight champ in UA's *Rocky*, which won the 1976 Oscars for best film, best direction (by John G. Avildsen) and best editing.

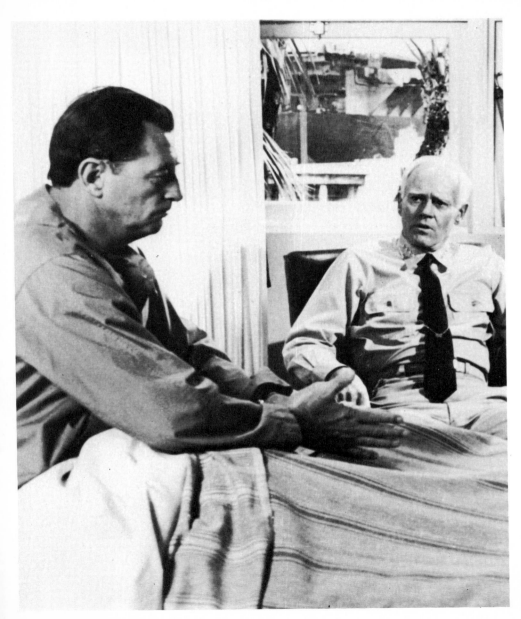

Hospitalised Robert Mitchum discusses tactics with Henry Fonda before the sea battle which was to have such an effect on America's war against the Japanese, in *The Battle of Midway*, a Universal–CIC spectacular made more impressive by the use of Sensurround.

Gulliver (Richard Harris) being fed by the little people of Lilliput in the combined cartoon and live action remake of the famous Dean Swift fairy story *Gulliver's Travels* – released by EMI.

Barbra Streisand and Kris Kristofferson in her own production of the third adaptation to the screen of *A Star is Born*, this time the stars being of the pop rather than the movie world. A Warner release.

UA's *Bound for Glory* is the story of America's famous, if controversial, radical folk-singer Woody Guthrie (played by David Carradine).

Dutch doctor Spaander suggests to British Airborne Commander Urquhart that he will ask the Germans for a truce to evacuate the Allied casualties. Laurence Olivier and Sean Connery in Joseph Levine's film of the airborne assault on the Rhine bridges at Arnhem in 1944, *A Bridge Too Far*, a United Artists release.

James Brolin as the cop who confronts the killer car in Universal–CIC's *The Car*, a mysterious vehicle which goes on the rampage – apparently without a driver at the wheel! – and terrifies a small community.

In Universal–CIC's *Gray Lady Down*, a further addition to the Disaster cycle, Charlton Heston plays the Captain of an American nuclear sub which is accidentally sunk in treacherous waters some sixty miles from the nearest base.

Universal–CIC's *Slap Shot* is the story of an ice hockey star (Paul Newman; with Michael Ontkean as a fellow player) and though written by a woman, Nancy Dowd, is promised in terms of language at least, to be one of the roughest, toughest movies yet!

Court revels in the re-make of that old classic *The Prince and The Pauper*, a Fox period piece in which Rex Harrison plays the Duke of Norfolk.

Beau Bridges plays the French King Louis XIV (osculatory partner is Ursula Andress, playing Madame de la Vallière) in another historical story re-make, *Behind the Iron Mask.*

Having fun? Jane Fonda and George Segal are the two stars of Ted Kotcheff's Columbia film *Fun with Dick and Jane*, the story of what happened after happy ever after, when Dick and Jane lose their jobs and try to keep their standard of living up without money!

Manager Ernest Borgnine has something to say to the champ between rounds in Columbia's *The Greatest*, Muhammad Ali's own story with himself starring in it!

Ghouls and pretty girl in Columbia's *Sinbad and the Eye of the Tiger*, another Dynarama spectacular carrying on with the fantastic adventures of that busy sailor lad from the Arabian Nights.

London's 'Listed' Cinemas by Allen Eyles

Today it's only the film on the screen that counts when visiting a cinema. The sense of occasion has gone. No longer are there four or five different prices to match one's social level or aspirations (with often a humbler side entrance to the front stalls). No longer do queues form to be patrolled by doormen, managers beam a welcome in their evening best, and usherettes guide the patron by torch beam through the gloom. The newsreel has gone, and the organ interlude, and the lighting frills that lent character to the auditorium. The cinema café no longer serves sardines on toast to brighten the journey home. Once the cinemas offered an escape from drab surroundings; but with today's improved standards of living, people's homes are comfortable enough except in bedsitter areas where cinemas are noticeably popular still.

Fortunately, while archives seek to preserve the outstanding examples of past film production, something is also being done to keep some of the best remaining examples of cinema building intact, both as a tribute to the imagination of the architect and decorator, and as an indication of what going to the pictures meant for a past generation. The Department of the Environment operates a system of 'listing' buildings. Once placed on the list, their demolition cannot take place without special permission and alterations that are made have to conform with the character of the building. Perhaps under the impetus of some notable cinemas disappearing, much more attention has been given recently to buildings of this century. London has taken the lead in examining

cinemas and listing the best of them. Almost all those buildings that have achieved listing have been under some sort of threat to their continued existence, and most have ceased screening films. Outside London, little has been done, but the Birmingham area has been under survey this year and there is hope that some of that city's remaining cinemas like the magnificent Tudor-style Beaufort at Ward End and the style-setting Odeons at Kingstanding and Sutton Coldfield will be accorded listing. There is no master list of cinemas (or even places of entertainment) available from the Department of the Environment to indicate what cinemas may have been listed outside London but it is possible from other sources to indicate those in and around the capital that are safeguarded for the future. (I exclude from consideration buildings that were designed as live theatres like the Coronet at Notting Hill Gate, now part of a 'conservation area', even though they may have spent many years showing films.)

The first purpose-built cinemas were erected from 1905. They have become a rarity in anything like their original form: the Biograph at Victoria (1905) has been fatally modernised; the Globe at Putney (1911) underwent similar 'improvements' to emerge as the Cinecenta and has now closed down; the Curzon at Sutton (1911) has been totally transformed into three smaller units; the Classic at Brixton (the Electric Pavilion of 1911) has been shuttered and there is talk of a supermarket. A few years ago it looked as though nothing could save the Electric in Portobello Road (1910). The

cinema showed double-bills of old films at rock-bottom prices. Finding it in its obscure location amidst a street market was an art; seeing films in its peeling, smelly auditorium with cramped seating conditions was a torture (films ran continuously with no intervals to reveal the full horror of the surroundings). But it has gained a new lease of life as a listed building which (like the 1911 Electric Palace at Harwich) provides a good impression of the early type of cinema building. The auditorium was (and is) a plain rectangle on a sloping floor with a barrel-vault ceiling and decorative plasterwork; the pay-box was situated in a recessed entrance, open to the street. Now it has been slowly restored to provide acceptable viewing conditions for members of the Electric Cinema Club. Unfortunately, the 1914 Grange at Kilburn – perhaps the largest British cinema at its time of opening (with over two thousand seats) and well-designed on an island site by Edward Stone (who was to become a leading cinema architect) – has not been listed even though it was active as a cinema until June 1975. (Even more surprising, perhaps, is the absence of the vast Gaumont State across the road from the protected list.) The 1914 Gaumont at Richmond, Surrey, enjoys a measure of protection since an original eighteenth-century Georgian house was adapted to form the foyer. Whether the auditorium behind is protected seems doubtful (and it does not have a great deal of character now), but it would be agreeable to see this cinema last as a rare bearer of the once omnipresent Gaumont name and as a home of slightly more imaginative

Detail of wall at the Electric, Portobello Road, showing early style of plasterwork detail.

The Electric, Portobello Road, in 1971.

programming than most big-circuit cinemas.

From the 1920s, two cinemas designed by Frank Verity have been listed, but both too late to save their interiors which have been entirely transformed. One is the Shepherd's Bush Pavilion (now the Odeon), dating from 1923 (when it won an architectural award for its façade). Its huge 2,776 seating capacity was heavily reduced in a drastic interior modernisation of 1955, and that has now given way to the building's subdivision into bingo club and cinema, the latter reached by escalator. Externally, the brickwork and stone could do with a good scrub-down, but the façade is otherwise barely changed. The second cinema, the Plaza in Lower Regent Street (1926), had its original sumptuous interior intact until 1967, but has now been divided internally at considerable expense. The façade, however, is little altered with the massive corner dome intact.

Late in the decade, the American idea of atmospheric or landscape settings was introduced, most spectacularly at the Astoria Brixton (1929) and the Astoria Finsbury Park (1930), both listed and both designed by Edward Stone (with T. R. Somerford and Evan Barr). At Brixton, audiences gained the impression of being seated in an Italian garden with the sides of buildings and cypress trees around them and with the sky overhead – the ceiling in which lights twinkled like stars while projected cloud patterns moved across. However, by the time the Department of the Environment took an interest in the Brixton Astoria, it had undergone a shortlived conversion to a dance and concert hall and been boarded

up. Thus it remains, a huge, mournful hulk sadly in need of some purpose to re-open. At Finsbury Park, the atmosphere was of a Moorish walled city with balconies, roofs, domes, turrets and palm trees surrounding the audience as they faced the screen which was set in an arch like a main gate to the city. This Astoria, too, has given up films and is now the Rainbow Theatre. The two lions that flanked the screen on tall, slender columns have disappeared; and reports of as many as two hundred seats being wrecked and thrown about at a recent punk rock concert do not inspire confidence in the future welfare of the building.

An even bolder stab at a fantasy setting was undertaken at the New Victoria (1930) where the Gaumont chief architect W. E. Trent and his associate E. Walmsley Lewis created an undersea cavern setting, the feeling of descent augmented by the stairs down to the stalls and by appropriate lighting. The exterior was kept rigorously simple and matched on the extensive frontages on Wilton Road and Vauxhall Bridge Road, with horizontal bands on the stonework being checked by the strong vertical lines above the two entrances. Redevelopment was threatened here as film attendances dropped, but when the cinema closed in November 1975 it became another venue for pop concerts.

Also in 1930, the Carlton, a huge cinema out on Essex Road, Islington, opened, designed by the noted cinema architect George Coles. Its façade made strong use of Egyptian features including lotus-bud capitals to the columns and vivid, intricately coloured friezes in the tiled

surface, while the interior was richly treated in Italian Renaissance style. For many years it was a highly successful cinema on the ABC circuit, but it suffered from rowdy audiences in the late 1950s, and slowly died in the 1960s as a result of its location (remote from the centre of Islington) and the marked apathy towards filmgoing that developed in working-class areas. The building is now a Mecca bingo club.

The Granada at Tooting Broadway, which opened in 1931, similarly came to grief in a poorer area of London. Once its opulent décor, in the manner of a Venetian Gothic palazzo, had enthralled audiences escaping from miserable surroundings; but it came to seem anachronistic and forbidding with its cathedral-like atmosphere, as well as even more cheerless with such small audiences assembled in its vast sea of seats. Its owners planned a fourteen-storey office block during the recent property boom but Wandsworth Borough Council made an unprecedented move by slapping a local preservation order on the building, to have it subsequently reinforced by one from the Department of the Environment. After much delay, Granada have reopened the building for bingo, maintaining the original décor (the work of Theodore Komisarjevsky in collaboration with the architects, Cecil Masey and R. H. Uren), adding new furniture to harmonise, and even emphasising the look of the place in promoting its début as a gaming hall. Out at Northfields, Ealing, one finds an atmospheric cinema dating from 1932 that is still happily open for films. Though not ideally located, the cinema

The cathedral-like interior of the
Granada, Tooting, in 1971.

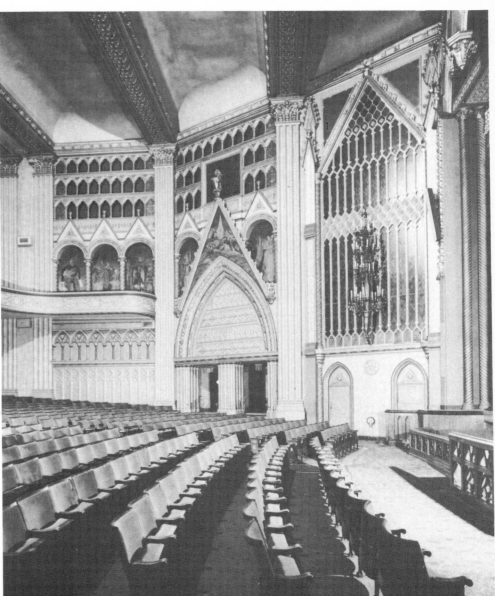

was fortunate in having a lower seating capacity (1,536 seats) than might be expected from the ambitiousness of its décor. Originally called the Avenue but long re-named the Odeon, it is in a Spanish style that unusually finds expression in both the exterior and the auditorium. Inside, the main ceiling is draped in red cloth, creating a tent-like impression, and once again tiled roofs, balconies, windows, shields, etc. on the side walls create an 'inside out' impression for the cinemagoer.

At Woolwich in south-east London, another vast Granada cinema (2,384 seats) has been listed although in many ways it duplicates the one at Tooting, being by the same team of architects and designer in the same Italian Gothic style. This one succumbed to bingo earlier than Tooting and the game is now played within false walls in the old stalls area. If one stands in the gutted balcony, the original walls can still be seen beyond. The cinema opened in 1937 to be followed a few months later by an Odeon opposite. This too has been listed. It is one of the many Odeons that brought a distinctive impact to the nation's High Streets with their vast, eye-catching expanse of cream-coloured tiles, their soaring vertical features, and their red neon signs. Unfortunately the Woolwich Odeon badly needs cleaning externally while the auditorium has been modernised, removing the troughs of concealed lighting set in the side walls and substituting a more economical flat surface that is merely bland. It is a pity that other Odeons at Muswell Hill and Balham, also by George Coles and much closer to their original condition,

184

should have been passed over for listing. One recent addition to the number of listed cinemas provides encouraging evidence that a sufficient volume of local protest at the threatened loss of a well-designed cinema can gain the support of officialdom in time. At Uxbridge, the Regal – designed by E. Norman Bailey and opened in 1932 – seemed set for demolition as part of a redevelopment scheme. Its exterior is rather unpromising but its auditorium is quite eye-catching with great troughs of concealed lighting running across the ceiling and

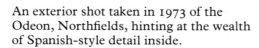

The beautifully-preserved Spanish-style interior of the Odeon, Northfields, still used for showing films.

An exterior shot taken in 1973 of the Odeon, Northfields, hinting at the wealth of Spanish-style detail inside.

within the unusually shaped proscenium arch. Seating is in the stadium style with the rear stalls stepped in lieu of an overhanging balcony. The impression the cinema makes is quite distinctive and bold. The listing of the Regal, which is still a popular cinema, shows what can be done to save a valuable and admired local amenity.

It may yet be possible to save more of London's cinemas from the wrecker's ball. Far too many dreary office blocks and nondescript supermarkets already occupy the sites of former landmark cinemas.

View from the stage of the Regal,
Uxbridge, the most recently listed
cinema in the London area. Note absence
of balcony.

The photographs illustrating this article
were kindly provided by the GLC
Historic Buildings Division.

Side-exit at the Regal, Uxbridge,
showing the unique style of interior
decoration.

Index

Page numbers in italics indicate pictorial references; titles in italics indicate reference to books.